Organized Crime

Organized Crime

The Fifth Estate

August Bequai

Lexington Books
D.C. Heath and Company
Lexington, Massachusetts
Toronto

Library of Congress Cataloging in Publication Data

Bequai, August.
    Organized crime.

    Bibliography: p.
    Includes index.
    1. Organized crime—United States.   I. Title.
HV6446.B46   364.1'06'073   77-18574
ISBN 0-669-02104-0

Copyright © 1979 by D.C. Heath and Company

Published simultaneously in Canada

Printed in the United States of America

International Standard Book Number: 0-669-02104-0

Library of Congress Catalog Card Number: 78-18574

For My Mother and Father

Contents

Preface

A study by the General Accounting Office found that arson for profit is increasing by 25 percent each year. The cost to the public and the insurance industry is billions of dollars each year. Two underworld informers testifying before Congress confirmed that arson for profit is a growing industry; they also said that professional arsonists (known as torches), sell their services for fees ranging from $500 to $1,500. One of the two witnesses summed it up as follows: "Many businessmen and speculators who know their way around can call an arsonist to provide instant liquidity of their property, the way the average person telephones a reservation to a restaurant."

In California police investigators uncovered a massive heroin smuggling ring that did more than $20 million in business each year. The group, composed mostly of Chicano racketeers, smuggled the heroin in from Mexico. While testifying before a congressional committee, the chief prosecutor of the Chicago Organized Crime Strike Force told his audience that the syndicate was now concentrating its efforts on union pension and benefit funds. In Rhode Island armed masked men hijacked a tractor-trailer loaded with gold and silver rolls.

Organized crime is big business in America; it rivals the auto industry in size and affluence. It is a power to be reckoned with. It abuses our constitutional rights daily, yet it has managed to escape the wrath of reformers. It is in essence a de facto government with its own private army and system of laws. Among its allies are men of power and wealth. It rules a far-flung empire that stretches both domestically and internationally. It is a conglomerate of numerous groups from numerous ethnic and racial backgrounds, preying on society at large. It is an American tragedy.

Acknowledgments

A book is the outgrowth of the efforts of many; an author relies heavily on his friends and associates. I would like to express my gratitude to Joe Kalet, my research assistant, to John Piazza, John V. Graziano, Philip Manuel, Dennis Goldman, E.J. Criscuoli, Jr., Lewis Schneider, Donald Duckworth, David Saari, Bruce H. Jones, Teuta Bequai, and many others.

There are no easy solutions to the problem of organized crime. After spending millions of dollars of the taxpayers' money on hundreds of studies, we know little more than we did in 1950. Organized crime poses a serious challenge, one that calls for serious revamping of our antiquated law enforcement machinery.

Introduction

Political scientists remind us that ours is a government of four estates. The legislative, executive, and judicial branches are the first three estates, while the press constitutes the fourth estate. The church, although powerful, finds itself constrained by constitutional limitations. There is, a fifth estate, however, which is not constrained by morality or governmental regulation. Organized crime can truly be called America's fifth estate.

Modern technology has given rise to the nuclear family. Our mobile lifestyle has uprooted millions. The individual, once dependent on the clan and tribe for protection, has come to rely on the state structure. The advent of the nation-state, has given rise to a social environment that increasingly supplants the family. The nuclear family finds itself increasingly dependent on the state apparatus for its security and well being.

When the body politic is riddled with corruption and ineptness and is highly fragmented, power falls into the hands of organized groups. The individual, now alone, easily falls prey. Freedom and liberty in such a body politic become a sham; organized violence takes on private rather than public channels. It matters little to the average citizen whether men of power employ the instrumentalities of the formal state or those of organized crime to take away his livelihood and constitutional rights. The tyranny of organized crime is no less hideous than the dictatorship of the state. Both have the power to injure and enslave. Ample safeguards have been established in our society to guard the rights of the citizenry against the government; few have been taken to guard him against organized crime.

Organized Crime

1 Defining Organized Crime

In 1963 Joseph Valachi, a onetime member of New York's underworld, in testimony before the U.S. Senate, told a shocked audience that for many years he had been a member of the Cosa Nostra.[1] This secret criminal cartel, according to Valachi, ruled a vast illicit empire and had its own private armies, code of ethics, and a ruling body known as the Commission. Valachi went on to tell how the Cosa Nostra recruited its manpower, who its leaders were, and how it eliminated its enemies. The public was shocked. Articles, books, and countless studies followed.

Organized crime is said to control union locals in more than twenty sectors of the economy. Many of these locals are affiliated with internationals that are either unwilling or unable to to interfere in the affairs of their locals. The net annual sales of this criminal combine are said to be as high as $50 billion. Experts estimate that its net worth may exceed $100 billion. Its untaxed profits may average as much as $600,000 per hour. In one city alone high officials of this criminal organization are said to exert control over more than eighty major businesses, with total assets of more than $500 million. Organized crime is a national power; it operates with impunity, free of any constitutional restraints. It is the fifth estate.[2]

Attempts to Define Organized Crime

Numerous attempts have been made, over more than a century, to define organized crime. In 1890 an Irish widow brought a suit against the Chicago Laundrymen's Association for racketeering activity, in the form of malicious interference with her business. In 1898 the Illinois Supreme Court declared that racketeering activities were illegal.[3] A 1915 Chicago crime commission, investigating racketeering activities in that city, found that well-organized criminal gangs, often in conjunction with legitimate business, were operating not only in Chicago but also in numerous other cities throughout the country. It also found that the activities of these criminal groups were often coordinated with those of criminal gangs in other cities. As early as 1891 Henry Cabot Lodge wrote on the New Orleans Mafia. Walter Lippman, writing in 1931, offered his observations on organized crime.[4] Numerous other scholars, commissions, and law enforcement agencies have offered explanations and definitions for organized crime.

1

Attempts to explain or define organized criminal activity fall into one or more of the following categories: (1) those put forth by law enforcement agencies, (2) those offered by criminologists, (3) those of former syndicate members, and (4) those espoused by economists. Criminologists and economists have been swayed in their interpretations of organized crime by the writings and testimony of law enforcement personnel and former criminals. These last two groups usually provide most of the sources in organized crime studies. This monopoly over data has given law enforcement a preeminent position in the development of policies and strategies regarding organized crime.

Police agencies have made numerous attempt to define organized crime. Perhaps one of the best known came in 1950, when U.S. Senate investigators of the Kefauver Committee uncovered evidence of a national secret criminal cartel known as the Mafia. Television, still in its infancy, enabled the committee to reach more than 20 million Americans. The Mafia, it was said, had its tentacles in dozens of American cities.[5] It controlled the most lucrative rackets of the underworld and had important international contracts. The committee noted that "there are indications of a centralized direction and control of these rackets" and that "leadership appears to be in a group rather than a single individual."[6]

The committee, however, has been criticized. Some have charged that there is no Mafia, that this secret criminal organization is largely a creation of law enforcement.[7] But events have shown that the committee's conclusions have some merit. If the committee is to be criticized, it must be for its attempt to define organized crime in America as a giant monolith, highly centralized and governed by a small ruling body of conspirators. The committee's analysis is in many respects similar to attempts to portray Communism as a giant monolith ruled from the Kremlin by a small group of fanatics. This search for a giant conspiracy, for Byzantine intrigue and centralization, drew attention from other ethnic crime groups. For the next twenty years organized crime and the Mafia were viewed as one and the same. The names of Poles, Germans, Jews, Greeks, and many other ethnic groups disappeared from the annals of organized crime. This attempt to define organized crime as a giant monolith influenced law enforcement's strategy for many years: Destroy the nucleus, law enforcement strategists often said, and you destroy organized crime.

In the early 1960s Governor Nelson Rockefeller of New York sponsored a series of conferences to identify and define organized criminal activity. The Oyster Bay Conferences, as they came to be called, defined organized crime as

the product of self-perpetuating criminal conspiracy to wring exorbitant profits from our society by any means—fair and foul, legal and illegal. . . . It survives on fear and corruption. . . . It is a totalitian organization . . . it imposes rigid discipline on underlings who do the dirty work while the top men . . . are generally insulated from the criminal act.[8]

The conferees described organized crime as a totalitarian system that sought to subvert the established governmental apparatus, using fear to maintain order within and outside its ranks. Its rigid discipline was said to be almost paramilitary.[9]

The conclusions reached by the Oyster Bay conferees were no different from those reached by students of political totalitarian systems. They viewed organized crime as a monolith, quasi-military in structure and discipline and ruled by a small central group of conspirators. Organized crime has been compared to totalitarian groups like the Bolsheviks and Nazis because of their highly centralized structures and their use of force to keep members and opponents in line. However, these groups differ markedly from organized crime in their ideological commitment, which lends them the cohesiveness that enables a small nucleus (the Party) to dominate the larger entity.[10] Organized crime lacks this quasi-religious ideology; it has neither utopian commitment nor revolutionary objectives. Organized crime more closely resembles the feudal bands of the Middle Ages; it is a confederation of criminal groups that come together because of economic and political need. It resembles the groups that existed before the nation-state epoch.

In 1967 the President's Commission on Law Enforcement and Administration of Justice lent further support to the findings of the Kefauver Committee and the Oyster Bay conferees. It concluded that organized crime is a

society that seeks to operate outside the control of the American people and their governments. It involves thousands of criminals, working within structures as complex as those of any large corporation, subject to laws more rigidly enforced than those of legitimate governments. Its actions are not impulsive, but rather the result of intricate conspiracies, carried on over many years and aimed at gaining control over whole fields of activity in order to amass huge profits.[11]

The president's commission portrayed organized crime as an ongoing conspiracy, a highly structured organization having branches in many cities and ruled by a national body called the Commission.[12] Equipped with its own code of behavior, the organization enforces its will not only on its own members but also on an army of auxiliaries. This portrayal of organized crime as a tightly knit conspiratorial group run by a small nucleus of bosses continues to dominate the law enforcement policies and strategies. The strategy is thus simple: imprison the leadership, and organized crime will topple. However, when Lucky Luciano was imprisoned and Vito Genovese forced into exile, the structure did not crumble but continued to operate efficiently and aggressively.

The late J. Edgar Hoover, borrowing heavily from the Valachi hearings, defined organized crime as follows:

> La Cosa Nostra is the largest organization of the criminal underworld in this country, very closely organized and strictly disciplined. They have committed almost every crime under the sun. . . . [La Cosa Nostra] operates on a nationwide basis, with international implications.[13]

Several years later the National Advisory Committee on Criminal Justice Standards and Goals offered its own definition of organized crime, adding little new and reiterating the old theme.

> Organized crime is a type of conspiratorial crime, sometimes involving hierarchical coordination of a number of persons in the planning and execution of illegal acts. . . . Organized crime involves the continuous commitment by key members.[14]

In 1969 federal authorities released the De Cavalcante tapes. These tapes were made when microphones were placed by federal investigators in the headquarters of a New Jersey Mafia figure. Parts of these tapes, released in a federal prosecution, disclosed that a national network of more than a dozen crime groups had been operating for a number of years in several large eastern cities. These groups often coordinated their efforts; they appeared to be well organized and in constant contact with one another. However, the De Cavalcante tapes fall short of supporting an analogy between these criminal groups and the Bolsheviks in czarist Russia.[15]

Criminologists since the eighteenth century have concentrated on crimes committed by the lower classes. Although secret societies are not a modern phenomenon, nineteenth century criminologists were not concerned with the Carbonari (a secret society of Italian nationalists), the Camorra, or the Mafia. Criminal gangs were also known to nineteenth-century American criminologists; yet even American criminologists paid scant attention to them and left their description to journalists. In 1931 the Wickersham Commission noted the need for a comprehensive, national study of organized criminal activity. Several years later the noted criminologist Edward H. Sutherland turned his attention to America's growing national criminal cartel. He saw organized crime as a social parasite that grew in the absence of a strong government. He also viewed it as a criminal grouping that divided labor, established territories, and selected its leadership from within its own ranks. It found unity in common opposition to the established structure of society. Sutherland was influenced by his studies of organized criminal activity in Asia and Southeastern Europe.[16]

Modern criminologists, relying heavily on the data released by law enforcement agencies, have offered their own explanations and definitions for modern organized crime. Some scholars have compared the modern criminal cartel to a corporation; its ruling body has been compared to a corporate board of directors. Like the corporation, it continues to exist despite changes in leadership; it enjoys perpetual existence. Its bosses have been compared to the executives of corporations; like a corporation, it enjoys working relationships with other corporate (criminal) bodies.[17] One criminologist defined the corporate theory of organized crime as follows:

> Like the large legitimate corporations which it resembles, Cosa Nostra has both kinds of positions, making it both a business organization and a government. . . . [It] exists independently of its current personnel, as does any big business or government.[18]

The corporate model, however, has been criticized by those who view organized crime as a social system. This theory views organized crime as the outgrowth of traditional social systems that are less responsive to cultural change. Its organizational structure is viewed as a fluid network of interrelationships based on kinship ties, friendships, and other social bonds. Unlike the stagnant corporate structure, which lacks fluidity, organized crime to this group of criminologists is almost a living organism.[19] Other criminologists are influenced by Marxism; they view organized crime as a component of the class struggle. For them, it is an instrument of the establishment (the employer) to keep the downtrodden classes in line; it is a mechanism for control. For the Marxist criminologist, then, organized crime is essentially an adjunct of the establishment.[20]

Criminals themselves have contributed to our understanding and definitions of organized crime. Joseph Valachi supported law enforcement's explanations and theories of organized crime. Valachi spoke of a national criminal cartel, highly centralized and ruled by a body called the Commission. He told his listeners that this cartel was divided into more than a dozen groups called families. At the head of each family was its ruler or boss; below him were his soldiers. Valachi also explained how these groups recruited their members, resolved their conflicts, and punished their enemies. Vincent Teresa, a former associate of organized crime, has indicated that Valachi's story may have been tailored by law enforcement agencies.[21]

Economists have also offered their own theories of organized crime. Some economists view organized criminal activity as an extension of the illegal trade practices of the robber barons of late nineteenth-century America. They note that it tends to flourish in industries subject to excessive competition and that racketeers make their way into small, unstable, and disorganized sectors of the economy. The criminal brings economic stability through monopolistic tools; competition is curtailed, and economic territiories are assigned to different groups. Organized crime is seen as a conspiracy to destroy economic competition through fear and political corruption. It is viewed as a natural outgrowth of the corrupt economic practices of late nineteenth-century America and as an extension of the robber baron mentality. The racketeer is viewed as heir to these corrupt traditions.[22]

Confederation of Necessity

Organized crime goes by different names. In Chicago it is known as the syndicate or the outfit. In many western states it is called the people; in upstate New York it is the arm. Some police agencies refer to it simply as the confederation. More often it is called the mob.[23] During the course of this book, I will often refer to it as the syndicate or the mob. The Mafia is but a component of this criminal confederation, though it is an important factor within organized crime in America. Given its vast economic resources, powerful political friends, and international contacts, the Mafia can rightly be called the reigning monarch of America's underworld.

Organized crime itself must be viewed as a loose confederation of ethnic and regional crime groups, bound by economic and political necessity. Some of these groups operate within fixed geographical areas. The Dixie Mafia crime groups are understood to operate mainly in the South. The Chicano crime families are more often found in California, Arizona, and other states with significant Chicano communities. The Italian, Jewish, and Irish crime groups are found across the nation. The Mafia groups, as well as the Cuban crime groups, operate internationally. The strength and geographic concentrations of these groups have varied with time and with their changing fortunes. Some have preserved their past identity, while others have taken on new forms and established new alliances.

In many respects organized crime resembles the feudal system of medieval Europe. It is a system of alliances and joint ventures, based in part on kinship ties and in large part on the dictates of necessity. The syndicate is the outgrowth of the economic and political needs of the underworld. No one criminal group can meet all the needs of a diversified illicit market such as that found in continental America. There is a need for a pooling of resources, often dictated by economic and political realities. Alliances and informal understandings guarantee peace. Violence, although becoming less frequent, is dictated by a system of values that has evolved over several generations. America's underworld is an orderly society, a hierarchy based on necessity and power relations. It is sophisticated and atuned to a changing society. Like the four other estates, it justifies its existence and power base through its own system of ethics.

Most studies of organized crime have concentrated on the Mafia and its components. Unfortunately we know little about its working relationships with other groups, such as the Chicano crime families and the gangsters of Balkan extraction. We also know little about how blacks, Chinese, and other ethnic crime groups fit into the mosaic of organized crime. Our knowledge of these other groups is limited; we know even less about their interactions with international criminal groups and still less about their involvement in white-collar crime. In fact, for the last thirty years we have only scratched the surface; much remains to be discovered. A sixteenth-century scientist, when asked by one of his students what made birds fly, replied that he did not know; he only knew that whatever it was, it worked well. The same can be said of organized crime: we know more about what it does than about what it is and how it works.

Notes

1. Francis A.J. Ianni and Elizabeth Reuss-Ianni, *A Family Business* (New York: New American Library, 1973), pp. 1-3.
2. Chamber of Commerce of the United States, *Deskbook on Organized Crime* (Washington, D.C., 1972), pp. 6-7,35.
3. Gus Tyler, *Organized Crime in America: A Book of Readings* (Ann Arbor, Mich.: University of Michigan Press, 1962), pp. 48-50.
4. Henry Cabot Lodge, "The New Orleans Mafia Lynchings," in *Crime Society,* ed. Francis A.J. Ianni and Elizabeth Reuss-Ianni (New York: New American Library, 1976), p. 86; Walter Lippman, "The Underworld as Servant," in *Crime Society,* p. 162.
5. Kefauver Committee, "Official Corruption and Organized Crime," in *Crime Society,* pp. 292-293.
6. President's Commission on Law Enforcement and Administration of Justice, *Task Force Report: Organized Crime* (Washington, D.C.: U.S. Government Printing Office, 1967), p.1.
7. Rufus King, *The Drug Hang-Up* (Springfield, Ill.: Charles C. Thomas, 1972), pp. 113-114.
8. Office of the Counsel to the Governor of New York, *Combatting Organized Crime: A Report of the Oyster Bay New York Conference on Organized Crime* (Albany, N.Y., 1965), p. 19.
9. Donald R. Cressey, *Theft of the Nation* (New York: Harper & Row, 1969), pp. 314-315.
10. Carl J. Friedrich and Zbigniew K. Brzezinski, *Totalitarian Dictatorship and Autocracy* (New York: Frederick A. Praeger, 1966), p. 19.
11. President's Commission on Law Enforcement, *Task Force Report,* p.1.

12. For a discussion of organized crime, see ibid., pp. 6-10.

13. Ianni and Reuss-Ianni, *A Family Business,* p. 5; see also Cressey, *Theft of the Nation,* pp. 20-24; and the President's Commission on Law Enforcement and Administration of Justice, *The Challenge of Crime in a Free Society* (Washington, D.C.: U.S. Government Printing Office, 1967), p. 192.

14. National Advisory Committee on Criminal Justice Standards and Goals, *Report of the Task Force on Organized Crime* (Washington, D.C.: U.S. Government Printing Office, 1976), p. 7.

15. Henry A. Zeiger, *The Jersey Mob* (New York: New American Library, 1975), pp. 1-5.

16. Edwin H. Sutherland, "Organization of Criminals," in *Crime Society,* pp. 5-7.

17. Cressey, *Theft of the Nation,* pp. 110-113.

18. Ibid., p. 110.

19. "What Is Organized Crime," in *Crime Society,* pp. 3, 4; for a review of the history and rise of organized crime in America, see Edward J. Allen, *Merchants of Menace—The Mafia: A Study of Organized Crime* (Springfield, Ill.: Charles C. Thomas, 1962), and Will Oussler, *The Murderers* (New York: Farrar, Strauss and Cudahy, 1961).

20. William J. Chamblis, "Functional and Conflict Theories of Crime," in *Whose Law, What Order,* ed. William J. Chambliss and Milton Mankoff (New York: John Wiley & Sons, 1976), pp. 8-11.

21. Peter Maas, *The Valachi Papers* (New York: Bantam Books, 1969), pp. 101-111; Vincent Teresa, with Thomas C. Renner, *My Life in the Mafia* (Garden City, N.Y.: Doubleday & Co., 1973), p. 322.

22. Walter Lippman, "The Underworld as Servant," in *Crime Society,* p. 165; Thomas C. Schelling, "What Is the Business of Organized Crime," in *Crime Society,* p. 69; Jones M. Buchanan, "A Defense of Organized Crime," in *The Economics of Crime and Punishment,* ed. Simon Rothenberg (Washington, D.C.: American Enterprise Institute for Public Policy Research, 1973), pp. 120-130.

23. Cressey, *Theft of the Nation,* pp. 19-21.

2

The History of Organized Crime

In the Sulu Sea a Panamanian freighter is attacked by armed boats; only with the aid of the Philippine Air Force is her crew able to turn back the attackers. In the Straits of Malacca supercharged speedboats armed with automatic rifles and M-79 grenade launchers attack numerous ships.[1] In both instances well-organized Asian criminal groups have turned to piracy. Philippino authorities arrest more than twenty individuals, said to be members of a criminal syndicate that specializes in gunrunning.[2] In the Golden Triangle of Asia Chinese criminals (with the assistance of a private army of five thousand men) transport opium through the jungles.[3]

Organized criminal endeavors are not merely an American phenomenon. Secret criminal societies are found in every country. Their roots often lie in political opposition to the ruling elites in their countries. Nomadic groups, found today in many parts of Africa and Asia, have historically preyed on their urban neighbors; for them crime is a profession. In many countries the absence of a strong state structure has led groups to take the law into their own hands. However, the mass technology of the twentieth century has provided a new impetus to organized crime. Mass communications enable these groups to maintain contacts with associates in other countries; modern banking facilitates international criminal transactions; and the modern revolution in electronics has given criminal groups access to new tools with which to steal billions of dollars. Our modern era has both armed and enabled the criminal groups in many countries to unite forces and has facilitated their ability to prey on organized society.

Brigands and Criminals in Antiquity

In the fifth century A.D. the Roman Empire was on the brink of its fall; the provinces were under attack by brigands and barbarians alike. Roman nobles surrounded themselves with powerful retainers, private armies known as the buccellarii.[4] Many of these armed groups turned to banditry to supplement their income and allied themselves with neighboring private armies.

The Romans considered the Huns brigands and barbarians. The Huns had no state; they led a nomadic existence and preyed on neighboring peoples. Until the time of Attila, the Huns had no kings and were ruled by tribal chieftains. Banditry was their way of life. Tribal raiding parties often joined forces and raided the Roman Empire. On many occasions the Romans were forced to pay the Huns tribute in return for peace. The Huns were not unified, and after Attila's death they disappeared into history. However, for several centuries, the Huns preyed on their neighbors and lived on their tribute.

The Mongols, like the Huns, were a nomadic people. They held no allegiance to any state, and until the time of Genghis Khan they had no unified state. For most of their early existence, the Mongols lived on tribute from their weaker neighbors, who regarded them as brigands and thieves. Each Mongol owed his allegiance first to his family and second to his clan. Each clan was ruled by a chief, and the clans gathered in a tribal council, which formulated policy and mediated conflicts among the clans. Each clan had its own rituals, and membership was based on blood ties.

Europe, too, had organized bands of criminals. Many of these groups began during the Crusades. Many of the knightly orders, although established for political and religious objectives, soon turned to brigandage and crime. The Knights of Saint John, organized in the eighth century to fight the Moslem armies in the Iberian peninsula, soon turned to pillaging their fellow Christians. The Teutonic Knights, first organized in the twelfth century to fight in the Holy Land, soon turned to conquest in eastern Europe. Although established to fight the heathens, they pillaged Lithuanians and Poles. The Knights, led by a grand master, survived as an order until the nineteenth century.

The Moslem world also gave rise to numerous religious orders that soon turned their attention to economic objectives. One of the better known groups began in the eleventh century when a Berber religious zealot, on the shores of the Niger river, started the movement of the Almoravides. At first a revolutionary Moslem sect, the Almoravides soon spawned factions that turned to brigandage and attacked not only the Christian West but also the Moslem East. In the twelfth century another Moslem religious movement, the Almohades, began. Like the Almoravides, the Almohades had revolutionary ideals of purifying Islam of corruption. As their revolutionary zeal waned, the Almohades turned to economic gain and stole from Moslem and Christian alike.

One of the more secretive Moslem sects was the Ismailis. In 1090 the discontented prophet Hasan Sabbah founded a new sect. Islam at that time was torn by schisms; the Shiate Abbasid Caliphate in power in Persia was at odds with the Fatimid rulers of Egypt. Hasan Sabbah was tired of both and, like many before him, sought to purify Islam. The movement that resulted came to be known as the Ash-sha-shins (or Assassins). Many of its members used hashish, and gave the drug its name. The movement, although revolutionary in its objectives, soon turned to the pursuit of power and wealth.

Assassin suicide squads were used as killers for hire by both Christian and Moslem rulers. King Richard the Lionhearted is said to have employed them to assassinate one of his European enemies. The sect, secret and ruled by a leader known as the Old Man of the Mountain, finally withered in the thirteenth century.

Throughout the Middle Ages numerous criminal groups came and went. Bands of former soldiers turned to banditry and in some cases were joined by landless knights. During the seventeenth century Germany was torn by the Thirty Years' War; the conflict offered a new opportunity for brigands and criminals. The early seventeenth century also saw the rise of the India Companies. The better known of these were the Dutch East and West India companies. Chartered by their respective countries, these companies soon raised private armies and preyed on many of the non-European peoples. Historians often compare them to piratical naval states with their own private armies and leaders, independent of the very countries that chartered them.

Eighteenth- and nineteenth-century Europe was a boiling cauldron of revolutionary groups. Some withered with the attainment of their political objectives, others were suppressed, and still others turned to criminal objectives. One such group was the Carbonari (charcoal burners), an outgrowth of the ideals of the French Revolution and Italian nationalism. The Carbonari were strong in Naples and expanded to other parts of Italy.[5] In 1820 they led a revolt against the king of Naples in an attempt to force constitutional reforms from him. In 1821 the Carbonari led a revolt in northern Italy. Both revolts were soon put down by Austrian and French armies. The Italian revolutionary Mazzini was also responsible for the founding of two revolutionary societies: the Young Italy movement in 1831 and the Young Europe movement in 1834.

Southern Italy, less advanced than the North and ruled by foreigners for most of its history, also had its secret societies. The South, ruled at different times by Carthaginians, Greeks, Romans, Germans, Arabs, Normans, Spaniards, and French, was strongly influenced by Mediterranean culture. Numerous peoples settled in and colonized southern Italy. One of the largest migrations to the South was that of the Albanian tribes. Driven from Albania by the oncoming Ottoman Turkish invasion, Albanian tribesmen at the invitation of the rulers of southern Italy began migrating there in the fifteenth century.[6] Many Albanian immigrants settled in the provinces of Calabria and Sicily. Today they constitute the largest minority in Italy and are known as Arbresheri (Italo-Albanians). A number of Mafia villages in western Sicily were settled by the Arbresheri.[7] These Albanian tribes, coming from a feudal and warlike society, sometimes turned to brigandage. Their full impact on the culture of southern Italy (the mezzogiorno) culture and their role in the formation of secret societies remains to be studied.[8]

The Culture of the Arbresheri

The Albanian tribes that settled in southern Italy brought with them a long history of tribalism and warfare. Their descendants, more than two hundred thousand, still live in Italy's southern villages and maintain a proud and ancient tradition, a tenacious loyalty to family and clan. The Albanian brought with him a disdain for and distrust of organized government, a powerful clannish structure, and the code of the vendetta.

The Albanian came armed with an ancient code of laws; the common law that regulated and shaped the daily life of the Albanian. It was an amalgamation of traditions and customs that had evolved in Albania's mountain villages over several centuries.[9] The Albanian also brought with him a tradition of brigandage and tribal government. Disputes were settled within the tribe by a system of elders; an injury to the tribe, clan, or family was avenged with similar injury. One's word of honor (besa) remains to this day almost sacred. One who gives his word and places his honor on the line is expected to carry through.

The Albanian settling in southern Italy found little opposition to his way of life and culture. Settlements were established in mountainous and isolated areas of Calabria, Sicily, and Lucania, making it difficult for the authorities to exert any control over them. Some of the Albanian clans later assisted Garibaldi. The Albanian adapted easily to his new environment; his culture and his rebellious nature reinforced the elements in the mezzogiorno that gave rise to southern Italy's secret societies. To this day the Arbresheri serves as a key link between the Italian-American and Albanian-American communities in the northeastern United States.

Secret Societies in Southern Italy

The South, unlike the northern areas of Italy, remained feudal and agrarian well into the nineteenth century. There was no centralized state, only a motley of local powerbrokers paying nominal respect to the kings based in Naples. The social fiber was family oriented; one called on one's family and friends for assistance. Government was viewed as alien and hostile, and the nation-state concept, which had taken hold in France and England, had not yet permeated southern Italy. Loyalty was given to one's relatives, friends, and associates rather than to the state. The state was constantly rocked by rebellions, and its authority was at best unstable. Honor and duty to one's family ranked first; offenses were to be repaid in kind. Power was a confirmation of the family's standing in its community. The nineteenth century South was an authoritarian and patriarchal society marked by an almost quasi-religious obsession with the family. It was in this environment that the Mafia and Camorra came into being.

In Calabria, a mountainous and remote province in southern Italy, numerous bandit groups and secret societies arose in the eighteenth and nineteenth centuries, to protect Calabria's culture and traditions. One such group was the Society of Honor (Onorta Societa).[10] The society had its own rituals and secret passwords, and it engaged in extortion and banditry. Whether the society survived into the twentieth century remains a mystery. However, the banditry of the secret societies of the nineteenth century continued well into the twentieth century. Calabria today has a network of Mafia crime families with close ties to their Sicilian counterparts.

In the early nineteenth century a secret criminal brotherhood, which came to be known as the Camorra, appeared in Naples and its surrounding countryside. The Camorra first took shape in the prisons of Naples as a protective society for prisoners.[11] By the mid-nineteenth century it had spread from the prisons into the city and its surroundings. It developed into twelve families or groups, and members of one family were often related to one another. Each family had a boss, and the bosses of the twelve families met on occasion to coordinate strategy and policy. The Camorrist viewed himself as a man of honor. By 1860 it had become fashionable for affluent groups of Neopolitan society to join the Camorra. Attempts by the House of Savoy to destroy the Camorra proved fruitless; its ability to get the vote out, once the franchise was instituted in Italy, ensured it political support. By the turn of the century the Camorra was the de facto government in Naples. Mussolini made several attempts to destroy it. Many Camorrists are said to have come to this country. Those who stayed behind were jailed or killed. Whether the Camorra survived the Fascist regime is still disputed. Certainly the forces that gave rise to it have survived. Criminal groups are still found in Naples, and Neopolitan organized criminals (sometimes referred to as the Neopolitan Mafia) continue to extort money from businessmen and to engage in a lucrative narcotics trade.

The Sicilian Mafia, more than any other secret criminal society, has stirred the imagination of writers and government officials for more than a century. In one year alone the Mafia and its associates were said to have been responsible for more than forty kidnappings in Italy, with more than $15 million in ransom paid by the families of the victims. The problem has become so serious that the late Pope Paul VI denounced the Mafia personally.[12] In Rome Mafia chieftain Basilo Surace was arrested by the authorities and charged with frauds alleged to total $1 million.[13] Surace was alleged to have ties with the Calabrian Mafia and was said to be linked to numerous kidnappings. In Sicily gunmen speeding in stolen cars shot and killed Giuseppe Sirchia, the reputed Mafia chieftain of Palermo, as he was visiting his parole officer.[14] Also killed was his wife, Giacomina. Sirchia had been a lieutenant of the well-known Palermo Mafia chieftain Michele Cavataio, who had himself been assassinated in 1969 by a rival Mafia family.

Sicily's history has been marred by violence and rebellion since the days of ancient Rome. Revolts by slaves were common in conquered Sicily; a herdsman by the name of Cleon led one such revolt in western Sicily. The slave Salvius also led a revolt against Rome. The uprisings were well organized and supported by the local population. The revolts were sparked largely by the antagonism of the local populace to acquisition of large estates by Roman noblemen. The Romans put down the revolts with extreme harshness; in the process more than twenty thousand Sicilians were crucified.[15] A pattern of occupation and rebellion emerged. The Mafia and other secret societies had their roots in this repressive climate.

There can be little doubt that the environment for the rise of the Mafia had its roots in Sicily's ancient past. However, when and how the Mafia came into being is still disputed by many historians. Some maintain that the Mafia had its roots in the ninth century, that it was a secret organization opposed to Arab rule of Sicily. Another view is that the Mafia is the outgrowth of a rebellion in 1282 against the Normans and that the battle cry was "Morte Alla Francia, Italia Anela" (MAFIA).[16] The more popular and accepted view is that the Mafia is an outgrowth of nineteenth-century Sicilian feudalism under the Bourbon kings.[17] It was at first a tool of the landed nobility. Mafia gangs arose from the armed bands of landowners who employed them to keep the peasants down and to keep banditry in check. In the face of a weak government and uprisings by the peasants, the landed nobles turned to armed retainers for assistance. These private armies were the nucleus of the future Mafia families.[18]

By 1860 the Mafia families had come into their own. In return for service the nobles gave them land and political protection. With the unification of the Italian state in 1870, the Mafia rose as a powerbroker; Mafia chieftains could now deliver the vote of peasants to the highest bidder. Attempts by the Italian government to crack down on the Mafia in 1878 failed. The prefect of police, Malusardi, was given power to imprison Mafiosi without any trial. Some Mafia chieftains went underground, others went to America; and those who were politically well connected enjoyed immunity from prosecution. The political instability of the Italian government and later its involvement in World War I weakened government attempts to curtail or destroy the Mafia. This task was left to Mussolini, but his attempts also failed. After the defeat of the Fascist regime, the Mafia reappeared. The Mafia is an outgrowth of Sicilian society and mentality. In many respects it is a way of life whose survival is tied to that of Sicilian society and tradition.

Unlike the Camorra, the Mafia is a loose association of crime families. In the nineteenth century most groups averaged fifteen to twenty members and were headed by a chief (capo). A group of families formed a cosca; several cosche formed a consorteria. The average Mafia family consisted of relatives through birth or marriage and close friends from the same village; thus it was a series of alliances reinforced through marriages. Many of the nineteenth-century Mafia groups operated in the countryside. By the turn of the century some of these groups moved into the cities, especially Palermo. Some of the better-known groups were the Amoroso, Fratellanza, Mala Vita, and Stoppaglieri. Feuds between these groups were common and often led to bloodshed. A code of conduct (the omerta), dictated the conduct of the Mafists. The code called for cooperation between the families in case of need. Absolute obedience to the chief was essential, and an offense against any member of the family was an offense against the entire group. The Mafist was not to appeal to the authorities for assistance, nor was he to reveal the names of those in his group.

The Mafist, however, was not a bandit. He served both a political and economic need; he kept the peasants on the lands. Through force, violence, and reward, the Mafia chieftain ruled the noble's estates as if they were his own. He saw himself as a man of honor engaged in an important and necessary profession. He met with other Mafist chieftains at country fairs, and he made alliances and treaties with neighboring Mafia powerbrokers. Through force, fear, and the respect of the peasants and villagers, he ruled his region like a feudal magnate; in essence he was a powerbroker between the nobles of Palermo and Naples and the peasants who toiled for them. Once the Mafia moved into the urban centers of Sicily, the Mafia families also moved into the lucrative commerce and businesses in those cities. In the post-World War II era, a new generation of Mafiosi made their way into power within the Sicilian Mafia and through increased contacts with their American counterparts gave rise to the new Mafia. The post-World War II Sicilian Mafia shifted its focus from the country to the city. It soon became involved in commercial crimes and national politics. With its American counterparts, it would play a key role in the international narcotics traffic.

In 1961, following a series of assassinations, the Italian Parliament established the Anti-Mafia Commission to study the problem of organized crime in Italy. The commission consisted of thirty-one members of Parliament, among them legislators from all parties. In 1971 it published its report. It concluded that the old Sicilian Mafia had changed into a national, sophisticated crime cartel with international contacts and heavy involvement in the narcotics trade. It also noted that three members of Parliament were connected to this criminal cartel, among them a former cabinet minister. Identified as one of the new Palermitan Mafia chieftains was Angelo Barbera. The Barbera group was said to have adopted the gangster tactics of American racketeers and to have waged a successful war against the more traditional Mafia families. Also identified was the Greco Mafia family, a rival of the Barberas. In addition, the Plaja family was said to have contacts with American racketeers and to have played a dominant role within the Castellammare Mafia network. Another Mafioso with key American contacts was Geraldo Alberti. Salvatore Zizzo was identified as boss of the Trapani Mafia. Gaetano Badalamenti, Calogero Sacco, and Gaetano Accradi were also identified as key Sicilian Mafiosi.

On February 15, 1978, Ignazio Selta, a Palermitan Mafia chieftain, was found shot to death. He and two of his bodyguards were killed while sitting in their automobile. On February 17, John LiVoti, alleged to be an American Mafia figure, turned up in Palermo, Sicily. Italian police suspect that LiVoti attended a meeting of Mafia chieftains in Leganano. The meeting was also to be attended by Girolando Alberti, an alleged Mafia chieftain from Naples.[19] The purpose of the Leganano meeting, authorities suspect, was to mediate the differences between various Mafia families. It also amply documented the close ties between American and Italian Mafia families.[20]

Organized Crime Outside the United States

Just as southern Italy gave rise to the Camorra and the Mafia, Corsica gave rise to the Union Corse (UC). And like southern Italy, Corsica had also been subjugated by foreign rule. The island had been overrun by Carthaginians, Greeks, and Romans. In the ninth century it fell under Arab rule. In the eleventh century it became a papal fiefdom and later fell under Genoese rule. In 1730 a revolt against Italian rule broke out in Corsica. The revolt, led by a Corsican leader named Pasquale Paoli, had the support of Corsica's numerous clans. The Genoese, unable to keep the rebels in check, called on the French in 1736. The French intervened, and in 1768 Corsica was annexed and became part of France.

Foreign rule led the islanders to distrust government and to associate it with outsiders. Thus the Corsicans, like the Sicilians, developed their own institutions. The vendetta, honor, and machismo became part of Corsica's social fiber. As with Sicily, political rebellion led to criminal activity. The UC now consists of some fifteen Corsican crime families. Like the Mafia, it is a confederation motivated by necessity. The crime families have their own territories, chiefs, and power bases. Among the better-known UC crime families are the Francisci, Venturi, Guerini, and Orsini. At the top of the crime family is the boss, followed by a series of lieutenants, and finally the soldiers or "milieu." The UC, like the Mafia, has a code similar to that of the omerta. Honor plays a key role in this code of conduct, and differences between the crime families are usually mediated through arbitration.

The UC has ties on several continents and has been rumored to have close working contacts with the French intelligence community. Many Corsicans during World War II remained loyal to the old republic. In the post-war era they were often employed, as were the Mafia in Sicily, to assassinate communists and socialists. UC crime families in turn developed strong ties to the police and intelligence community. Roger de Louette, convicted in this country in April 1972 for smuggling millions of dollars of narcotics, is said to have been with the French intelligence service (the Service de Documentation Exterieure et de Contre-Espionage) and also tied to the UC. Auguste Ricord, a Paraguayan gangster heavily involved in narcotic trafficking into the United States, is also said to have had ties to the UC crime families. Corsican crime families are assumed to have ties with Asiatic gangsters and to play a significant role in the smuggling of narcotics from Asia into Europe and the United States. UC crime families are said to work closely with American gangsters in international narcotics transactions. In the early 1960s UC gangsters and Mafia chieftains from the United States met in Hong Kong and Ecuador.[21] One of those present may have been Santos Traficante, Jr., the alleged Florida Mafia chieftain. UC crime figures are also said to have close ties with the American Bonanno and Gambino Mafia families.

Like the Sicilian Mafia, the UC survives because of its political contacts. Through bribery and the ability to get the vote out, UC crime families have developed a series of powerful political alliances. One UC chieftain, for example, was an elected official from Corsica; another UC chieftain had ties to one of France's former presidential candidates. The UC labored hard to get their candidate elected, but they failed. UC crime families own extensive real estate holdings in Europe and have investments in casinos in England. UC crime figures have also infiltrated the French labor movement and have proven adept at changing with the political environment. The UC, like the Mafia, is a way of life. Those who join its ranks view themselves as men of honor. It survives because it has learned to be politically useful; it exploits the needs of those in power. Surrounded by legend and secrecy, it operates internationally. Marseille is to the UC as Palermo is to the Mafia.

On the evening of January 22, 1978, Paolo Violi was killed by two assailants in Montreal.[22] Violi listed himself as a businessman with interests in several Montreal pizza shops. In 1974 the Montreal Police Commission named him the head of that city's underworld. His death was connected to a gangland war that had been tearing that city for weeks.

Canadian organized crime, like its American counterpart, is a motley of ethnic groups, among them Italians, French-Canadians, Greeks, Yugoslavs, and the Irish. One of the key crime families is Cotroni, based in Montreal. The Cotroni group is said to work closely with American gangsters, and they are heavily involved in narcotic smuggling operations. Some Cotroni group members have gambling interests in Florida.[23] The Cotroni are also said to have good ties with the Corsican underworld.

The Mediterranean basin has spawned numerous secret societies and armed feudal bands. Much of the turmoil in Lebanon has been caused by these warring feudal factions. Some are motivated by politcal ideology, some by economic incentive. Lebanon, like southern Italy, has been overrun by numerous powers. Loyalty has traditionally been reserved for the family and clan rather than the state. Lebanese and Turkish gangsters have played a key role in the smuggling of narcotics into Europe. Since French is widely spoken in Lebanon, Corsican gangsters have found it easy to make their contacts with the Lebanese underworld. Even some of Lebanon's political groups have been compared to warring gangs in search of booty.[24]

In 221 B.C. China was unified under the Chin dynasty. The Chin rulers were succeeded by the Hans (202 B.C.-220 A.D.). China has had numerous monarchs, some foreign.[25] China has also had a history of barbarian invasions; some of these (the Mongols) even established their own dynasties. In this political climate a series of secret societies took form. Some started with political goals; others had criminal objectives. When Chinese immigrants left their homeland for other Asiatic countries and North America, they brought with them these secret societies. Among these are the tongs and triad groups which are found in American cities and in many parts of Asia where large Chinese communities reside. Historically the tongs have extorted money from businessmen; there are some similarities betwen them and the Sicilian and Corsican criminal groups. The triads, however, tend to control the Asian narcotics trade. These Chinese criminal syndicates, like their Mediterranean counterparts, are centered around family and friends.

Chinese criminal bands operate in a number of Asiatic countries. Some of them have been able to gain control of the opium trade in Burma, Malaysia, and Thailand. In Burma the Ka Kwe Ye (KKY), a Chinese-dominated militia, openly controls the opium trade. The Burmese government, in need of its military support, has tolerated it for many years. Remnants of Chiang Kai-shek's Kuomintang army form the core of organized criminal activity in several Asian countries. On at least one occasion the Thai government was forced to pay the leaders of these bands large sums of money to get them out of the opium trade.[27]

Narcotics rings also operate from a number of Latin American countries. In Ecuador, Peru, and Bolivia well-organized criminal syndicates operate a large network of narcotics-smuggling operations, in some instances with open assistance from corrupt government officials. In Brazil a well-organized criminal network, with large holdings in real estate, operates a lucrative cocaine trade. In Colombia illegal drug trafficking is a multibillion-dollar industry; government officials and gangsters often work together.[28] The Corsican underworld, as well as American gangster groups operating mostly from Florida, provide the needed funds and expertise to their Latin American associates. Drug trafficking is big business for Latin American criminal syndicates; it has even been rumored that Fidel Castro may have substantial investments in this lucrative trade.[29] In Los Angeles the reputed head of a Mexican-based criminal syndicate and several of his associates were convicted of conspiring to distribute more than $10 million of heroin in the United States.[30]

There is no country today without some form of organized criminal activity. Even the Communist nations often complain of criminal rings running black markets in scarce Western goods and currency. In many instances crime has been a way of life for more than a century; it has been a response to a corrupt and inefficient government, sometimes dominated by foreigners. The secret societies of Asia and the Mediterranean proliferated and migrated to the Americas, bringing with them their centuries-old traditions and their foreign connections. These soon took hold in the New World.

America's Criminal Groups

In 1933 President Franklin D. Roosevelt is said to have asked one of the guests at a Tammany Hall banquet to visit him at the White House. The guest was Joseph Bonanno, alleged to be one of the most powerful men in America's crime society. With Carlos Marcello of Louisiana and Santo Trafficante of Florida, Joseph Bonanno is alleged to be a major financial backer of most major narcotics operations in Latin America.[31] In Buffalo the son of a reputed Mafia figure was found shot to death.[32] In Miami police fished the body of John Rosselli out of the ocean.[33] Rosselli, a long-time member of the Mafia, was assassinated after testifying before a U.S. Senate committee. His murder is said to have been approved by the National Crime Commission itself.

The American Mafia has its roots in Sicily. Sicilian criminal gangs known as Black Hand societies were common in many eastern cities at the turn of the century. Twenty-four Mafia crime groups are said to constitute the core of organized crime in the United States. These twenty-four groups are believed to operate out of large urban centers predominantly in Florida, Illinois, New York, New Jersey, Louisiana, and Nevada. Each of these twenty-four crime groups is known as a family; membership is usually restricted to those of Italian extraction. The size of each family varies from as few as twenty members to as many as a thousand. Each family is headed by a boss; he in turn is served by an underboss and a counselor (consiglieri). The underboss, in the absence of the boss, takes command of the family; he insulates the boss from the lower echelons of the family and relays orders and instructions to family members. The counselor serves as an adviser to the boss and underboss; he is usually an older and well-respected member of his crime family.[34]

Below the underboss are the lieutenants (caporegime). They further insulate the boss from the lower echelons of the family and carry out the instructions of the underboss. Each family lieutenant has charge of a unit of soldiers. Some lieutenants are assigned specific roles in addition to the usual ones common to all lieutenants. Each lieutenant has responsibility for his unit, and all commands, information, and complaints flow through him. The lieutenant is usually served by one or two soldiers who function as assistants.[35] They usually help the lieutenant direct, control, and relay orders to the soldiers within the unit. The soldiers constitute the lowest level within the crime family. Soldiers usually operate their own illicit ventures. Partnerships between soldiers within the same family are common, as are joint ventures between a soldier and his lieutenant. Beneath the soldiers is a large army of associates and agents of the family.

The ruling body of this confederation of twenty-four crime families is the Commission. It combines judicial, executive, and legislative functions.[36] On the Commission sit the heads of the most powerful families (the numbers vary from nine to twelve men). The interests of the other families are usually represented on the Commission by one or more of the sitting bosses. The Commission has traditionally been dominated by New York's five crime families and those of Detroit, Chicago, and Philadelphia. Until the death of Carlo Gambino, his crime family was reputed to be the strongest of the five New York families. The Gambino group was first headed by Philip and Vincent Mangano. In 1951 Albert Anastasia assumed control of the group after he ordered the assassination of Philip Mangano. Vincent Mangano disappeared at about the same time and is presumed dead. Anastasia was killed in October 1957 and was replaced by Carlo Gambino. In 1976, with the death of Gambino, his underboss Aniello Della Croce was understood to have made way for Joseph N. Gallo. Della Croce retired to Florida. It was feared that Gambino's death would spark a war among the crime families. These fears found support when a Long Island man was found at a Kennedy airport parking lot, shot in the head (the sixth victim in a wave of killings).[37]

The well-established Genovese crime family has enjoyed a reputation as one of New York's more powerful criminal groups. Its first boss was Lucky Luciano (Salvatore Luciano), one of the key architects of America's modern criminal cartel. In 1936 Luciano was sentenced to thirty to fifty years on white slavery charges. The following year his underboss Vito Genovese fled to Italy to escape prosecution in the United States. In Italy Genovese quickly made powerful friends and donated $250,000 to the Fascist party; Mussolini awarded him Italy's highest civilian medal. When the Allies invaded Italy, Genovese was finally arrested by an army sergeant, Orange C. Dickey, who was with the Army's Criminal Investigation Division. With Luciano in prison and Genovese in exile, Frank Costello (the prime minister of crime) took the reigns of power. When Genovese finally returned to the United States, the government's witnesses had either disappeared or been assassinated. Peter La Tempa, a key government witness, was poisoned. On June 10, 1946, Genovese was once again a free man; Sergeant Dickey's attempts to bring him to prosecution had failed. Between 1946 and 1957 Genovese wrestled with Costello for control of the Luciano family. Finally, in 1957, Genovese regained control and maintained his leadership until his death in prison in 1969. Gerardo Catena became the family's acting boss while Genovese was in prison. Catena was himself imprisoned in 1970. Power then fell into the hands of Thomas Elboli, who was murdered in 1972. The reigns then fell to Frank Tieri.

Another of the powerful New York-based crime families is the Bonanno group, headed initially by Joseph Bonanno, who in 1964 was deposed by the Commission. Bonanno's underboss, Carmine Galante, had been imprisoned in 1960 for trafficking in heroin; he was released from prison in 1974. Frank Labruzzo inherited Bonanno's mantle, only to be deposed in 1965 by the members of the Commission. Gaspar Di Gregorio's reign was also short-lived; he retired in 1966 after suffering a heart attack. Paul Sciacca's reign came to an end in 1970, when he made for Natale Evola. Evola died in 1973 of natural causes and was followed by Philip Rastelli, his underboss. In 1974 Rastelli stepped down from power after his stepson was killed in gangland style. Power fell to Carmine Galante, who was out of prison on parole.

Two other powerful New York crime groups are the Profaci and Lucchese families. The Profaci group, one of the oldest of the crime families, was first headed by Joseph Profaci, one of the elder statesmen of America's organized crime. Profaci died of natural causes in 1962 and was replaced in 1963 by Joseph Colombo, Sr. The latter's rise to power was assisted by Carlo Gambino, who at the time, was locked in a power struggle with Joseph Bonanno and Joseph Magliocco. Colombo had been approached by Magliocco to assist in the assassination of Gambino, but Colombo soon turned the table on the conspirators and informed Gambino of the assassination plot. When he assumed command, Colombo began an aggressive expansion of illicit activities in labor racketeering, bookmaking, loansharking, and construction. In 1969 Colombo was identified by law enforcement sources as a member of the Commission.

Colombo soon became one of the organized crime's more flamboyant modern chiefs. He was instrumental in organizing the Italian-American Civil Rights League, which lobbied to have the title Cosa Nostra eliminated from government references to organized crime. In 1971, while attending an Italian-American Day rally in Manhattan's Columbus Circle, Colombo was shot by Jerome Johnson, a twenty-four-year old black man. Johnson was killed on the spot, and the shooting of Colombo was soon linked to Joseph Gallo (also known as Crazy Joe). In 1972 Joe Gallo was shot to death while dining with his wife in a Manhattan restaurant. The 1971 shooting incident left Colombo paralyzed; leadership of the family then changed hands. Joseph Yacovelli (Joe Yak) took the reigns of power briefly. Vincent Aloi followed him. In 1973, when Aloi went to prison for perjury, Thomas DiBello took over the leadership of the family. He in turn was replaced by Charles Panarella, who continued to head the Colombo family when Colombo died in 1978.

New York's fifth crime family, the Lucchese group, was first headed by Gaetano Gagliano. Gagliano was another of the founding fathers of organized crime in America, and at his death (of natural causes) in 1953, he was succeeded by his underboss Thomas Lucchese. The latter also died of natural causes, in 1967, and the family's reigns of power fell to Carmine Tramunti. Law enforcement sources have recently speculated that a new crime group may have become New York's sixth family. The group, known as the Purple Gang (not to be confused with Detroit's Purple Gang), is said to have been behind a rash of murders involving important members of organized crime.[38] The Purple Gang is said to have ties to the Genovese family, and to use silencer-equipped .22-caliber pistols for close-range killings. There is wide speculation about the members of this new gang. Some believe that they are killers imported from Italy. Others speculate that they may be Viet Nam War veterans. The Purples are said to be heavily involved in narcotics, and they are referred to as cowboys because of their violent nature.

The Mafia has moved out of its traditional northeastern and midwestern power bases and into the western and southern states. California prosecutors have linked more than two hundred state residents to the traditional organized crime groups.[39] At least twenty killings have been connected to these criminals, and it is said that they are doing more than $6 billion worth of illegal business annually. These organized crime groups have also moved into white-collar crime and have left the more traditional (and riskier) criminal endeavors to the newer and less sophisticated criminal groups (for example, blacks and Latins).[40]

In September 1977 a gangland shooting in San Francisco's Chinatown left five persons dead and fifteen wounded.[41] The bloodshed was the result of a struggle between San Francisco's Chinatown gangs for control of the extortion rackets in Chinese-American neighborhoods. In New York two Chinese-Americans were arrested by narcotics agents in connection with a large heroin deal.[42] One of the two was known to federal agents as the General; the other went by the nickname of Mayor. In Maryland five members of a Chinese-American gang known as the Ghost Shadows were indicted by a grand jury in connection with an attempt to extort money from local merchants.[43] The group was also said to have attempted to extort money from Washington, D.C., merchants.

These examples illustrate that organized criminal groups are widely found within the Chinese-American communities throughout this country.

The view of many in law enforcement that the Chinese-American communities are peaceful has been shattered in the last several years. There has been mounting and visible violence within America's Chinatowns. In large part this violence has been an outgrowth of attempts by the younger Chinese to gain access to the lucrative gambling empires and narcotics trade, long controlled by the Chinese-American tongs.

Like many other ethnic groups, the Chinese found themselves in a hostile environment when they came to this country. The large Chinese migrations of the late nineteenth century gave rise to an anti-Chinese furor in many states. In California attempts were made to exclude the Chinese from testifying against whites in court. The California Supreme Court in 1854, in the case of *People* v. *Hall*, held that the testimony of a Chinese witness against whites was inadmissible in a court of law.[44] It was not until 1873 that Chinese-Americans could testify in a California court against whites. This hostile social and legal structure, which treated Chinese-Americans as outcasts, led to their isolation. The traditions and culture of the Chinese-American reinforced this isolation. By clinging to the ways of old China, the Chinese-American turned his Chinatowns into islands, insulated from American society. Like the Sicilian immigrants, the Chinese turned to their traditional ways and structures. The tongs, part of that tradition, came to play a key role in America's Chinatowns.

Many of the pre-World War II Chinese immigrants came from the province of Kwangtung. With them they brought family ties, business associations, and secret criminal groups known as the tongs. These Kwangtung immigrants came from a rural and primitive environment; many were illiterate and had traditionally paid tribute to the criminal tong groups. Like the Sicilian Mafia, the tongs extorted tribute; they constituted an invisible government. In a China torn by revolt and turmoil, the tongs provided the only semblance of law and order in many provinces. Both oppressed and oppressor turned to them for assistance. In periods of weaknesses even the government called on them to put down dissent. The tongs, the traditional ways of rural China, and a distrust for government all accompanied the Chinese immigrants to America.

Today tong groups are found in the many Chinatowns of America. The tongs of New York's Chinese community are said to control a gambling empire with an income that approaches $100 million a year. In San Francisco raids by undercover policemen in three gambling dens alone netted more than $50,000. The tongs control their vast gambling empires through the growing number of Chinese youth gangs. These gangs act as enforcers and in return receive payments and are allowed to share in the underworld activities of the tongs. In New York's Chinese communities gambling establishments are said to pay the tongs $30,000 per week per gambling house as tribute for allowing their operations. The youth gangs receive an average of $800 per week per gambling house for services to the tongs. These services take the form of protection and enforcement.

Gambling, prostitution, and narcotics are well-organized rackets in New York's Chinatown under the control of the local tongs. To ensure that others do not infringe on their operations, the tongs employ well-organized youth gangs as enforcers. The gangs enjoy a reputation for violence and have been involved in a number of killings. Among the better-known groups are the Ghost Shadows, the White Eagles, and the Flying Dragons. The San Francisco tongs are said to employ the Wah Ching gang, the Joe Boys, and the Golden Dragons. The gangs often quarrel among themselves, and the tongs play one against another whenever one of the gangs becomes too powerful. The gangs are also allowed to extort money from store owners in a tong's territory. For example, in some cities, these payments average between $50 and $500 per month.

The tongs are also said to be heavily involved in the smuggling of narcotics. Since the Chinese are a close-knit society, with family ties in numerous Asian countries, the tongs can call on their associates in Asia for assistance in the importation of narcotics. The triads, mob-style drug rings found in a number of Asian cities including Hong Kong, control much of the Asian narcotics traffic. Their roots are deep in China's history. Neither the Imperial governments of China nor present Asian law enforcement agencies have been able to eliminate the triads. The tongs and triads are also said to have the silent backing of the Nationalist Chinese government in Taiwan which, in an attempt to curtail the influence of its Communist rivals on the Chinese mainland, is said to have entered into alliances of political convenience with the tongs and triad groups.

Many of the same forces that propelled the Chinese and Sicilians into crime also gave rise to what have come to be known as the Chicano Mafia families. Although these groups had their beginnings in California's prisons in the 1950s, they did not come to the notice of law enforcement until the early 1970s. Like the Camorra, the Chicano Mafia families were first established as self-protection groups within California's prisons, where they assumed their structures and developed their code of behavior. They have since expanded beyond the prison and now control a lucrative trade in drugs in the California area. Some of these gangs have also expanded their operations to Arizona. Prisoners in that state have complained to the authorities of attempts by the Chicano Mafia families to extort payments from them and their relatives.

The two key Chicano crime groups are the Nuestra Familia (NF) and the EME. The NF is composed mostly of rural Chicanos from California's central valley. The EME, its archrival, draws its membership mostly from the urban Chicano neighborhoods of East Los Angeles. In 1975 and 1976 open warfare between these Chicano crime groups left more than one hundred persons dead in California alone.

These Chicano crime groups average between twenty and one hundred family members. Like the Sicilian Mafia families, they usually recruit from a large pool of relatives and friends. Unlike the Mafia, however, their power base had its beginnings in the prisons. In this respect they bear greater similarity to the Neopolitan Camorra. At the head of the family is the boss, known as the general. Below him is the underboss, known as the captain, followed by the lieutenants and finally the soldiers. The family also has associates who, although not family members, work with family soldiers in a number of illicit ventures.

The NF and EME have chapters in a number of California cities. They have traditionally been involved in the narcotics trade, but they have now expanded their operations into white-collar crime. The multibillion-dollar federal welfare and drug rehabilitation programs have become prime targets of the Chicano Mafia groups. Halfway houses and prepaid health programs have been forced to pay protection money to NF and EME members. These gangs have also developed a lucrative black market in methadone. It has been suggested that some high EME officers have links to the American Mafia.

California's prisons also gave rise, in the early 1960s, to the Aryan Brotherhood (AB), originally formed as a self-protection society. The AB soon spread to prisons in other states and inevitably outside the prison walls. The AB is said to be a rival of the NF and EME in a number of illicit drug operations in California and Arizona. AB members have also resorted to extortion. The Arizona State House Committee was told by more than a dozen witnesses that AB members forced fellow inmates to make protection payments averaging hundreds of dollars each and that those who refused sometimes met violent ends.[45] In one Arizona prison more than eight inmates were killed and fifteen wounded in an eleven-month period.[46]

In the 1950s elusive groups of criminals known as the Dixie Mafia arose. The Dixie Mafia is said to be a loose confederation of traveling groups of criminals operating in seventeen states. Each traveling group has its own leader, and there are groups operating in both urban and rural settings. The rural groups are said to be somewhat backward and not as well organized as their urban counterparts. As many as twelve of these groups may operate in one state at any one time, and in some states more than 50 percent of organized criminal activities are an outgrowth of the Dixie Mafia's involvement. These criminal groups often concentrate on hijacking trucks, fencing, prostitution, gambling, and narcotics. Dixie Mafia groups are also said to be involved in arson schemes, pornography, and contract murders.[47] In growing number, they have begun to infiltrate white-collar crime. The groups have also invested in legitimate fronts such as nightclubs and restaurants. Their corruption and bribery of local law enforcement officials assures them immunity from prosecution.

Blacks, Cubans, Balkans, and numbers of other ethnic groups have also played a sizable role in organized criminal activity.[48] Black crime groups, some patterned after the Sicilian Mafia families, have been identified in Detroit and New York. Cuban criminals have been operating from Florida, New York, and New Jersey. The Cuban crime groups are also said to play a key role, because of their Latin American connections, in the illicit multibillion-dollar cocaine trade. Many of the Cuban groups, trained in the 1960s by the Central Intelligence Agency to subvert Castro's Cuba, have now turned from politics to racketeering. Gypsy groups are also said to be involved in organized crimes, especially those of a commercial nature.[49] Balkans are also making their way into many of the lucrative gambling operations of the New York and New Jersey areas. The tight family structure and the importance of kinship ties make these groups somewhat similar to the Italian-American ones. Their similar cultural backgrounds and value systems have led them to form alliances with Italian-American crime groups in the areas of gambling.

Organized crime is an international as well as domestic problem. Criminal groups have taken on numerous forms throughout history. The pirates of the Barbary Coast have given way to the modern cargo hijackers. The smuggling of tobacco and spices has given way to the smuggling of narcotics and other contrabands. Criminal groups have demonstrated an uncanny ability to survive and adapt to a changing environment. Modern technology has armed these groups with awesome powers, yet law enforcement has failed to keep abreast. In this country, save for the Italian-American crime groups, few other ethnic crime groups have come under close scrutiny. We know little of the Balkan groups, the Gypsies, or the Cubans. To deal effectively with this confederation of crime, we must better understand its components and their working relationships. Further studies are needed to determine the role of other ethnic crime groups within organized crime.

Notes

1. "The Jolly Roger Still Flies," *Time*, July 31, 1978, p. 35.

2. "Gunrunning in the Philippines," *Washington Post*, June 13, 1978, p. A-22.

3. "Victory over Opium," *Time*, July 30, 1973, p. 33.

4. Otto J. Maenchen-Helfen, *The World of the Huns* (Berkeley, Calif.: University of California Press, 1973), p. 475.

5. William L. Langer, ed., *An Encyclopedia of World History* (Boston: Houghton Mifflin Company, 1952), pp. 650-651.

6. George N. Nasse, *The Italo-Albanian Villages of Southern Italy* (Washington, D.C.: National Academy of Sciences, 1964), pp. 1-3.

7. Anton Blok, *The Mafia of a Sicilian Village: 1860-1960* (New York: Harper & Row, 1975), p. 30.

8. *Francis A.J. Ianni and Elizabeth Reuss-Ianni, A Family Business* (New York: New American Library, 1973), p. 18.

9. Stavro Skendi, *The Albanian National Awakening: 1878-1912* (Princeton, N.J.: Princeton University Press, 1967), p. 15.

10. Ianni and Reuss-Ianni, *A Family Business*, p. 24.

11. Ibid., p. 25.

12. Joseph Fried, "Pope Assails Mafia in New Year Message," *Daily News*, January 2, 1975, p. 6.

13. "Italian Police Arrest Mafia Suspect," *Washington Post*, May 27, 1976, p. A-15.

14. "Godfather Slain at Sicilian Jail," *Washington Post*, May 24, 1978, p. A-30.

15. S.G.F. Brandon, ed., *Ancient Empires* (New York: Newsweek Books, 1973), pp. 115, 116.

16. Gus Tyler, *Organized Crime in America* (Ann Arbor, Mich.: University of Michigan Press, 1962), p. 28.

17. Blok, *The Mafia,* pp. 1-5, 17; also see Ianni and Reuss-Ianni, *A Family Business*, pp. 30-36.

18. Tyler, *Organized Crime in America*, p. 348.

19. Jack Anderson, "Sicilian Mafia-U.S. Crime Link," *Washington Post*, April 19, 1978, p. B-11.

20. Based on author's interviews with various law enforcement sources.

21. Jack Anderson and Les Whitten, "Opium Policy: Apathy to Threats," *Washington Post*, July 23, 1975, p. E-15; see also Dieter Hentrup, "The Drug War Revisited," *Atlas World Press Review*, September 1978, p. 55.

22. "Montreal Gangland Figure Slain," *Washington Post*, January 23, 1978, p. A-4.

23. Florida, Organized Crime Control Council, *1976 Annual Report* (Tallahassee, Fla., 1977), pp. 2-10, 2-11.

24. William Branigin, "Slayings Plunge Lebanon into Worsening Crisis," *Washington Post*, June 15, 1978, p. A-25.

25. Dun J. Li, *The Ageless Chinese* (New York: Charles Scribner's Sons, 1965), pp. 556-563.

26. U.S., State Department, Cabinet Committee on International Narcotics Control, *World Opium Survey* (Washington, D.C., 1972), p. 30.

27. "Victory over Opium," pp. 33-34.

28. "Drug Trafficking Indictment of Torrijos Brother Cited," *Washington Post,* February 17, 1978, p. A-4.

29. "Cuban Figure Arrested," *Washington Post*, March 7, 1978, p. A-5.

30. The ring, allegedly headed by one Jose Valenzuela, is said to have had close ties with Latin criminals in the New York area and is reputed to have done more than $1 million in business in a two-day period.

31. Michael Satchell, "Mafia Figure Joe Bonanno: My Conscience Is Clear," *Parade,* February 12, 1978, pp. 4, 5.

32. The deceased was Albert M. Billiteri, twenty-three-year-old son of Albert Billiteri, who was serving a prison sentence in Lewisburg, Pennsylvania, at the time of his son's death.

33. Nicholas Gage, "The Story of John Rosselli's Rise and Fall within the Mafia," *Washington Star*, February 25, 1977, p. A-4.

34. President's Commission on Law Enforcement and Administration of Justice, *Task Force Report: Organized Crime* (Washington, D.C.: U.S. Government Printing Office, 1967), pp. 6, 7.

35. Ibid., p. 8.

36. Ibid., p. 8.

37. "Mob War Feared," *Washington Post*, March 26, 1978, p. B-8.

38. Jack Anderson and Les Whitten, ".22 Pistols Used in Gang Slayings," *Washington Post*, December 6, 1977, p. B-15.

39. "Organized Crime in California," *Washington Post*, May 3, 1978, p. A-13.

40. Gus Tyler, "Sociodynamics of Organized Crime," in *The Crime Society*, ed. Francis A.J. Ianni and Elizabeth Reuss-Ianni (New York: New American Library, 1976), p. 127.

41. "Chinatown Arrest," *Washington Post*, March 26, 1978, p. B-8.

42. "Search and Destroy War on Drugs," *Time*, September 4, 1972, p. 22.

43. Barbara J. Katz, "Five Men Are Indicted in Chinese Restaurant Extortion Attempt," *Washington Post*, December 29, 1977, p. C-1.

44. 4 Cal. Rep. 399 (1854).

45. "Arizona Probes Prisons," *Washington Post*, April 29, 1978, p. A-5.

46. "Hooded Witnesses," *Washington Post*, January 13, 1978, p. E-1.

47. National Advisory Committee on Criminal Justice Standards and Goals, *Report of the Task Force on Organized Crime* (Washington, D.C.: U.S. Government Printing Office, 1976), p. 11.

48. "Black Mafia," *Newsweek*, June 17, 1974, p. 98.

49. Peter Maas, *King of the Gypsies* (New York: Bantam Books, 1975), pp. 47-93.

3 Organized Crime in America

Federal investigators have uncovered evidence that some of the largest casinos in Las Vegas, with gambling holdings in the billions of dollars, may be owned by members of the Chicago underworld.[1] A statewide investigation in Michigan has led to the filing of charges against dozens of law enforcement officials, labor leaders, and politicians.[2] In a quiet New York City nightclub two underworld assassins shot and killed two patrons, one of whom had been marked for death by New York's underworld.[3] A wide-ranging investigation of one of this nation's largest pornography publishing firms has led law enforcement officials to conclude that the company may have been funded by vending machine companies owned by the syndicate.[4]

These examples illustrate the growing power of organized crime in America. This economic and political power base has grown over a period of many years; it is the product of a long and bloody evolutionary process. The growth of organized crime in this country was made possible, in large part, by the fragmented political structure of the United States and by the technological and historical forces that formed modern America. The historical turmoil of our cities, the corruption of local political machines, and a legacy of corporate violence and illegal competitive practices all served as models for organized crime. America's modern syndicate is an outgrowth of these forces. It is the old fused with the new.

Early History of Organized Crime

Americans by tradition and history tend to look on the criminal as a modern Robin Hood. Such a romanticized fantasy is ingrained in the minds of many citizens. In the colonial period it was common practice to obtain land grants by bribing legislators.[5] During the early eighteenth century Pennsylvania lands were illegally occupied by bands of Scotch-Irish settlers. French settlers and trappers set up the first illegal distilleries in what is now Chicago. America's urban centers slowly witnessed the rise of organized criminal activity. Though England had Moll Cutpurse (1584-1659) and Jonathan Wild (1683-1725), New York had Rosanna Peers and her Forty Thieves.[6] Rosanna's vegetable market in the early 1820s became the center of activity for Edward Coleman's gang (the Forty Thieves), which engaged in robbery, murder, and theft. Rosanna's place also gave rise to a second gang, the Kerryonians, which recruited many of its members from New York's Irish community, most of whom had been born in County Kerry.

The Irish immigrants came to this country in droves and settled in New York's poorer and crowded neighborhoods. The Five Points area (Lower East Side) of New York became an Irish neighborhood within a short period of time. For the next century the Irish gangs preyed on and terrorized New York's citizens. Some of the better-known ones were the Bowery B'hoys, Roach Guards, Patsy Conroys, Shirt Tails, Atlantic Guards, Daybreak Boys, Hookers, Swamp Angels, and Buckoos. Tammany Hall, especially under Tom Foley, began to employ the gangs to get the vote out. In return Tammany Hall provided the gangs with political protection. The nineteenth century also saw the rise of gangsters such as New York's Butcher Bill Poole and Lew Baker. In 1855 Baker shot Poole in a gang-related quarrel. New York's gangs enjoyed national notoriety thoughout the nineteenth century and were imitated in many cities.

In the middle of the nineteenth century Chicago was a prairie town, a trading post where cowboys, Indians, and traders conducted business. One of the first brothels in the city was owned by the superintendent of police. Organized crime soon made its way into this prairie town. Michael Cassius McDonald more than any one else played a key role in organizing Chicago's criminals. McDonald was a notorious gambler who, from the end of the Civil War until the turn of the century, built a powerful criminal base from which he expanded his power into local Chicago politics. His gambling casino, known as the Store, became the unofficial city hall. With the aid of the Hankins brothers and Hal Varnell (the Prince), he established the city's first well-organized criminal syndicate. When the local city Democrats became troublesome, McDonald organized his own party, Mike's Democrats.

McDonald never saw himself as a criminal, however; he saw himself as a businessman. In those years, with the robber barons pillaging the cities and countryside, perhaps he was right. McDonald later purchased the *Chicago Globe* newspaper and used it to strengthen his power base. By the end of the nineteenth century McDonald and his associates had become Chicago's most respected citizens. Over a period of more than thirty years he had managed to legitimize his ill-gotten gains. By the time that Al Capone came on the scene, McDonald's heirs were respectable citizens of Chicago.

The West also had its criminals. San Francisco became a haven for numerous criminal groups. Among San Francisco's early gangs were the Hounds, organized during the post-Mexican War period. The Hounds engaged in extortion and murder and were often employed by the local politicians to get the vote out. Nonwhites, primarily the growing Chinese community, were often the targets of this violence. When the Hounds began to turn on the business and political establishment that so often protected them from prosecution, they met swift justice. The Hounds were either jailed or forced to leave town. Two other San Francisco gangs that were often feared and came to play a key role in that city's underworld were the Hoodlums and the Sydney Ducks. Like the New York gangs, San Francisco's underworld was often employed by the local political machine to get the vote out and scare the opposition. In return they were allowed to share the spoils of the system.

Rural America also had a history of violence and gangs. The Johnson County (Wyoming) War attracted the interest of the public and law enforcement. Cattlemen's associations hired private armies to battle their business competitors, often small cattle ranchers. While the press gave daily accounts of these wars, law enforcement sat idly by, unable to intervene. The James brothers also made headlines. Their exploits became legendary. The late Carl Sandburg compared Jesse James to Robin Hood. James's stature as a folk hero was based largely on the rob-the-rich notion.[7] His train robberies, in Iowa in July 1873 and in Missouri in January 1874 won him national attention.

During the nineteenth century the robber barons, the princes of industry and commerce, arose. The fortunes of the Four Hundred were built by illegal means.[8] Extortion, blackmail, and the use of large private armies were as common to the robber barons as they were to the city political machines, who often used local gangs. Wealth became an end in itself; its acquisition was all-important. Violence found sufficient justification in this environment. The state, too fragmented to interfere, was often employed in the machinations of these men of power. This environment later proved fertile ground for America's fifth estate, organized crime. The growth of America's gangs into a national crime cartel came as no surprise to either law enforcement or the public.

Rise of the Modern Syndicate

After the Civil War the southern Italians and eastern Europeans came to America's eastern cities, and with them came the secret criminal societies and traditions that laid some of the groundwork for the present criminal syndicate. In the 1890s Sicilian criminals began to infiltrate New York's waterfront.[9] About this same time, elements of the Sicilian Mafia made inroads in New Orleans. On October 15, 1890, David Hennessey, chief of police for New Orleans, was assassinated. Before his death he had warned that a criminal organization known as the Mafia was attempting to organize America's underworld into a national criminal confederation.[10] A New Orlean's grand jury investigating Hennessey's murder concluded that ''[the] range of our research has developed the existence of the secret organization styled Mafia.'' Black Hand extortion rackets sprang up in numerous eastern cities; the victim was often contacted through the mails:

> You will be so good as to send me $2,000 if your life is dear to you. . . . I beg you warmly to put them on your door within four days. . . . If not, I swear this week's time not even the dust of your family will exist. . . . With regards.

By 1900 Germans, Poles, Jews, and Levantines had joined the ranks of the underworld. New York, Chicago, Detroit, Cleveland, New Orleans, St. Louis, and Tampa had become centers of organized criminal activity. The gangs engaged mostly in illegal gambling activities, prostitution, protection rackets, and vote fixing. The gangs were still the servants of the local political machines, but this relationship changed with Prohibition, when gangsters amassed large fortunes. After Prohibition the political centrifugal forces placed Washington, D.C., on the center of the national stage. With the New Deal came a growing shift toward the national political arena, leaving the cities and their political machines to the gangsters. The political fundraisers now concentrated on Washington.[11] Local politicians turned to the new millionaires for financial assistance for their elections.

In the early 1900s a young, unknown thug by the name of Johnny Torrio became the head of New York's Five Points gang. The gang was made up mostly of young men of numerous ethnic backgrounds. The gang engaged in robberies and extortion, and they assisted the local Lower East Side political machine in getting out the vote. The underworld was still fragmented; there was no national criminal cartel. The Five Pointers often worked jointly with the other gangs in the city. One other group was that of Frank Uale (also known as Frank Yale), a Sicilian thug who operated from Brooklyn. Johnny Torrio was a Neopolitan, like his future partner Alphonse Capone. Both Capone and Charles (Lucky) Luciano (whose Italian name was Salvatore Luciana) later joined the Five Pointers. Capone was born in New York City in 1899. He joined Torrio in 1919 in Chicago and turned that city into one of America's crime capitals. Luciano was born near Palermo in 1897 and was destined to play a key role in the history of organized crime in America.

Two key crime figures in Chicago also arose in the early 1900s. One was Maurice Enright, who developed labor racketeering into an art; the other was Sunny Jim Cosmano, boss of the Chicago Black Hand. Chicago's gangs, like those of New York, were engaged in illegal gambling activities as well as prostitution, extortion, and election fixing. Cosmano and Enright were sooned joined by (Big) Jim Colosimo, who rose from janitor to become one of the city's biggest brothel operators. In 1902 Colosimo married the owner of a large city brothel. He also befriended Michael Kenna and John Coughlin, two Chicago aldermen who enjoyed a citywide reputation for corruption.

In 1907 a small group of Italian-Americans founded the White Hand Society to counter the growing influence of the Black Hand. The attempt proved a dismal failure. About the same time the Sicilian community of New York founded the Unione Siciliana; branches were soon established in a number of other cities, including Chicago. The Unione Siciliana in Chicago alone had more than thirty thousand members. The society soon fell under the control of the criminal elements within the Italian-American community.

Jim Colosimo, under growing threats from Cosmano's Black Hand group, called on his nephew Johnny Torrio. Torrio left New York's Five Points Gang and joined his uncle in Chicago. With him he brought valuable New York criminal contacts and a cunning intellect. Within a short time gang wars erupted between the Colosimo and Cosmano groups. Three Black Handers were killed, and Cosmano was seriously wounded. Although Cosmano survived, the balance of power shifted to the Colosimo-Torrio group. By 1911 Chicago's gangs had begun to take shape. There were the Irish gangs, headed by men like George (Bugs) Moran, William O'Donnell, and Frankie Lake (who controlled one of the oldest groups), and a motley of other gangs such as those of Hymie Weiss, Joe Moresco, Frank McErlane, Ed O'Donnell, and Joey D'Andrea.

In New York the growing problem of gang warfare led to attempts by citizens to curb it. The Society for the Suppression of Crime was formed at the turn of the century, but like the White Hand Society, it soon fell into oblivion. In New York Arnold Rothstein (the Prince of Broadway, as the press referred to him) had laid the groundwork for the modern syndicate. Rothstein was at first heavily involved in gambling and loanshark operations; once the Harrison Anti-Narcotic Act was passed, he expanded into narcotics smuggling. Rothstein, born in 1883 to an affluent New York family, knew the value of powerful political contacts. In 1902 he befriended (Big) Tim Sullivan, the head of New York's Tammany Hall. In 1909 Rothstein married a young actress and opened a gambling house with Willie Shea, a former ward leader. Rothstein later provided Luciano and other young criminal chieftains with a blueprint for growth. Whereas Cosmano and the other gang bosses were happy to be left to their old ways, Rothstein provided the younger criminals with a blueprint for a national criminal cartel. But Luciano and the other future notables of crime were still minor members of the underworld. Alphonse Capone, a future czar of the underworld, was a bartender-bouncer in New York. Paolo Antonini Viccarelli had replaced Torrio as chieftain of the Five Pointers. Ciro Terranova controlled many of the Brooklyn rackets. John Lupo (the Wolf) was still a powerful Black Hand boss. And Frank Uale had become president of the Unione Siciliana. The picture was not radically different in other cities in 1920, when Congress enacted the Volstead Act and thus opened the Prohibition era.

Gangland and Prohibition

The turning point in the history of organized crime in the United States came with the passage of the Volstead Act in 1920. With Prohibition a new criminal society was born. Before 1920 America's underworld consisted of a motley of criminal groups, competing with one another and killing each other's members. The pre-Prohibition era can be compared to the Dark Ages. It was a period of numerous warring gangs, each parochial in its perception of its role. The underworld was highly fragmented, torn by ethnic animosities and rivalries over territories. Prohibition required the underworld to supply a national market and deliver large supplies of liquor to hundreds of thousands of speakeasies. In 1920 New York City had more than twenty thousand such establishments. The criminal had to become a businessman. He needed accountants, managers, business counselors, and lawyers. This multibillion-dollar industry also called for peace and diplomacy. The conflicts of the past had to be resolved through nonviolent means. Although still far from a national organization, the underworld was becoming more sophisticated.

Chicago and the other eastern cities were far from peaceful in 1920. Prohibition at first increased the violence of the past. Territories were ill-defined, and no one criminal group was able to impose its will on the others. The Italian-American gangsters were still subservient to the Irish and Jewish criminal groups. New York City's Dutch Schultz (born Arthur Flegenheimer) still reigned as undisputed lord of the Bronx. By the 1930s Schultz had taken over the black-run Harlem numbers operation. He was also heavily involved in bootlegging, and he specialized in restaurant protection rackets. Schultz was also said to have played a role in the murders of Arnold Rothstein and Eddie (Legs) Diamond, a New York City racketeer and bootlegger killed in 1934.

In the early 1920s a new wave of violence erupted. The beer wars began. In Chicago the Black Hand's chieftain had labor racketeer Mossy Enright murdered. Torrio and Capone, eager to take control of Colosimo's underworld empire, had him assassinated. The Torrio-Capone group allied itself to the Druggan-Lake gang and began dividing territories among themselves. The Genna brothers (Angelo, Michael, Tony, Sam, Peter, and Jim), also known as the Terrible Gennas, began to carve out their own territory in Chicago. Within several years the Gennas were able to develop a multimillion-dollar empire involving thousands of tenement distilleries. Their expansion brought them into open warfare with the Torrio-Capone syndicate. The Gennas, known for their violence, soon fell into open conflict with the Irish group led by Dion O'Bannion.

Organized crime was taking shape in other cities as well. In Cleveland Alfred (Big Al) Polizzi, a tough Sicilian gangster, had gained control over most of that city's bootlegging operations. Cleveland's Italian and Jewish gangsters had also developed a close working relationship; the ethnic animosities of the past were giving way. In Detroit Peter Licavoli was establishing a powerful foothold in illegal gambling and rum smuggling. In the state of New York criminal notables were proliferating. Stefano Magaddino was establishing a powerful base in the Buffalo area; Frank Labruzzo, Vito Genovese, Joseph Profaci, and Frank Garofalo were active in New York City. Labruzzo later became a brother-in-law of Joseph Bonanno. Joseph Masseria and Salvatore Maranzano had become powers within the city's Italian-American underworld, and Lucky Luciano had built close ties to Meyer Lansky, Louis (Lepke) Buchalter, and Jake (Gurrah) Shapiro. These Jewish racketeers later proved valuable to Luciano's bid for power. Joe Lupo, long powerful in Black Hand rackets, in 1925, received a twenty-five-year prison sentence, thus departing from the crime scene.

Mayor Bill Thompson, long a favorite of Chicago's underworld, made a bid for the presidency in 1927. With gangland support his protege Len Small had been elected governor of Illinois. While Thompson ran for president, Chicago witnessed the bloody War of the Sicilian Succession, a battle between the Capone group and the Genna brothers for control of Chicago's Unione Siciliana. The struggle took on national dimensions, as gangs from around the country sent in their assassins to assist one or the other of the warring groups. The Capone group, although victorious, was forced to move its headquarters to Cicero from where it rules to this day. Among the top Capone officers were Frank Nitti, Tony Accardo, Fellice de Lucia, James de Mora, and Sam Giancana. This group continued to rule Chicago's underworld long after the imprisonment and death of Capone. The 1920s were a turbulent era for organized crime. They were also formative years.

In January 1928 Herbert Hoover, the newly elected president, began his administration by instructing Secretary of the Treasury Andrew Mellon to find a way to put Capone in prison. Capone, with an annual income in the millions, was a silent partner in a number of corporations and even banks. Capone was also an enemy of Frank Uale, who was then president of the Unione Siciliana. The Unione, with chapters in cities throughout the country, had become an important political and economic vehicle. Uale was assassinated on a street in New York, and Johnny Torrio replaced him as president of the Unione Siciliana. The election of Torrio to this powerful post marked two key developments in the history of organized crime: the coming together of the Chicago and New York crime groups and the beginning of a union between Sicilian and other Italian (primarily Neopolitan) criminal elements. Torrio was not Sicilian; the animosity that had long existed between the Sicilian and the other southern Italian groups was coming to an end. The factionalism that had long prevented a unified approach to national criminal endeavors was now coming to an end. At the same time, Capone was cementing his relations with the Purple gang of Detroit, a group that was tied to New York's criminal underworld. The Purple gang played a key role in smuggling liquor across the Canadian-American boundary. The Purples were not Italians, and Capone's working relationship with them marked a growing alliance between various ethnic crime groups. This alliance was dictated by the needs of a national, multibillion-dollar illicit liquor market.

These forces, in large part set in motion by Prohibition, came to the surface on December 5, 1928, at the Statler Hotel in Cleveland. Sicilian-American gangsters from numerous localities met to discuss and develop joint strategies and to mediate their differences through nonviolent channels. Johnny Torrio, a key architect in organized crime's formative years, had for many years been calling for bosses of the major crime groups to develop and implement a national unified crime policy. The 1928 meeting was small and was restricted mostly to Sicilian-American gangsters, but a more important meeting took place in Atlantic City on May 13-15, 1929. This second meeting was not restricted to Sicilian gangsters. The key architects of this national crime conference were Lucky Luciano and Abner (Longy) Zwillman, a major force in New Jersey's underworld. The Luciano-Zwillman alliance marked a shift from parochialism within the hierarchy of organized crime. Luciano and Zwillman represented the modern mobster. More than twenty crime chieftains were present at the Atlantic City conference; among them were Sam (Swifty) Lazar from Philadelphia, Dutch Schultz from New York, and Capone from Chicago. The conferees formally recognized the geographic power bases of the groups present and declared Miami an open city. Costello and Luciano outlined the need for a national body (the Commission) to mediate differences between crime groups and to help formulate policy.

By the end of 1929 the Masseria-Maranzano conflict, later dubbed the Castellammare War, was beginning, and it did not end until Masseria died in 1931. In early 1930 Masseria declared Peter Morello boss of all Italian crime groups in New York City. Morello had a long history of involvement with Black Hand criminal activities. Although liked and respected within the underworld, the non-Italian gangs as well as the Sicilian Castellammare criminal groups (headed by Salvatore Maranzano) opposed the selection of Morello to head New York's Italian underworld. Many saw this appointment as a ploy by Masseria to control the rackets in New York. The clannish

Castellammare crime groups, with a long history of Mafia involvement in Sicily, were not willing to allow Masseria to rule them that easily.

Masseria aggravated the situation by requesting that all the crime groups, including Maranzano's, pay him tribute. Masseria had the backing of Capone, Luciano, Vito Genovese, Carlo Gambino, Albert Anastasia, and Frank Costello. In Maranzano's ranks were Joe Bonanno, Peter Magaddino, and Stefano Magaddino, who later became Mafia chieftain of Buffalo and expanded his operations into Canada and Ohio. Maranzano also had support from Joseph Profaci, Joseph Magliocco, and Tommy (Three Finger Brown) Lucchese. The warring factions were clearly lined up for the impending conflict. It began violently in March 1930 and ended in April 1931 with the death of Masseria. The war was fought primarily between Italian-American criminal factions, but it also involved other ethnic groups. Dutch Schultz and Meyer Lansky threw their support to Masseria. Masseria appeared to have the upper hand at first, but soon Maranzano was favored. The latter, a literate man, perceived that Masseria's young lieutenants were far from happy with the old "mustache pete"; he was also aware that Masseria's non-Italian allies were not happy with his shabby treatment of them. Maranzano promised these wavering Masseria factions a less parochial crime network, an idea that sat well with their views of a national network of crime groups working together. It represented a new order.

On April 20, 1931, Joe Masseria, while dining in a New York City restaurant, was killed by assassins recruited by Luciano. Soon afterward the war came to an end. Maranzano became boss-of-bosses (*Capo de tuti capi*), and the present crime families began to take shape. Maranzano, an astute man, recognized that criminal groups had sprung up in a number of cities throughout the country. Joseph Valachi later credited Maranzano with establishing the modern Cosa Nostra. By 1931 the present crime cartel had taken form; Maranzano just formalized what was already in existence. According to Valachi, Maranzano divided New York into five crime families—the Bonanno, Luciano, Mangano, Gagliano, and Profaci groups—and outlined a code of behavior for the emerging crime families. Each family was to have a boss, underboss, counselor, lieutenants, and soldiers. A soldier had to be loyal to his family. He could not approach his boss directly but had to work his way through the chain of command. Further, a family member was not to attack another family member in anger or violate that member's wife.[12]

Maranzano's victory was short-lived, however. He had alienated many of the powerful non-Italian crime chieftains. Dutch Schultz, overlord of the Bronx, had no intention of bowing to Maranzano. Maranzano also met powerful opposition from Meyer Lansky, Louis (Lepke) Buchalter, and Jake Shapiro. A new showdown was in the making. Maranzano had also alienated William Moretti, the New Jersey crime boss. Luciano and the younger generation of Italian criminals found Maranzano too conservative, and too committed to the old ways. Luciano and the younger Italian gangsters, many of whom had been in Masseria's camp, now turned against Maranzano and joined forces with the non-Italian criminal groups. On September 11, 1931, five assassins impersonating police officers raided Maranzano's headquarters and killed him. A new age had arrived. There was no longer to be a boss-of-bosses, and the clannishness of the old Italian gangs gave way to cooperation between Italian and non-Italian gangsters. Zwillman, Lansky, and Schultz, with Luciano, had played a key role in the assassination of Maranzano. Crime in America became national. Jewish, Polish, Irish, and Italian racketeers, joined by other ethnic groups, formed a national criminal confederation based on need. Luciano revived the idea of a national crime commission long espoused by Johnny Torrio and the more progressive elements within the underworld.

On October 24, 1931, Capone received an eleven-year prison sentence for tax evasion. Some studies of organized crime have suggested that Capone's downfall was engineered by the more progressive groups within organized crime because he had brought too much law enforcement pressure and public attention to the syndicate. After 1931 Capone faded from history, and the Lucianos took over. Organized crime was beginning to assume its modern form. In St. Louis the Hogans and Egans (Irish gangs) were coming to the forefront; they worked closely with the Green Dagoes (Italian) and the Cuckoos (mostly Levantine). In central Illinois the Shelton crime group had become the dominant power. It often worked closely with both the St. Louis and the Kansas City crime groups.

Even Washington, D.C., had its criminals. Jimmy La Fontaine had built an illicit gambling empire. Organized crime was going national. Those who opposed it did not always fare well. Anton Cermak, who had been elected mayor of Chicago on a reform platform, was assassinated in 1933 in Miami by Giuseppe Zangara. On his deathbed, Zangara told the authorities that the syndicate had ordered the mayor's assassination.

In 1934 the country's most powerful underworld chieftains met in New York. Like many other national conferences, this one was also master-minded by Johnny Torrio, Lucky Luciano, and Frank Costello. The conferees lent their support to the newly formed National Crime Commission and acknowledged the territorial claims of twenty-four crime families that had sprung up in a number of cities. The New York conference was follow-ed by one in Kansas City, also organized by Torrio and Luciano. This one attracted many of the midwestern crime groups, among them the Mayfield gang of Cleveland, the Purples of Detroit, the Capone mob, and represen-tatives from New Orleans and St. Louis. With Capone in prison, leadership in the Chicago syndicate had fallen to Ralph Capone, Tony Accardo, and

Jake Guzik. In 1936 Dutch Schultz, who for a number of years had been in difficulty with the authorities, was murdered by the syndicate in a New Jersey restaurant. Two things sparked his murder: his plans to kill Tom Dewey, a New York prosecutor, and the attraction of his lucrative rackets, which upon his death were divided among the other crime groups. The very next year, Lucky Luciano was sentenced to thirty to fifty years of imprisonment on white slavery (prostitution) charges. In 1937 Vito Genovese fled the country in fear of prosecution and made his home in Italy.

In the late 1930s the syndicate made its way to California. Bugsy Siegel, an associate of Meyer Lansky, was sent to the West Coast to oversee the syndicate's interests in California. At the same time the growing crime cartel began to look at narcotics as a new market, since the end of Prohibition deprived the nation's criminals of a lucrative source of revenue. Joseph De Luca established a narcotics-smuggling network, which was based in Kansas City and supplied the midwestern states. Similar networks sprang up in the New York-New Jersey area as well as the Florida region. In St. Louis Thomas Buffa and Tony Lapiparo, both crime chieftains, began to turn their attention to narcotics. The newly formed syndicate turned its attention to gambling. Al Polizzi, a Mafia chieftain from Cleveland, invested in the Continental Press, a new service that provided racing news for the national network of bookmakers that had emerged.

During the war years the syndicate moved into white-collar crime, and Cuba began to play an increasingly important role in the strategy of the syndicate. Mafia families had sprung up in New Orleans (under Carlos Marcello) and Tampa (under Santos Trafficante). Costello had sent Philip Kastel to oversee gambling operations in New Orleans and to coordinate them with Marcello's group. Lansky, Costello, and Joe Adonis began to turn their attention to Las Vegas as a possible gambling center. California's affluent movie industry also attracted the attention of America's organized underworld. Gangsters infiltrated industry-related labor unions and used these to extort money from the movie moguls. George Browne, president of the International Association of Theatrical Stage Employees, was implicated in a Hollywood extortion racket run by the syndicate. The war years also saw the rise of a gambling empire in the Miami area, run by Jules Levitt and Charles Friedman. With Luciano in prison, Genovese in Italy, and the United States involved in World War II, the syndicate continued its momentum and made inroads into the economic sectors. The gun gave way to the pen, and narcotics began to assume a more important role in the syndicate's business. Cuba became a key staging point for the growing narcotics trade.

The war years also gave organized crime a badly needed respite from the adverse publicity and prosecutions of the late 1930s. The nation's police agencies were so concerned with the threat of sabotage and internal subversion that efforts against organized crime took on secondary importance. Organized crime, it is said, even assisted in guarding the nation's piers and factories from foreign sabotage. While the country was battling for survival, organized crime grew and consolidated its gains. It would come out of the war years stronger and wiser.

Crime in Postwar America

The Prohibition era marked a shift for organized crime. During the 1920s the small and isolated criminal gangs, often under the thumb of local political machines, were able to build enormous financial empires. Capone is reputed to have owned banks, real estate firms, hotels, and numerous other investments worth more than $20 million. Prohibition demonstrated to the ethnic criminal groups that national cooperation was necessary for illicit liquor operations. It also taught them that the arts of finance and management were indeed needed to run vast financial empires. During the war years the syndicate became more involved in the growing black market and in white-collar crime, which for many years had been the exclusive province of the professional classes. Costello and Lansky were quick to see the potential value of legalized gambling. The gangs of the 1920s now found respectability behind the corporate veil. The Capones gave way to the Costellos. William O'Dwyer, a former New York City mayor, best summed it up when he said, "It doesn't matter whether it is a banker, businessman or gangster, his pocketbook is always attractive."

The postwar years saw the rise of syndicate-owned businesses in entertainment, legal gambling (Las Vegas and Cuba), auto agencies, hotel chains, restaurants, taverns, labor unions, jukebox concerns, laundries, clothing manufacturers, racing and sports news, as well as penetration of Wall Street by syndicate agents. The new mob, given its affluence, national character, and growing sophistication, was quick to learn that commercial crime promised small risks and enormous profits. For example, during the war years the syndicate had made large profits by selling stolen or counterfeit gas ration stamps to legitimate businessmen; few, if any, syndicate men were prosecuted. The Prohibition era had given rise to a new business aristocracy; America's Puritan tradition continued to create new markets for the syndicate. Attempts to legislate morality only resulted in successful efforts to evade these laws.

Jack Zuta, a well-known Chicago gangster of the 1920s, kept detailed records of payoffs he had made to politicians, judges, and even businessmen. When he died, the police uncovered his records and the press soon gained access to them. The Zuta papers, as they came to be called, highlighted the deep involvement of the syndicate in Chicago's political and financial world. For example, Zuta recorded payoffs of thousands of dollars to Judge Joseph W. Schulman of the Municipal Court of Chicago for the period 1921-1925. He also recorded payoffs to Judge Emanuel Eller, as well as to state senator George Van Lent, head of the Illinois Republican party. The Zuta papers provided evidence of a growing liason between the syndicate and members of the Illinois political and business establishments.

Frank Costello, a key syndicate strategist, had always recognized the value of political contacts. During the 1930s and 1940s he had developed contacts with Jimmy Hines, leader of New York's West Side Tammany Hall, and with Governor Huey Long of Louisiana, who personally asked him to install slot machines in his state. It was Costello who helped nominate Thomas Aurelio to be New York Supreme Court Justice in 1943. The postwar syndicate, with its billions of dollars, continued to play an important role in politics. Masseria and the other mustache petes had given way to the businessman-gangster.

During the postwar era crime families became powerful. The New York-New Jersey area was dominated by six crime groups. Joseph Profaci, Joseph Bonanno, and Vincent Mangano had established their power bases in Brooklyn and had investments in other areas of New York City, in upstate New York, and in northern New Jersey. The Luciano group (although its boss was in prison and its underboss, Vito Genovese, had fled to Italy) was established in Manhattan and had interests in other areas of the city and in several other states. Longy Zwillman ran New Jersey. Costello was the acknowledged head of the Luciano group in the postwar years and held that post until 1957, when he was forced out by Genovese. The Gaetano Gagliano crime family had its power base in Brooklyn, and the Chicago underworld came to be ruled by the Accardo-Guzik-Fischetti triumvirate (all three had been top Capone lieutenants), which had investments in Kansas City, Dallas, Miami, Las Vegas, and California, as well as in Chicago. A Costello-Addonis-Lansky national network had also developed, with investments in Saratoga, Bergen County, New Orleans, Miami, Las Vegas, Los Angeles, and Havana. A national criminal cartel, with international contacts, had taken shape. These crime groups were often tied to one another not only by business necessity but also through intermarriages. For example, two of Joe Profaci's daughters were married to the sons of William (Black Bill) Toco and Joseph Zerilli, both powerful Michigan crime bosses. The Joseph Bonanno crime family was allied to the Zerilli crime group through intermarriage. The son of Nick Licata, a West Coast mob chief, was married to a daughter of William Toco. Thus the criminal aristocracy that arose during the postwar years was held together by bonds of necessity and marriage and ruled in part by a national crime commission.[13]

A well-entrenched, organized criminal structure had taken hold nationally in numerous cities. California, for many years virgin territory, became the center of much syndicate attention in the postwar years. Many of the West Coast movie studios began to pay tribute to the syndicate in order to avoid labor problems with syndicate-controlled unions. Twentieth Century Fox is said to have paid $50,000 a year for labor peace; the smaller studios are said to have paid an average of $25,000 per year.[14] Bugsy Siegel, tied to the Lansky group, had been able to gain control over several Hollywood unions during the war years and had been able to use these to gain a foothold for the syndicate in Hollywood. Mickey Cohen, a Cleveland gangster, also made his way to California and for many years was an active syndicate agent in that state. Jack Dragna was able, by the early 1950s, to become boss of the Los Angeles underworld.

Important organized criminal networks also took shape in Cleveland and Kansas City. The Cleveland group included Samuel (Gameboy) Miller, Morris Kleinman, Moe Dalitz, Louis Rothkopf, Samuel Tucker, James Licavoli, Jerry Milano and Thomas J. McGinty. In Kansas City an extremely well organized criminal network arose. The city's underworld had a long history, dating back to the early 1900s. By the late 1940s a confederation of American Mafia types and other ethnic crime groups had constructed a powerful political-economic structure. In the 1930s the Kansas City mob had attempted on several occasions to fix the local elections. In 1934 the attempt left more than ten individuals dead or wounded. During the 1940s Charles Binaggio became one of the city's most powerful crime bosses. He was murdered in 1950 by his rivals, but only after he had managed to establish an informal alliance with local law enforcement. In return for payoffs the police agreed to allow the syndicate to operate freely. In Dallas James Civello had begun to consolidate various crime groups under his leadership.

By the time the Kefauver Committee (Senate Special Committee to Investigate Organized Crime in Interstate Commerce, chaired by Senator Estes Kefauver of Tennessee) was formed in 1950 to look into organized criminal activity, the syndicate had developed branches in many parts of the country. A network of crime families and their associates, consituting a national confederation of criminal groups, was dominating crime in numerous cities. The committee's investigators soon found links between the crime families of New York, Chicago, Miami, Tampa, Cleveland, Kansas City, Dallas, Los Angeles, and even Havana. It found what was essentially a national criminal cartel whose members often cooperated in joint ventures and employed assassins to eliminate its enemies. The nation was stunned to learn that this criminal cartel had its own police force, Murder, Inc., and that between 1930 and 1940, this enforcement arm had murdered more than one hundred individuals targeted by the syndicate as its enemies. The committee also uncovered a well-organized international drug-smuggling network. America was stunned to learn that it now had a fifth estate.

The Kefauver Committee Findings

Senator Kefauver took his hearings to numerous cities and through them educated millions of American citizens. In Kansas City committee investigators asked a well-known underworld figure whether he belonged to the Mafia; his reply was, "What is the Mafia?" A powerful New Jersey mobster, when asked the same question, replied: "I am sorry, I don't know what you are talking about." Both witnesses were later identified as members of Mafia groups in their respective states. In New Orleans committee investigators uncovered illegal gambling interests linking the Costello, Lansky, Addonis, and Carlos Marcello groups. Marcello himself, a Tunisian-born Sicilian, had come to the United States as a child and allegedly had risen to become Mafia chieftain of New Orleans. In Cleveland the committee's investigators uncovered widespread corruption. The Cleveland syndicate had expanded its base into neighboring Kentucky; where towns like Newport and Coventry were mob controlled. The Cleveland syndicate also had close working arrangements with the Miami, Detroit, Las Vegas, and Los Angeles crime groups. In Tampa committee staffers were able to document a close working relationship between Mafia figures and a large and powerful group of Cuban gangsters. Santos Trafficante, Jr., was said to be one of the powerful Tampa crime bosses. Tampa, New York, and New Orleans had become key ports in the smuggling of narcotics into this country.

The committee, after one year of traveling to numerous cities throughout the country, concluded that the growing power of organized crime was directly connected to the corruption and connivance of governmental officials. The committee uncovered a national pattern of bribery and protection payments to law enforcement officials and payoffs to political figures to ensure protection from prosecution. Some public officials were not only the recipients of bribes and payoffs, but also direct participants in businesses controlled by the syndicate. In Philadelphia, for example, committee investigators uncovered widespread corruption in all of the city's thirty-eight police precincts. In Dade County, Florida, local police officials were employed as bagmen for the mob. In Jackson County, Missouri, the committee found that many local police officials were on the payrolls of distributors of slot machines, in direct violation of the law. In Los Angeles police officials were borrowing money from mob-connected bookmakers. A top police official in East St. Louis had large interests in real estate, restaurants, and other businesses; yet investigators estimated that his salary was less than $6,000 per year.[15]

The committee found widespread corruption involving local and state political figures. In New York City, it found, the Luciano crime family exerted great influence over the Manhattan Democratic political machine, while Brooklyn mobster Joe Addonis was exercising great influence over that borough's political machine. In Kansas City the syndicate attempted to install its own man as chief of police, with the assistance of corrupt local politicians. The mayor of Granite City, Illinois, was said to have ordered his police officials not to interfere with the city's syndicate operation. Miami political figures were said to have received payoffs from the S and G Syndicate, a local bookmaking operation started in 1946 by Harold Salvey, Sam Cohen, and Charles Friedman. The committee also found that the Capone syndicate had made large campaign contributions to governor Fuller Warren of Florida. Committee investigators uncovered widespread involvement by organized crime in local political races, as well as numerous working arrangements between members of the mob and public officials.[16]

The Post-Kefauver Committee Era

Although the Kefauver Committee hearings disclosed widespread corruption and concluded that organized crime continued to grow and survive only with the illicit cooperation of both police and elected officials, business continued as usual for the syndicate. In 1953 New York crime boss Gaetano Gagliano died of natural causes and was replaced by Tommy Lucchese. Vincent Mangano, another New York crime boss, had suspiciously disappeared, and his crime group was now headed by Albert Anastasia, who was suspected of having played a role in that disappearance. Joseph Bonanno and Joseph Profaci were still secure in their seats of power, and Costello continued to head the Luciano group, with Genovese second in command. The latter was growing impatient and soon made his move to replace Costello.

After the termination of the Kefauver Committee hearings, Senator John L. McClellan began to turn his attention to labor racketeering. As chairman of the Senate Subcommittee on Investigations (of the Senate Government Operations Committtee) and with Robert F. Kennedy as general counsel to that subcommittee, he embarked on a widespread investigation of syndicate involvement in the labor movement. Jimmy Hoffa, the controversial head of the Teamsters Union, became the target of the subcommittee's investigators. Later the subcommittee focused on the involvement of organized crime in the smuggling of narcotics. It was this subcommittee that later brought Joseph Valachi to the attention of the American public. Although the subcommittee's investigators uncovered widespread examples of fraud and syndicate involvement in the labor movement, the syndicate continued to hold its own.

The late 1950s was a period of growth and consolidation for the syndicate. Great strides were made in white-collar crime, and mob figures began to assume new roles. They made large investments in numerous businesses and became more heavily involved in local political races. Frank Costello typified the new mobster. He lived in an expensive apartment on New York's Central Park West. He mingled with judges, politicians, businessmen, and other notables. On weekends he played golf on the fashionable South Shore of Long Island. In short, he was "accorded all the freedoms of a prosperous and successful man."[17] The violence of the 1920s and 1930s gave way to the businesslike atmosphere of the 1950s. Although the Anastasias and Genoveses were still part of crime's leadership, their violence and crude tactics were beginning to give way. Costello personified the modern gangster chieftain. He provided a model for the younger and upcoming leadership of the underworld.

Luciano was deported to his native Italy in 1946, but he still continued to exercise a dominant control over his crime family from abroad. In the early 1950s he took up residence in Cuba and kept control over his interests through Costello. The Batista government, one of the more corrupt in the Caribbean, proved both a willing ally and an important associate. Gambling, narcotics, and prostitution flourished; the American syndicate operated with impunity. In 1959, when Fidel Castro came to power, the political environment changed. Castro was not willing to allow business to continue as usual. Castro's vision of a new Cuba allowed no role for the syndicate. Soon the mob went into exile. Luciano was forced to retreat to Italy.

Even before Castro's takeover in Cuba, Genovese began to make his power moves against Costello. The latter was the target of a tax evasion investigation; in 1954 he was sentenced to five years in federal prison. In 1956 he finally entered prison, and Genovese took the reigns of power. Genovese had also arranged in 1953 for the assassination of William Moretti, a stalwart supporter of Costello. In the summer of 1956 Bill Bonanno (son of Joe Bonanno) married Rosalie Profaci (a niece of Joe Profaci), further solidifying the alliance of these two powerful crime families. The other crime families, although concerned, could do little.

In 1957 Frank Costello was released from prison. Genovese's fear that Costello might oust him from power led him to act decisively. Vincent Gigante, a former boxer, was given the task of assassinating Costello. The attempt failed and Costello was only wounded, but the message was clear. Costello soon announced his retirement, thus leaving Genovese in undisputed control of the Luciano family. Several months later Genovese played a key role in planning the assassination of Albert Anastasia, a close Costello ally. Genovese feared that Anastasia, who was known for his bad temper, might retaliate for having ousted Costello from power. Anastasia had made enemies in the National Crime Commission with his high-handed tactics. Many also suspected him of having engineered the disappearance of his boss, Vincent Mangano. On October 25, 1957, Anastasia was murdered in a midtown New York barber shop. Carlo Gambino then assumed the leadership of Anastasia's group. Gambino had the support of Genovese, Lucchese, and the other powerful chieftains of the underworld.

The death of Anastasia firmly established Genovese in power. It also served as a reminder that organized crime was a confederation of numerous crime groups and that its chieftains were neither ready nor willing to allow a reversion to Maranzano's centralization. Anastasia had alienated his peers, and for this he paid with his life. In the autumn of 1957 one of the largest meetings of syndicate chieftains in the history of modern crime took place in upstate New York. More than sixty prominent crime figures converged on the estate of Joseph Barbara, a member of the Buffalo crime family of Stefano Magaddino, a sitting member of the National Crime Commission. Although the authorities raided the estate and arrested dozens of crime figures, little but publicity came out of this event. America was once again reminded that organized crime was alive and doing well. In the fall of 1957 Johnny Torrio, one of the underworld's most brilliant strategists, died of natural causes. Torrio had outlived Capone by more than a dozen years.

In 1959 Genovese, along with more than a dozen other crime figures, was tried for narcotics violations. After a lengthy trial he was convicted and received a fifteen-year prison sentence. A year later Joseph Valachi, until then a third-rate figure within the underworld, was brought to trial and received a fifteen-year sentence. Although now in prison, Genovese continued to control his crime family through Tommy Ryan Elboli and Gerardo Catena. Elboli represented Genovese at two future gangland meetings, one in 1965 in a Long Island restaurant and the second in 1966 in a Queens nightclub. In 1972 Elboli was assassinated. Genovese never saw the outside world again; in 1969 he died in prison of natural causes.

The Gallo Revolt and After

The Gallo group, relatively unknown in the 1950s, had been brought into the Profaci crime family in 1954. Joey (Crazy Joe) Gallo was the better known than the other two Gallo brothers, Albert and Lawrence. These young and aggressive Gallos were angered by what they felt was the unequal division of spoils within the Profaci crime family; they felt slighted when Profaci gave his friends and relatives a larger share of the booty. The Gallos were also covertly encouraged by Genovese and Carlo Gambino, who feared that the close ties between the Profaci and Bonanno groups could lead to a union of the two crime families, thus dwarfing the other groups. In 1961 the Gallos kidnapped the Profaci lieutenant Joseph Magliocco and thus set off the Gallo-Profaci war, which left dozens of individuals dead and led to the downfall of the Gallos themselves several years later. Profaci appealed to the other chieftains of the underworld for aid. Gambino, Magaddino, Genovese, Sam Giancana (of Chicago), and Angelo Bruno (of Philadelphia) refused. Tommy Lucchese, after hesitating at first, also refused to assist Profaci. The other chieftains were fearful that Profaci and his ally Joe Bonanno had grown too close and posed a threat to the other crime groups. They saw the war as an opportunity to cut Profaci's power base from under him. Ten years later Gambino and the other chieftains again employed the Gallos to cut the power base of Joseph Colombo, then boss of the Profaci crime family.[18]

The Gallo-Profaci struggle continued well into 1963. With the death of Profaci in 1962, it fell on his underboss Magliocco to carry on the war. In late 1963 Magliocco died and was succeeded by Joe Colombo, until then a minor lieutenant within the Profaci crime family. Colombo had the support of Gambino, Lucchese, and the other crime chieftains who wanted someone outside the Bonanno group to sit on the Profaci throne. Soon after Colombo made peace with the Gallos, a struggle for power within the Bonanno family erupted. Bonanno had angered many of the other crime bosses by ignoring the orders of the National Crime Commission. Although he was a member of that body, he often sent his underboss to its meetings instead of going himself. This offended many of the other powerful crime bosses. His ties to the Profaci crime family had led the other crime families to fear a union between these two powerful crime groups. The elevation of Colombo to the Profaci throne had averted such a union, but Bonanno continued to expand his operations both domestically and internationally, giving rise to suspicions that he wanted to build a national crime empire and thus dwarf his competitors. In addition, Magaddino was angered when his brother-in-law, Gaspar DiGregorio, a captain in the Bonanno crime family, was passed over by Joe Bonanno's son as possible heir to the Bonanno throne.

In 1965 Giancana, Elboli, and Carmine Traumanti (a high lieutenant in the Lucchese crime family and one of its future bosses) met in a Long Island restaurant to discuss Joe Bonanno. An open struggle now began to take shape within the Bonanno crime family between a rebel group led by DiGregorio and the forces loyal to Joe Bonanno. A second gangland meeting took place in 1966 in Queens. The syndicate chieftains discussed the open warfare going on within the Bonanno crime family. Those present included Gambino, Colombo, Santo Trafficante, and Carlos Marcello. The conferees were concerned with who was going to head the Lucchese crime group once the old chief died. It was widely known within the underworld that Thomas Lucchese was dying of a brain tumor, and the syndicate bosses wanted to avert another Gallo-Profaci war.

The internecine struggle within the Bonanno crime family came to an end in early 1969. Soon after, Vito Genovese died in prison. Luciano's death several years before and Frank Costello's retirement had left a power vacuum. About this time Carlo Gambino is known to have made a bid for the leadership of New York's crime syndicate.[19] Some have said that Gambino was able to assert his power over the other New York crime groups and become the legendary boss-of-bosses. Whether this is true or not, Gambino was a powerbroker within organized crime. He shied away from publicity and had a disdain for rebels. The wars of the last several years had brought undue publicity to organized crime. Many of the old loyalties had been shaken, and new bosses had come to the forefront. The younger leadership proved restless. The prestige of the National Crime Commission, on the wane since the early 1960s, had to be restored.[20] Joe Colombo, young and aggressive, posed a threat to the old chieftains. Joe Gallo, in prison for several years, was now out and recruiting blacks and other minority members to replenish his lost power base. These underlying forces soon came to the surface in the summer of 1971.

In 1970 Joe Colombo was charged with income tax evasion and his son was charged with melting coins into silver ingots. Soon after, Colombo crime family members and their relatives began to picket the New York offices of the Federal Bureau of Investigation. After several months the Italian-American Civil Rights League was born, an instrument of Colombo and the other crime chieftains. The league continued picketing the federal agencies, and its leaders attempted to portray it as a civil rights organization. It conducted an intense campaign against federal prosecutors and corporations that used Italian stereotypes. Colombo's activities, different from those that the older generation of bosses had been accustomed to, incurred the wrath of the syndicate's establishment. Gambino saw an opportunity to rid himself of Colombo and reassert his power. In this he had the support of the National Crime Commission, which viewed Colombo as an upstart and considered the league's notoriety adverse to the syndicate's interest. In late June 1971 Jerome Johnson attempted to assassinate Colombo at a league celebration in Columbus Circle. Suspicions soon turned to the Gallos, and it was rumored that the Gallos had trained Johnson, a black former convict, for his assassin's role. Gambino was also suspected of being behind the Gallos in this new power play.

Although Johnson failed to kill Colombo, the latter ceased being effective in the daily affairs of the syndicate. He was left a cripple until his death several years later. Joey Gallo was assassinated in a little restaurant on the Lower East Side. The finger fell on the Colombo crime family; this was their revenge.[21] Implicated in the Gallo murder were Joseph (Joe Pesh) Luparelli and Carmine (Sonny Pinto) Di Biase, both members of the Colombo crime family. The death of Joey Gallo led to a second war between the Gallo group and the Profaci (now known as the Colombo) crime family. In mid 1972 Tommy Elboli was assassinated in New York, and Gambino was soon acknowledged by Carmine Traumanti (now boss of the

Lucchese family) as head of New York's crime syndicate, a position that he held until his death (of natural causes) in October 1976.

In 1963 Mayor Wagner of New York City called on syndicate bosses to end racial violence in the streets of the city. Two years later his successor did the same. In other parts of the city business for the syndicate goes on as usual. In the South Bronx Jewish gangsters continue to control the numbers operations. In black Harlem independent black crime bosses work hand in hand with organized crime, as do their Puerto Rican counterparts in upper Manhattan. Queens bookmakers and numbers operators leave their businesses to their sons, who in turn expect to leave them to their heirs. In New York a Southern District federal court found Leroy (Nicky) Barnes and eleven associates guilty of selling millions of dollars worth of narcotics in Harlem. Barnes (known as Mr. Untouchable) was soon replaced by other black crime figures, and the syndicate and its associates continued their daily business. Organized crime in America is now big business. It is a power to be reckoned with, and one that is underestimated by many of its critics. The Torrios, Capones, Lucianos, and Gambinos have constructed an organization that can truly be called one of America's five estates. It is changing, growing, and threatening our very freedoms.

Notes

1. "Chicago Gangsters Linked to Ownership of Nevada Casinos," *Washington Post*, July 14, 1978, p. A-7.

2. "Addenda," *Washington Post*, July 14, 1978, p. A-7.

3. Frank Faso and Paul Meskill, "Club's Late Show: Hit-Men Execute Two," *Daily News*, October 24, 1974, p. 3.

4. "Flynt Connections Alleged," *Washington Post*, July 7, 1978, p. A-6.

5. Gus Tyler, *Organized Crime in America: A Book of Readings* (Ann Arbor, Mich.: University of Michigan Press, 1962), p. 44.

6. Edward Robb Ellis, *The Epic of New York City* (New York: Coward-McCann, 1966), pp. 230-231.

7. William A. Settle, Jr., "Jesse James," in *The Super Crooks*, ed. Roger M. Williams (Chicago: Playboy Press, 1973), pp. 45-46.

8. Tyler, *Organized Crime in America: A Book of Readings*, p. 45.

9. Peter Maas, *The Valachi Papers* (New York: Bantam Books, 1969), p. 60.

10. Francis A.J. Ianni and Elizabeth Reuss-Ianni, *A Family Business* (New York: New American Library, 1973), p. 2.

11. G. William Domhoff, *Who Rules America* (Englewood Cliffs, N.J.: Prentice-Hall, 1967), pp. 132-138.

12. Maas, *The Valachi Papers*, pp. 105-106, 154.

13. Ianni and Reuss-Ianni, *A Family Business*, pp. 190-191.

14. Tyler, *Organized Crime in America: A Book of Readings*, p. 203.

15. "Official Corruption and Organized Crime," in *The Crime Society*, et. Francis A.J. Ianni and Elizabeth Reuss-Ianni (New York: New American Library, 1976), pp. 293-295.

16. Ibid., pp. 293-296.

17. President's Commission on Law Enforcement and Administration of Justice, *Task Force Report: Organized Crime* (Washington, D.C.: U.S. Government Printing Office, 1967), pp. 2-3.

18. "The Mafia: Back to the Bad Old Days," *Time*, July 12, 1971, pp. 14-18.

19. "Carlo Gambino, New York Mafia Boss Dies," *Washington Post*, October 16, 1976, p. D-6.

20. "Back to the Bad Old Days," p. 18.

21. Donald Goddard, "An Incredible Evening with Joe Gallo," *New York Magazine*, March 18, 1974, p. 44. A series of articles by Paul Meskill on the assassination of Joe Gallo appeared in the *Daily News*: "Gallo, A Swaggering Target But Hard to Nail," November 26, 1974, pp. 3, 21; "A Mobster Talks: They're Out to Kill Me," November 24, 1974, pp. 30, 82; "His Flight Begins with Order: Kill Your Wife," November 27, 1974, pp. 4, 34.

4 Labor Racketeering

In a lonely street in one of Chicago's suburbs a key government witness was recently gunned down by syndicate hit men. He was to testify in a federal case involving a $1.4 million loan from a labor union pension fund to a New Mexico firm with organized crime links. In Cleveland the secretary-treasurer of a union local was killed when a bomb was set off by remote control. He had been involved in a power struggle for control of union locals by organized crime members.[1]

In New York dissident Teamsters called for a federal investigation of New York Teamsters funds.[2] The group alleged that more than $500,000 from local Teamster funds had made its way into organized crime-controlled businesses. A six-month investigation into labor racketeering in Queens County resulted in the indictment of two union leaders.[3] One of the defendents was alleged to have had ties to organized crime. The defendants were charged with threatening bodily harm against the employees of a firm they were trying to unionize. In Washington, D.C., a high U.S. Labor Department official was charged with operating a fraudulent scheme.[4]

These are examples of labor racketeering, what has come to be called an American tragedy. The United States may be unique in Western society in its corruption of labor. Powerful labor unions, with millions of members and billions of dollars in treasuries, are presently manipulated by criminal syndicates. Union welfare and pension funds are open to looting, and federal and state governments have done little to stop it. Labor racketeering provides criminal cartels with large amounts of interest-free capital to invest in business ventures and powerful voting blocks that give them leverage with national and local political figures. It is a serious and growing problem. It threatens not only the labor movement and the world of business but also our very democratic fiber.

The Rise of Labor

Organized labor is not a modern phenomenon, nor is it found solely in America. More than three thousand years ago in Egypt and Mesopotamia, arbitration was often employed to settle disputes between employers and employees. Disputes between workers and their employers were also common during the Greek period of Homer. Professional arbitrators were

51

employed in the fifth century B.C. to deal with labor disputes. Guilds of artisans were common throughout the Roman era, and they controlled various facets of the Roman economy. In ancient Byzantium guilds of grocers, bakers, butchers, and fishmongers regulated the distribution of food necessities for the eastern Roman Empire.[5]

Guilds were also common during the Middle Ages in Europe. These associations of merchants were found in numerous European towns. The guilds were generally given powers by the town's governmental unit to hold courts and establish rules for regulating their industry.[6] These associations were outgrowths of an agrarian world and bore little resemblance to modern labor. They met the needs of a nonindustrial society and have parallels in many of today's Third World countries.

The guilds were not open to everyone who wanted to join them. They were exclusive clubs. Serfs, even those who had fled to the towns, could not join local guilds. As Europe entered a more advanced economic stage, more specialized guilds began to emerge along the lines of occupation. Thus the artisans broke with the merchants and established their own guilds. Each guild nevertheless attempted to maintain its monopoly in the marketplace of its own town and continued to exert exclusive control over the availability of labor. An apprenticeship system was established, and those who sought to enter a specific profession or occupation first had to serve under a master. Ater serving this fixed time of apprenticeship, the individual applied to the guild for entry. An apprentice who was turned down was unable to practice his occupation within the town. Some moved to other towns. If the apprentice was allowed to enter the guild, he became a journeyman, and the guild usually guaranteed him a job. Wages, working conditions, and even holidays were controlled and negotiated by the guild.

The guilds also played a social function. They cared for members who were ill and for their widows and children, and they even established a system of schools and hospitals for the families of their members. As labor became more specialized, political differences began to arise between labor and employers. Craft guilds, for example, often had differences with the powerful merchants who ran a town's economy and government. Sometimes these differences were arbitrated; sometimes they resulted in work stoppages and even in outright violence. In Flanders, for example, the craft guilds revolted against the merchants and the kings of France.[7] Labor violence is neither new nor indigenous to the American social fabric.

The guilds died, not at the hands of the merchants or kings, but as a result of their inability to adapt to a changing economy. By the eighteenth century Europe's mercantilism was being replaced by the rising technology that paved the way for modern industrial societies. Guild regulations prohibited members from adapting this new technology to their occupations and from working for merchants who used it. The rise of technology and the modern banking institutions led to the end of the guild system. Those who used this new technology simply moved their shops to the countryside or to new towns where the guilds exerted little or no power. The new technology gave rise to a new system of manufacture that made use of semiskilled or unskilled labor. Thus the guilds became obsolete. A new class of labor began to emerge, and new associations were needed to fill the void left by the guilds.

The first attempts to organize a modern labor union in this country took place in Pennsylvania in the early nineteenth century. In 1827 associations of workers resembling the old guilds attempted to negotiate wages and working conditions with Philadelphia employers. These initial attempts to organize modern labor met with opposition from both government and business. Some employers resorted to violence; armies of thugs were hired to put down organized efforts to unite labor. From the first the labor movement in this country met hostility and violence. A dangerous precedent had been set, one that later facilitated the rise of organized crime within the American labor union movement. As the Teamsters later showed, labor could also form alliances with armies of thugs to fight back. The criminals in turn exacted their price.

In the pre-Civil War years labor groups began to take shape. Printers formed several unions and began to negotiate contracts with their employers. In 1866 labor groups meeting in Baltimore instructed their members to establish committees to negotiate contracts with their respective employers.[8] During the post-Civil War era large corporate empires rose, and a class of robber barons began to emerge. In response, numerous labor groups proliferated in many cities. The Noble Order of the Knights of Labor in 1869 declared as its policy the principle of a negotiated working contract between employees (its members) and employers. Numerous other labor groups, some Marxist and anarchist in orientation, also took shape. The employers, now armed with large reserves of wealth, struck back politically and with violence. Numerous pitched battles were fought between these labor groups and armed guards hired by their employers. The roots of the labor movement were firmly embedded in violence.

Labor movements in Europe fared no better. Labor unions in France, Germany, and Italy fell under the sway of political radical groups. In Europe many labor groups took to the streets in revolt. The latter half of the nineteenth century was marked by labor violence in both the United States and Europe.

The Knights of Labor was a reformist group whose leadership wanted to attack the evils of industrial America. This group included unskilled laborers, small merchants, farmers, and even professionals. In many ways this group resembled its European counterparts. Its struggle took on a moral tone. By the 1880s it had more than five hundred thousand members and represented all sectors of the economy. It advocated political reform and social equality. Whereas the guilds of medieval Europe were concerned with improving only the lot of their members, the Knights of Labor had utopian visions of bettering mankind. However, in the final analysis, the goals and organization of the Knights of Labor proved to be their weakness and led to their downfall.

By the late 1890s the Knights had declined to about a hundred thousand, and by the early 1900s their movement had withered away. This confederation of farmers and workers fell because the needs of these groups were too divergent to be met by one organization. The Knights were a loose confederation of different national labor unions. Often conflicts erupted between these national groups and the leadership of the confederation. During this same period a new national labor federation appeared. This was the American Federation of Labor (AFL), made up of skilled, national craft unions.

By 1890 the AFL had a membership of more than two hundred thousand and an able president in Samuel Gompers, who ruled it with a firm hand for more than thirty-five years. Unlike the Knights of Labor, the AFL had no socialistic leanings; it had no utopian visions of reforming and reshaping American society. Like the medieval guilds, it merely sought to better the lot of its members. Radical politics were rejected, and the AFL engaged in lobbying activities. The AFL gave each national union exclusive jurisdiction over its own craft. With the jurisdiction of every national union well defined and enforced, the internal difficulties that had destroyed the Knights of Labor were circumvented. By the time America entered World War I, the AFL had more than 2 million members concentrated in key industries. Only skilled laborers could join it; no attempts were made to recruit the unskilled.

Employers did not immediately accept the AFL or other labor groups. Between 1918 and 1930 numerous company unions were founded. Their combined membership reached more than a million. Violence was common and often used as a tool. Criminal gangs were hired to assassinate labor leaders, who in turn struck bargains with these criminal groups. Some criminal syndicates eventually founded their own labor unions as fronts to exort money from employers. When Franklin D. Roosevelt was elected president, labor had a friend in the White House; labor had played a key role in the national election. In 1937 several national unions that had broken with the AFL formed the Congress of Industrial Organizations (CIO) which, unlike the AFL, opened its ranks to the millions of unskilled Americans who sought to join a labor organization. By 1953 the CIO and AFL had laid their differences aside, and in 1955 the AFL-CIO was formed. The Teamsters and several other large national unions do not belong to this national labor confederation. Whereas labor unions in Europe allied themselves with political parties and in some instances formed their own, labor groups in this country maintained a politically neutral posture. Some of the national unions fell under the control of criminal groups, especially in the post-World War II era. The Teamsters, with more than a million members, was reputed to be one such group.

Labor Unions and the Courts

Attempts to contain union-employer violence began to arouse political interest in the 1880s. Maryland passed one of the first labor laws in the country; it provided for arbitration of labor disputes. Pennsylvania, Ohio, and Kansas enacted similar legislation. In 1886 New York established the State Board of Arbitrators to mediate labor disputes, thus averting violence. Unfortunately the board proved of little value; of more than four hundred labor disputes brought before it, only twenty-one were successfully arbitrated.[9]

Employers found friends in government. In 1806 in the *Philadelphia Cordewainers' Case,* the court held that the banding of employees into a union was illegal. In 1896 a Massachusetts court held that union picketing interfered with the right of an employer to conduct his business.[10] "No one can lawfully prevent," the court noted "employers or persons wishing to be employed from the exercise of their rights." In 1893 the Pullman Palace Car Company was faced with a strike. The attorney general of the United States intervened against the American Railway Union (heading the strike) and obtained an injunction against the strikers.[11] The United States Supreme Court, on appeal, upheld the federal government's intervention. In 1908 the *Danbury Hatters* case came before the U.S. Supreme Court. The union had been engaged in a boycott. The Court held that the union was an illegal combination.[12]

Union membership was not affected by these adverse court rulings; labor unions grew in strength and power. In 1919 more than three hundred thousand steelworkers went on strike. The employers resorted to violence. By the 1930s it had become apparent that labor was a growing power. The New Deal initiated a series of laws that legitimized its standing in American society. In 1935 Congress enacted the Wagner Act, also known as the National Labor Relations Act, which established the principle that employees have a right to organize into unions and that this right should be protected by the government. The act made it an unfair labor practice for employers to interfere with this right. The act also made it illegal for employers to dominate a labor organization. Interference with a labor organization by an employer, whether direct or indirect, was made illegal by the act.

In 1947 Congress enacted the Taft-Hartley Act. Unlike the Wagner Act, which directed itself against abuses by employers, the Taft-Hartley Act sought to curtail unfair labor practices by the unions themselves. The Taft-Hartley Act made it illegal for a labor union to restrain or coerce an employer in the selection of his bargaining representative. The act, in part, was a response to the growing infiltration of unions by criminals; it was also a product of a conservative backlash against labor. This act made it illegal for a union to encourage employees to stop work in order to induce an employer or other person to do business with any other person; the act also forbade a union from encouraging employees to stop work in order to induce an employer to recognize and bargain with the union where another union had been certified as the bargaining agent. In 1959 the act was amended, making it illegal for a union to picket for recognition under certain circumstances. The amendments also legalized prehire and seven-day union shop contracts.

That same year Congress enacted the Labor-Management Reporting and Disclosure Act. This act was an outgrowth of the McClellan committee hearings on the infiltration of organized crime into the labor movement. The act sets a code of conduct for unions, union officials, employers, and consultants. This legislation requires that every union have a constitution and bylaws and that every union file annual financial reports with the secretary of labor. These reports must also be disclosed to the membership. Reports on trusteeships must also be made to the Department of Labor; union officials are required to report conflict-of-interest transactions. Employers and labor relations consultants are required to file reports with the Department of Labor on expenditures and other arrangements that affects the bargaining rights of employees. The secretary of labor, through his agents, is given policing powers to ensure compliance with the act's requirements.

Another key statute, also a response to racketeering activities in the labor movement, is the Hobbs Antiracketeering Act, which prohibits criminal conspiracies that imped interstate commerce through use of extortion or robbery. The act also forbids the coercion of broadcasting companies to hire employees whose services are not needed. The Welfare and Pension Plans Disclosure Act, enacted a year before passage of the Landrum-Griffin Act, requires administrators of employee welfare and pension plans to make detailed reports to the secretary of labor. In 1962 the act was amended to give the Department of Labor investigative powers. Kickbacks, bribes, false reporting, embezzlement, and arrangements involving conflicts of interest were made criminal offenses. The states have enacted similar legislation aimed at dealing with criminal conduct by labor officials.

Enforcement of these statutes by the Department of Labor has proven lax and lacking in prosecutorial vigor. In fact, the department has shown itself a captive of the very constituency it was empowered to police. The legitimate labor sector has hampered stringent enforcement of labor laws for fear that antilabor groups might use these laws to stifle the legitimate labor movement. In the process criminals have benefited. For example, union locals in more than twenty industries are now under the control of criminal elements. One major supermarket chain was approached by a labor consultant, who in return for labor peace, suggested that the company purchase products from a firm he controlled.[13] He was later identified as a major underworld figure.

Regulation of Labor Unions

A key official in a national union was indicted by federal authorities for accepting more than $50,000 in cash payments from a large corporate employer.[14] The money was paid by the company to have its cargo unloaded at major ports despite a strike. The head of a union local, which has more than a thousand policemen as members, is said to have embezzled over $100,000 of union funds for personal expenditures.[15] The missing funds were reported as legal expenses. A West Coast businessman with ties to organized crime is said to have borrowed more than $2 million from a union pension fund, with another loan of more than $60 million in the making.[16] The money was to be used to purchase several Las Vegas casinos. In a separate case the Labor Department intervened to block a loan of more than $15 million from a union's pension plan, said to constitute about 36 percent of its own assets, to an individual with no known residence or occupation.[17] Federal attorneys informed the court that such a loan was subject to an "unreasonable risk of loss."

Such irresponsible and criminal behavior by union officers and officials has led to the enactment of legislation to regulate the conduct of unions and their agents. These rules and regulations cover everything from the establishment of labor groups and the election of union officials to financial reporting requirements.[18] Despite this legislation, criminal elements continue to pillage many unions with impunity. The problem is not too few laws but too little enforcement. The record of the Labor Department in this area has been dismal.

The Labor Management Relations Act provides the National Labor Relations Board (NLRB) with authority to determine which bargaining body will represent the employees of a given employer. An individual may petition the NLRB for an election to determine which union is to represent the employees. The petition must be supported by at least 30 percent of the other employees at the plant, and the petitioner cannot be a member of management. An employer can petition the NLRB for a union election if a union seeks exclusive bargaining power over his employees. In addition, a labor union itself can petition the NLRB for an election if an employer refuses to recognize it as the bargaining agent of his employees or if the union simply wants formal recognition from the NLRB as the exclusive bargaining agent of the employees at that plant or company.

The NLRB has power to supervise elections of a bargaining unit. If the petition for elections is approved, the NLRB directs one of its regional directors to supervise the election. A day and specific hours are selected to hold the election. The location of polling places is determined by agents of the NLRB, and the employees at the plant are given sufficient notice of the election. These precautions have been taken to ensure a democratic selection for a bargaining unit. Each of the parties that have an interest in the outcome of the election, including the federal authorities, appoint observers, who also assist in counting the ballots. The NLRB representative determines which ballots are valid and ensures that the process is free of corrupting influences. If no objections are raised concerning the outcome of the election, the NLRB certifies the winner as the representative bargaining agent for the employees at the company. The employer in turn must bargain only with the certified union. Rival unions may not coerce an employer into bargaining with them, nor is an employer allowed to deal with any other union. An individual, an employer, or another union may petition the NLRB for a decertification election if there is good cause, for example, if foul play in the certification process is suspected.

The Landrum-Griffin Act requires that a union's bylaws establish procedures for replacing officers. If cause can be shown, an election for the removal of a union official must be held, and the election must be in accord with the union's constitution. The Labor Department is charged with policing the removal process. Charges of electioneering fraud must also be investigated by the department. If probable cause is found, then the secretary of labor is required to bring civil action. In addition, the department must supervise a new election, if the court finds that the first election was a sham. The Landrum-Griffin Act prohibits criminals and certain ex-felons from holding union offices. The latter are barred for at least five years, although the ban can be lifted if the United States Board of Parole (in instances of federal crimes) determines that the paroled felon would pose no threat to the union if he held office. Obviously this procedure opens the process to political manipulation. For example, it is alleged that the Teamster leadership pressed the Nixon White House into prohibiting James R. Hoffa, who had been jailed in 1967, from participating in union politics once released on parole.[19]

In a scheme involving an Arizona plastics manufacturer, union trustees and criminal elements bilked the union's pension fund of more than $1 million through a series of fraudulent loans.[20] In another case the son of one of the nation's most powerful labor officials and an associate of the son were charged with scheming to embezzle funds from a union trust fund.[21] The defendants were also accused of using union funds to buy life insurance policies for themselves and their friends. To curtail misuse of union funds by union trustees and officers, the Landrum-Griffin Act provides certain constraints for those in positions of trust and power. Union officials are required to spend a union's funds solely for the benefit of the union and its members. Union officials are required to refrain from dealing in any activity that might adversely affect the interests of the union. An official must account to the union for any profits he reaps as a result of his office. A union may not lend one of its officers or its employees more than $2,000. The act requires that union officials file with the Department of Labor, within ninety days of the end of the fiscal year, reports on their financial holdings and transactions. They must also file reports on any stock or other financial interest that they or members of their families have in any company represented or being organized by their union. The act prohibits any secret loans, payments, or expenditures.

The act requires that a member of the union being victimized by its officials bring the matter to the attention of the Labor Department. The initiative is left with the membership. In cases inolving organized crime few members would be willing to risk their lives to come forth as complainants. The member must first take his complaints to the union. If the union fails to act, he then directs his complaints to the Department of Labor. If the member has exhausted his remedies with the union, he may also file a civil action in a local court, asking the court to order his union to remedy the problem.

The Landrum-Griffin Act also provides for the parent union organization to police its locals. In instances of corruption or undemocratic behavior by local officials, the parent union may impose a trusteeship on the local. A report must be filed with the Labor Department within thirty days of the trusteeship and then every six months while the trusteeship remains active. If the parent union abuses its trusteeship and deviates from its bylaws and constitution in its application of the trusteeship status, the local or any of its members may ask the secretary of labor for appropriate relief. The secretary can bring civil action, or the local itself can bring similar action, if the trusteeship has been in existence more than eighteen months. The trusteeship is a tool that allows parent organizations to police their locals, but it is a two-edged sword. It has been employed by corrupt national leaders to control and pillage the funds of their locals.

The Landrum-Griffin Act also provides protections for the individual union member. No union member may be disciplined unless he is served with charges and given a resonable period of time to prepare his defense. All members have a right to assemble and speak freely about the administration of their union. They have a right to oppose, either verbally or through the ballot box, those in power within the union. No member can be disciplined for exercising these rights. A member has a right to go ask the courts to remedy any internal union problems after he has exhausted internal union remedies. Although numerous federal statutes, including the Landrum-Griffin Act, provide civil and criminal sanctions against those who abuse their positions of trust within the labor movement, labor racketeering still grows. Laws without adequate enforcement do not suffice.

Categories of Labor Corruption

Corrupt practices within the labor movement can take four major forms: rivalries for leadership, abuses involving the union-employer relationship, collusion between labor and organized crime, and frauds involving union welfare and pension funds. Labor racketeering may take any of these forms. Members of criminal syndicates are often involved in these corrupt practices. Labor is not always an unwilling victim. In great part labor racketeering is the result of corruption among labor leaders and lax enforcement of federal and state laws.

The Central States Pension Fund is said to have assets of more than $1 billion and investments in Las Vegas casinos, Florida hotels, and large restaurant chains.[22] Union welfare and pension funds are estimated to amount to more than $100 billion and to be growing by billions of dollars annually.[23] The leadership of the labor movement presently bears little relationship to the labor organizers of the late nineteenth century. The presidency of a union is highly prized; it provides a large salary and numerous fringe benefits, as well as political power. It is so highly prized that rivalries for the presidency sometimes culminate in violence. The United Mine Workers provide an example of such violence. In 1974 the president of this large and once powerful labor union was convicted of the murder of his rival.[24] On December 31, 1969, Joseph (Jack) Yablonski, his wife, and his daughter were shot to death while they lay asleep in their Pennsylvania home. Three UMW members later confessed to the murder and implicated the president of their union. The conspiracy was hatched in a Kentucky motel in November 1969.[25]

In Howell, Michigan, the candidate for the presidency of a local union, influential in Michigan labor and political circles, was found slumped over his car's steering wheel; he had been shot to death.[26] In 1967 James R. Hoffa, president of the Teamsters, one of the largest labor unions in the United States, entered federal prison, leaving his hand-picked successor to run the union. On July 30, 1975, Hoffa disappeared when he attempted to regain his presidency.[27] High union offices are highly prized. Labor leaders have access to large fortunes and numerous positions that they can fill with their allies and relatives. "Dirty tricks"—even murder—have been employed to discredit and defeat opponents. Rivalries for union leadership have allied some factions with criminal syndicates. Hoffa, it is said, first formed his alliance with organized crime when in search of support of his bid for power. However, these rivalries have sometimes had a serious impact on the rest of society. The United Mine Workers, disillusioned with their leadership and highly fragmented, brought this country to a standstill with a national strike that crippled America's energy needs for more than ninety days. The victim in this instance was not only the union but also the public.

In 1954 the United States Court of Appeals for the Eighth Circuit upheld the conviction of a labor leader who had obtained property from corporate employers through fear and the threat of violence.[28] The defendant had been charged with violating Section 1951 of Title 18 of the United States Code. The statue provides as follows:

> Whoever in any way or degree obstructs, delays or affects commerce or the movement of any article or commodity in commerce, by . . . extortion or attempts to conspire so to do . . . shall be fined not more than $10,000 or imprisoned not more than twenty years, or both.

At an ammunition plant in the Midwest, corrupt unions bilked their employer of more than $10 million in cost overruns.[29] Abuses involving the "union-employer relationship" are numerous. In many instances they are the outcome of a mutual understanding. Some employers give in for fear of labor strife. One employer told a state investigating commission the following:

Q. Before you joined the union, did an accident occur with regard to your premises, Mr. B?

A. Oh, my windows were broken.

Q. All of them?

A. All of them, yes.

Employers have been known to retain racketeers as labor consultants. Some firms have paid an average of $15,000 annually for their services. The consultant ensures labor peace through his contacts within the union. Some union officials receive kickbacks from those consultants. In other situations the payoffs take a more direct route. Federal investigators have uncovered a national practice of payoffs, ranging up to $50,000, at most posts.[30] Payoffs to corrupt union officials have become so common in these ports that

employers pass them off as a cost of doing business and include them in
their shipping rates. In New York a key official of the International
Longshoreman's Association was indicted by a grand jury for accepting
more than $50,000 in cash payments from a multinational corporation.[31] In
return, prosecutors allege, the employer was promised labor peace.

Employers are not always the victims of those union-employer abuses.
The vice-president of a national chain store was indicted for soliciting the
aid of organized crime to persuade unions to meet his company's demands.
Many employers willingly enter into sweetheart contracts with corrupt labor
officials. Under these agreements union members settle for lower wages and
fewer benefits, while their leaders pocket cash payoffs and other benefits
from the employers. Some corrupt union officials, with the aid of criminal
syndicates, establish dummy locals and through this vehicle negotiate
payoffs with employers. Phony welfare plans are used to elicit payoffs from
employers. These schemes are so common and so lucrative that some
racketeers specialize in setting up dummy union locals. Corrupt members of
management may also receive kickbacks from these union shells. Although
the corrupt practices take many forms, the losers are always the union
members and the stockholders of the firm. One corporate officer described
the union-employer relationship to government investigators as follows:

> *Q.* Actually you don't negotiate anything. They just bring a piece of
> paper to you which is a form and actually it is a Xerox copy,
> something like that. They fill in the names and sign it. Isn't that about
> the way it happened?
>
> *A.* . . . yes.

Although the Taft-Hartley Act makes it illegal for employers to pay labor
leaders, the practice continues and by all indications has increased
dramatically. In some instances the employer is an unwilling participant; in
others, a willing contributor. For a fixed fee many employers hope to avoid
labor strife and thus gain an edge over their competitors. One prosecutor
noted that if employers came forth, these practices would not continue.

The McClellan investigation disclosed that Anthony "Tony Ducks"
Corallo, a known Mafia leader, was in control of several Teamster locals.
Mr. Corallo was also alleged to have been a key figure in the narcotics
trade. When Hoffa was asked whether he had taken any steps against
Corallo and other racketeers who had penetrated Teamster locals, his
answer was "as of now, no." In 1972 Lloyd Hicks announced his candidacy
for president of Teamster Local 390 in Miami.[32] Two days later he was
gunned down. In New Jersey the sixty-year-old secretary-treasurer of a
powerful local union was reindicted on kickback-conspiracy charges.[33] The
defendant is alleged to have strong links to organized crime and is under

investigation on charges that he may have taken part in the murder of a well-known gangland figure in upstate New York in 1961. The working relations between organized crime and unions go back to the early part of this century. Many of these relationships have become institutionalized. One investigator remarked, "It's difficult to tell a labor leader from a member of organized crime."

In the early history of the labor movement employers hired gangs of thugs to intimidate workers or break strikes. The rising unions, in turn, employed gangs to assist them against their employers. Violence was met with violence. In the 1930s gangsters began to infiltrate the labor movement. By the 1940s their foothold was well established. In some industries racketeering and labor went hand in hand. Albert Anastasia, a leader in New York's underworld, selected his brother to head the Brooklyn longshoremen's union. The balkanized nature of the longshoremen's unions and other fragmented labor groups further facilitated the rise of organized crime within the labor movement. Corruption on New York's docks became so common that the Waterfront Commission was finally established in 1953 to clean it up. Numerous union officials have been convicted of racketeering activities. For example, a head of the New York longshoremen's union was indicted on fifty-one counts of misusing union funds.[34] But the payoffs, kickbacks, and thefts, continue.

In 1956 James R. Hoffa, in an attempt to gain control of the Teamsters, enlisted the assistance of organized crime. In 1975 these allies played a key role in his demise. His union fell, in large part, to their control. Through the Teamsters, these criminal syndicates were able to exert pressure even on the White House. With their pension funds and large membership, the Teamsters became tools of criminal cartels. In 1969 these criminal elements conceived a union insurance scheme that bilked Teamster locals of large sums of money. Under this scheme employers paid $40 per week to buy individual insurance policies for their employees; employers who refused to go along suffered the union's wrath. These funds were eventually drained away by organized crime in the form of large commissions and administration fees.[35]

For organized crime the labor movement represents a powerful political tool as well as a vehicle for monetary gains. Control over labor groups gives organized crime a powerful political voice and enables criminal elements to hire themselves out to employers as labor consultants who ensure labor peace in return for payoffs. In 1968 a grand jury indicted the president of a multibillion-dollar corporation on charges of perjury.[36] The defendant had lied about his attempts to enlist several members of the Mafia as labor consultants.

In late March 1978 Salvatore Briguglio, a syndicate-connected union leader, was shot to death by two hired assassins in New York.[37] During this time an official high in the Labor Department was reassuring an audience of concerned citizens that the federal government's crackdown on labor racketeering had proven a success. In Las Vegas federal sources were expressing concern that a key Mafia leader had made an attempt to gain control of some local unions.[38] Other government sources were expressing concern that one of the nation's largest labor unions might soon elect an exfelon as its president.[39] The individual involved is alleged to have strong links with organized crime, has been under investigation by federal authorities for more than a dozen years, was once convicted for obstruction of justice, and served a brief prison term. His second-in-command also has a history of criminal involvement and has been indicted three times by federal prosecutors.[40]

A Florida federal grand jury has been looking into kickbacks involving labor officials. Federal investigators have been looking into a $3 million union fund loan to several businessmen. One union official was said to have received a $100,000 kickback.[41] The administrator of a union welfare fund testified before a U.S. Senate subcommittee that the fund was under the total control of a known "mobster."[42] He also noted that the Labor Department had been dragging its feet. A multinational firm with organized crime ties is said to have obtained a $13 million loan from a union fund.[43]

Frauds involving union pension and welfare funds have become a serious problem. Many of these funds have been depleted by loans to anyone willing to give a kickback to corrupt union officials; organized crime-owned businesses have received loans under these terms. Funds have also been invested in elaborate securities schemes. Union funds have been used to hire racketeers as consultants at exorbitant salaries, as well as pay for boats, airplanes, and even private homes for corrupt labor officials. In 1974, under increasing criticism, the federal government established the little-known Pension Benefit Guaranty Corporation (PBGC). The program is financed by insurance premiums assessed against employers who operate private pension funds. The latter fall into two categories: single-employer funds, where one firm pays into the funds, and multiemployer funds, in which a number of employers pay into the same fund. The obligations of these private pension funds are now about $350 billion, while their assets are about $200 billion. About 12 percent of these private funds are experiencing serious difficulties. If they went broke, the PBGC would find it difficult to insure them all adequately, and many union members would go without compensation. The impact on the overall economy could be staggering.

In 1977 one pension fund lost about $7 million as a result of an insurance fraud that involved two hundred thousand of its members.[44] A police pension fund may have been defrauded of more than $500,000, and a pension fund in New Jersey went bankrupt as a result of possible fraud.

Millions of dollars of union members' pension and welfare funds are invested in fraudulent schemes. Corrupt union officials, in conjunction with criminal syndicates, are bilking their members. Many of these investments vanish in the air. Although corrupt union officials receive large kickbacks, their members stand to lose all their benefits. For example, corrupt officials of one union decided without consulting their members to make a multimillion-dollar loan to a firm owned by organized crime. The meeting went as follows:

> *Mr. W.*: I so move, Mr. Chairman.
>
> *Mr. S.*: Second the motion.
>
> *Chairman*: You have heard the motion and seconded. Are you ready for the question? . . . The motion was put to a vote and carried without dissent . . . . It is so ordered.[45]

This brief discussion awarded an organized crime agent more than $100 million, over a ten-year period, in union pension funds. Unless the federal government acts decisively, union welfare and pension funds will continue to be pillaged. The PBGC is far from adequate for dealing with criminal syndicates and corrupt labor leaders bent on bankrupting union treasuries.

The Regulators

A high Justice Department official recently told the U.S. Senate Judiciary Committee that efforts to get the Labor Department to take an aggressive posture toward labor racketeering, "including the infiltration of labor unions" by organized crime, had not proven successful.[46] The Labor Department has conceded that it has committed only thirty investigators to labor racketeering. Plans to reduce that force to fifteen investigators were cancelled when the Congress and Justice Department voiced their opposition. More than three hundred local unions, belonging to five international unions, are presently under federal investigation.[47]

The Labor Department, charged with administering and policing the federal labor laws,[48] was created by act of Congress in 1913. It assumed the role first played by the Bureau of Labor, which had been created in 1884 and had been incorporated within the Interior Department. In 1903 the bureau was placed under the Department of Commerce. The creation of a ninth executive department was convincing proof of the growing role and power of organized labor in this country. The chief officer of the Department of Labor is the secretary, who is assisted by a number of deputy undersecretaries and a staff of executive assistants. The department has its home offices in Washington, D.C., and has ten regional offices, each headed by a regional director. The department has no direct criminal jurisdiction. All criminal cases are referred to the Justice Department for prosecution. The Labor Department has only direct civil jurisdiction; it can only go to court and ask for an injunction. An injunction hardly suffices to deter organized criminal activity in the labor movement.

Under growing criticism, the Labor Department has taken some civil action against several unions. In Ohio the department obtained a court order removing the administrator and trustees of a union health and welfare fund. The department charged that the administrator had been paid "far in excess of reasonable compensation."[49] The department also announced plans to sue a number of former trustees of a $1 billion pension fund.[50] The former trustees have been accused of corrupt practices and mismanagement of the fund. The department initiated its investigation some fifteen years after the frauds began, and then only under congressional pressure. Other federal agencies had been urging the department for several years to act. Some charge it has acted too late.[51]

The Labor Department also supervises various public service jobs, including the Compehensive Education and Training Act (CETA). The program covers more than seven hundred thousand public service jobs and is funded by more than $11 billion. CETA is one of many programs established by Congress to help employ the unemployable, the poor, and minority groups. The program has come under attack, and there are now more than a hundred allegations of mismanagement and fraud. Critics charge that perhaps as much as $1 billion in CETA funds may have been misused and that the new programs have only opened new opportunities for criminal groups.

The department is undermanned. Its entire investigative team consists of only two hundred individuals, a number barely sufficient to meet the present needs of the department let alone investigate new areas of fraud. Without proper supervision the infusion of federal funds into the labor market and union area will only create additional opportunities for organized crime. Programs similar to CETA can easily fall prey to criminal attack as the many antipoverty programs have.

The real target of labor racketeers is no longer the traditional arena; these criminal elements, allied with corrupt union and government officials, are now focusing their attention on white-collar crime. Employers have been found to lease machinery from firms connected or associated with corrupt labor leaders or their relatives. For example, one union leader, with a criminal record dating back to 1925, was renting machinery to employers dealing with his union.[52] On the open market the machinery sells for about $50,000; renting it from the union boss costs about $45,000 a year. These new forms of union corruption, or sweetheart agreements, are the wave of the future.[53] Whether the Labor Department has the expertise and the will to commit resources in this arena remains to be seen.

Detecting Labor Corruption

A number of indicators could assist both the public and law enforcement in detecting labor racketeering. For example, where wages of workers in one union are much lower than those of other unions doing similar work, the difference could be due to union-employer abuses, employment of organized crime figures as labor consultants, or both. The employment of labor consultants known to have links to organized crime is also an indication of corrupt labor practices. For example, a company retains the services of the ABC, Inc., consulting firm to advise it on labor problems; the fee paid is extremely high, and Mr. X, president of the consulting company, is known to have links with criminal syndicates.

Buying from certain suppliers, even though the same products might be cheaper if purchased from other sources, is also an indicator of labor-related fraud. For example, Mr. X sells company YT machinery for $100,000; the same equipment is available from another source at $60,000. In addition, Mr. X is a relative of the president of the local union whose members are employed by YT. Another common practice is for union officials to openly ask for gratuities or for certain individuals to be hired over others. Work slowdown, wildcat strikes, sabotage, and other forms of violence against an employer are also indications of corrupt labor practices. Intimidation of a firm's clients or patrons may also indicate labor racketeering. A tolerance by employers of gambling and loansharking operations on their premises is also an indicator of some understanding between the employer and the union leadership or those who control it.

If a firm is under no pressure to unionize while other employers have been forced to do so, the employer and organized crime figures may have some agreement, or the firm itself may be controlled or owned by organized crime. Pressures on management to contribute to union affairs may also be an indication of some corrupt agreement between labor and management. For example, employers commonly contribute large sums of money to charities sponsored by unions known to have organized crime connections. Whether the funds ever reach the charity is dubious; the charity may be a funnel for illegal payments to union leaders. In addition, unions with officers known to have criminal records or criminal ties may also indicate corrupt practices within that union.

In 1977 a major national television network disclosed that federal investigators had evidence of a $250,000 illegal payment to the Nixon White House by the heads of one of the nation's largest unions in order to release their former president.[54] Soon after, he was paroled. Control of an airport local union in a large eastern city has given organized crime access to valuable freight.[55] These are but a few examples of the problems posed by labor racketeering. The labor movement, born in violence, has found itself the target of gangster elements. Through collusion with some dishonest employers and corrupt union officials, criminal syndicates have infiltrated a number of powerful national unions. The federal government has sat idle for too long; that laxity has in large part facilitated the infiltration of organized crime into every aspect and level of the American labor system.

Notes

1. The deceased, John Anardi, had been involved in Teamster affairs for many years and had an extensive history of criminal involvement in labor matters ("The Frank Fitzsimmons Invitational Golf Tournament," *Overdrive*, April 1975, p. 54).

2. "Teamster Group Asks for Probe of New York Fund," *Burlington Free Press*, August 25, 1977, p. 5A.

3. "Indictment Names Three of Teamsters in Case Involving Tiger Unit," *Wall Street Journal*, December 23, 1977, p. 3.

4. "U.S. Labor Deputy Charged in Fraud," *New York Times*, December 1, 1977, p. 63.

5. J.M. Hussey, *The Byzantine World* (New York: Harper & Bros., 1961), pp. 43, 87, 93, 136; for a review of labor arbitration, see Maurice S. Trotta, *Arbitration of Labor-Management Disputes* (New York: American Management Association, 1974), pp. 13-23.

6. Sydney Pointer, *Medieval Society* (Ithaca, N.Y.: Cornell Press, 1951), pp. 73, 79-84.

7. Ibid., p. 84.

8. Trotta, *Arbitration of Labor-Management Disputes*, p. 43.

9. Ibid., p. 14.

10. Vegelahn v. Guntner, 167 Mass. 92 (1896).

11. United States v. Debs, 64 F Supp. or 2d 724 (1894).

12. Loewe v. Lowlar, 208 U.S. 274 (1908).

13. Chamber of Commerce of the United States, *Deskbook on Organized Crime* (Washington, D.C., 1972), p. 35.

14. Marcia Kramer, "Accuse a Top Banana in ILA of 100 G Bribes," *Daily News*, December 11, 1976, p. 7.

15. Jack Anderson and Les Whitten, "A Look at a Teamster Local's Files," *Washington Post*, August 2, 1977, p. C-19.

16. "$90 Million of Teamster's Money Approved for 32 Year Old," *Overdrive*, September 1974, pp. 50-58.

17. "U.S. Would Block Teamster Loan for Casino," *Washington Post*, March 28, 1978, p. A-18.

18. Ronald A. Anderson and Walter A. Kumpf, *Business Law* (Chicago: Southwestern Publishing, 1967), pp. 889-903.

19. Jack Anderson and Les Whitten, "Sources Say Mob Eliminated Hoffa," *Washington Post*, August 21, 1975, p. F-21.

20. "Frank Fitzsimmons Invitational Golf Tournament," pp. 49-58.

21. "Fitzsimmons' Son Accused," *Washington Post*, April 16, 1978, p. C-7.

22. Anderson and Whitten, "Sources Say Mob Eliminated Hoffa," p. F-21; see also Donald R. Cressey, *Theft of the Nation* (New York: Harper & Row, 1969), pp. 95-99.

23. U.S. Chamber of Commerce, *Deskbook on Organized Crime*, p. 35.

24. "Boyle Set to Appeal Second Conviction in Yablonski Deaths," *Wall Street Journal*, February 21, 1978, p. 12.

25. "Ex-Aide Testifies Boyle Delayed, Then Ordered Yablonski Slaying," *Miami Herald*, February 3, 1978, p. 22-A.

26. "Teamster Leader Shot," *Washington Post*, December 14, 1977, p. A-6.

27. Jack Anderson and Les Whitten, "Chile Resorts to Book Burning," *Washington Post*, August 30, 1975, p. E-21.

28. Hulahan v. United States, 214 F 2d 441 (1954).

29. U.S. Chamber of Commerce, *Deskbook on Organized Crime*, p. 36.

30. Nicholas Gage, "Dock Payoffs Reported Found in Undercover Inquiry by FBI," *New York Times*, September 1, 1977, p. A-1.

31. Kramer, "Accuse a Top Banana in ILA of 100 G Bribes," p. 7.

32. Lester Velie, "The Mafia Tightens Its Grip on the Teamsters," *Readers Digest*, August 1974, p. 99.

33. "Provenzano Reindicted," *Washington Post*, December 20, 1977, p. A-3.

34. "On the Waterfront, Then and Now," *New York*, August 15, 1977, p. 42.

35. Velie, "The Mafia Tightens Its Grip on the Teamsters," pp. 100-102.

36. Cressey, *Theft of the Nation*, p. 98.

37. "N.J. Teamster Official Killed by Two Gunmen," *Washington Post*, March 23, 1978, p. A-8.

38. "Police Discredit Story of Possible Gang War," *Las Vegas Sun*, October 25, 1974, p. 6.

39. Jim Drinkhall, "Teamsters Chief May Soon Depart," *Washington Post*, October 29, 1977, p. A-3.

40. Jim Drinkhall, "Witness in Protective Custody Alleged Role in Kickback to Teamster Official," *Wall Street Journal*, August 18, 1977, p. 4.

41. Ibid., p. 4.

42. "Teamster Fund Controlled by Mobster, Official Says," *New York Times*, November 1, 1977, p. 23.

43. "Central States Pension Fund Loans Help Tell Tale of Teamsters Officials, Organized Crime and the Attorney General of the United States," *Overdrive*, June 1974, p. 46; see also "Meet 'Mr. Manipulator'—The Criminal Lawyer through Whose Fingers Has Poured 200 Million Teamster Dollars, Morris Shenker," *Overdrive*, January 1975, pp. 58-66.

44. Jim Drinkhall, "The Teamsters Accuse an Insurance Promoter of Defrauding Them," *Wall Street Journal*, October 24, 1977, pp. 1, 27; see also "Avalanche of Indictments Hit Organized Crime's Web of Pension Fraud," *Overdrive*, April 1974, pp. 48-50.

45. "The Intricate Financial Web of Allen Dorfman," *Overdrive*, February 1974, p. 55.

46. "Civiletti Chides Labor Department on Strike Force Cooperation," *Washington Post*, March 3, 1978, p. A-29.

47. J. Thomas, "Labor Agency, in Shifts, May Widen Crime Inquiries," *New York Times*, April 10, 1978, p. A-21.

48. 5 U.S.C. 611.

49. "Court Orders Teamsters Fund in Ohio to Remove Its Administrator, Trustees," *Wall Street Journal*, January 4, 1978, p. 8.

50. "Labor Department Seen Prepared to Sue Ex-Trustees of Teamsters' Pension Fund," *Wall Street Journal*, February 1, 1978, p. 7.

51. "Labor Agency Demands Detailed Records of Dorfman's Pact with Teamsters Fund," *Wall Street Journal*, July 26, 1977, p. 7.

52. "On the Waterfront, Then and Now," *New York*, August 15, 1977, p. 42.

53. Dang Ireland, "New York's Mr. Lucky," *New York*, August 15, 1977, pp. 40-43.

54. "Hoffa Prison Release Subject of New Probe," *Washington Post*, July 30, 1977, p. A-2.

55. Velie, "Mafia Tightens Its Grip on the Teamsters," p. 99; see also Public Citizens Staff Report, *White Collar Crime* (Washington, D.C.: Congress Watch, 1974), pp. 18-19.

5 Cargo Thefts

In New York City a housing policeman and an associate of an organized crime boss were charged with conspiring to hijack a liquor shipment valued at more than $30,000.[1] In France a twenty-five-ton truck carrying valuable uranium was attacked and its cargo stolen.[2] In Washington, D.C., federal sources disclosed that more than three thousand pounds of plutonium, enough to construct three hundred atomic bombs, was missing.[3] A key federal official conceded that theft was a possibility. In one large midwestern city a wiretap showed that both the police and the courts were protecting criminals engaged in major thefts. Many policemen wore stolen clothes, and many judges purchased stolen merchandise.[4]

Theft of cargo is a serious and ever-increasing problem. One U.S. Senate study has concluded that "many of these things [merchandise] are stolen for order and they are handled by organized crime."[5] Well-placed sources put the figure at more than $1 billion annually.[6] Cargo theft affects all modes of transportation. It requires an organization, and organized criminal cartels are playing a dominant role in the planning of the theft and the distribution of the stolen goods. With the rise of terrorism an increase in cargo thefts by these groups is expected in the near future. The proliferation of nuclear material may attract organized criminal attention. It should come as no surprise if criminal cartels and terrorist elements eventually work together in this arena. The vulnerability of both transient and stationary goods is inviting.[7]

The Problem of Cargo Theft

Stolen cargo may consist of valuable securities, drugs, precious metals, even cigarettes and shoes. The problem of cargo theft may involve carriers, shippers, insurers, labor unions, employers, and employees. Stolen cargo is a valuable commodity; through a chain of fences the thieves can quickly find buyers for their stolen wares. The resale value of these stolen goods is high; the ability of the market to absorb them is good. Further stolen merchandise is usually difficult to trace and identify.

Stolen cargo affects four key areas of the economy: air, rail, truck, and maritime. A study by the federal government places the annual losses of thefts of air cargo at $400 million, rail at $600 million, truck-related cargo

71

at $1.2 billion, and maritime-connected cargo at $300 million.[8] These thefts usually involve the cooperation of insiders. One well-known New England crime figure has told investigators that these insiders are known as ten percenters. In exchange for his valuable assistance the insider is given 10 percent of the proceeds after resale.[9] Packages of razor blades that sell in the marketplace for $1.95 were sold by these criminal groups for 50 cents, thus undercutting the legitimate businessman.

Hijacking has also been used in the theft of cargo and usually requires the cooperation of an insider. In this situation the driver surrenders possession of his truck and goods without a fight. The driver may park his truck on a street and leave to eat; his associates then move in and steal the truck and all its cargo.[10] A single theft of cigarettes usually exceeds $30,000, a truckload of appliances can exceed $500,000 in value, and camera equipment can exceed $200,000.[11] Organized crime members are usually not directly involved in cargo hijackings, but the planning, funding, and contacts would often be impossible without their assistance.[12] More than 20 million trucks in this country haul valuable cargo; thus the dimensions of the problem are staggering.

Airports are a favorite target of criminal groups. One well-organized gang over a period of four years was able to steal more than $100 million in stocks, bonds, furs, jewelry, traveler's checks, credit cards, and cash. As a result of their contacts in national criminal syndicates, the gang found easy outlets for their goods. Although independent of the national criminal groups, this smaller group could not function on such a large scale without syndicate assistance. The leader of this gang testified: "The most important of my partners was Phil. . . . [He] had very good connections with the principal mob people in New York and New Jersey. . . . Through him I met most of the principal fences we used."[13]

Many cargo thefts take place at either freight docks or piers. One common scheme is to "pad the truck." The driver and checker may count 500 cartons of a product on the truck but record only 300. The consignee, aware that he has received 500 cartons, signs for only 300 and files a claim for the difference. The 200 cartons eventually find their way into the illicit market. These thefts could not be perpetrated successfully without the assistance of insiders. In some instances even top company officials may be indirectly involved. In order to stave off union problems, management may close its eyes to these thefts and pass the cost to the insurance company and consumers. At other times in return for a percentage of the theft, top executives may openly assist the felons.

By manipulating records, by bribing, or by using force, national criminal syndicates prey on air, land, and water transport systems, both inside and outside the country. The increased use of the computer has encouraged the falsification of records. By manipulating a computer's programs or input data or through the use of a company's agents, organized crime can steal with impunity. The computer is a new tool for these criminals.[14]

Impact of Cargo Theft

Some dismiss thefts of cargo as a mode of doing business. One businessman confided that, after all, it is the insurance company and the public who "foot the bill". Company losses are passed to them in the form of insurance claims and higher prices. However, the businessman neglected to consider the indirect impact of cargo theft on the overall economy. Some carriers refuse to handle cargo that proves theftprone. A study of ninety-six carriers found that they were reluctant to handle all theftprone cargo.[15] The businessman may find that the carrier has dropped him, and he may find it difficult to find alternate transport. Some carriers not only are reluctant to handle theftprone cargo but also avoid theftprone areas; piers, docks, and airports with high rates of theft may be blacklisted.

Cargo thefts result in higher insurance premiums. Business or industries in a high-risk area often find their insurance premium rates increasing rapidly. The insurer may refuse to underwrite any new businesses, or he may blacklist a certain area. After a series of hijackings, for example, one firm found that its annual insurance premiums had increased by 1,000 percent. The firm declared bankruptcy soon after.

Thefts of cargo also result in lost sales and occasionally in bankruptcy. The victim may find it difficult or even impossible to replace the lost merchandise. Even if replacements are available, they may be costly, especially when seasonal merchandise is involved. Few small businessmen can afford the extra costs of replacement, and the delays involved in shipping the replacement merchandise may increase the victim's losses. The victim may even have to declare bankruptcy to stave off his creditors.

The threat of violence, always present in cargo thefts, may drive businesses from a city or a state. It may also result in the diversion of cargo. To minimize the theft of their cargo some firms may direct their shipments over routes that avoid the theftprone areas. This can result in higher prices to the shipper and to the consumer, since the shipper will usually pass these to the consumer. Lost cargo can also diminish the tax base. Businessmen are unable to pay taxes on goods they never received, and thieves pay no taxes. Thus the government recoups no taxes from the stolen cargo. The public loses confidence in both the government and the business sector. The economic impact of cargo theft far exceeds the direct loss suffered by its owner.

Role of Organized Crime

A carloader at a large rail terminal stole valuable raw furs valued at over $100,000 simply by removing their shipping tags and readdressing them to fences in several large cities. A gang of fewer than six individuals employed by a major airline made it a practice to steal cargo from the airline terminal. Among the cargo they stole were hundreds of cartons of revolvers. Employees, acting alone or in small bands, have been responsible for millions of dollars of lost cargo. Their activities are usually coordinated and funded by organized criminal combines. The lone wolf poses little problem for cargo security.

Organized crime groups play a key role in the theft of cargo. That role may take a direct form. In one large eastern city 15 to 20 percent of all cargo thefts are directly connected to organized crime members. As many as 75 percent of all hijackings in the same city were planned and executed by organized crime groups.[16] Many other offenses are a result of collusion between employees and organized crime associates.

The role of organized criminal groups in the theft of cargo may take an indirect form. Many times, however, it is direct and visible. Organized crime is usually involved in the planning and execution of a theft and in the distribution of stolen cargo. In one large midwestern state cargo theft is an important activity of organized crime.[17]

There are many reasons why organized criminal groups control so much of this area of criminal endeavor. Only they can provide a sophisticated network of large fences to dispose of the stolen goods. In many instances organized crime-controlled businesses are the consumers of those goods. With control over more than ten thousand businesses (many of these with national and international branches), organized crime has access to a large market for stolen merchandise. Organized criminal groups also exert powerful political pressure. Reliable sources note that organized crime can shut down one of the nation's largest airports if the airport authorities pose a problem.[18] The hold of organized crime over powerful labor unions in the trucking and shipping industries ensures that few will seriously challenge it.[19] Businesses not only close their eyes to these illegal activities but also make cash payments to maintain labor peace.[20]

The role of organized crime in this arena is facilitated by the very nature of the stolen cargo. Large and bulky cargo calls for a large distribution system. Stocks, bonds, diamonds, gold, and other precious metal require a sophisticated system of fences, as well as forgers and counterfeiters to prepare phony identification cards. Organized criminal syndicates, through their internal company contacts, can easily falsify internal company records. In this computer era, in which computer programmers and operators can be called on to manipulate computerized data, the role of organized crime may be expected to attain new growth levels. A computer operator who owes money to a loanshark can easily be persuaded to falsify computerized data. The growth and sophistication of cargo security has also marked the end of the lone thief; thefts are now better planned and funded. Organized criminal groups alone possess this capability. The changing technology and needs of a highly industrialized society demand specialized distribution systems. The hijacking of a gasoline truck poses few distribution problems, but the hijacking of valuable radioactive material requires a specialized fencing network with international contacts.

The role of organized crime in cargo theft is on the increase, because technology and the specialized nature of society have marked the decline of the individual thief. Cargo theft, especially cargoes of goods that are difficult to dispose of, requires the efforts of organized criminal groups. These groups determine who will do the job, how it will be executed, and how the stolen cargo will be transferred and fenced.

Need for Security

Those who have dealt with the problem of cargo theft concentrate their efforts in two areas: personnel security and physical security.[21] The objective of a security strategy is to reduce cargo exposure to criminal elements. The underlying philosophy of industrial security is the reduction of opportunities for theft and pilferage. Employees should be well screened and their references checked; the prospective employee should be made aware of this screening process. Some security personnel also suggest polygraph tests for applicants for sensitive jobs; voice analyzers have also been used in screening out undesirable applicants. In addition to these measures, the applicant may be required to list all arrests and other contacts with law enforcement and the courts.

Security personnel suggest other measures to tighten control. Access to sensitive areas should be only on a need-to-know basis. Badges and other forms of identification should be used where needed.[22] Security personnel should be posted, and entries by employees to controlled areas should be logged.[23] Personnel positions should be rotated, and complaints by employees should be fully investigated. When thefts involving employees are uncovered, prosecution should be swift; hesitation to prosecute one employee will only be an invitation to others. Key management personnel should be rotated, as should key personnel who have access to records. One firm that had been losing large amounts of its merchandise later discovered that the thefts were the result of collusion between drivers and the shipping department.[24]

Physical security is another method recommended as a tool for reducing cargo theft. This strategy includes the use of alarm systems, lighting, barriers, and communication devices. Physical security strategists have even suggested using helicopters to move cargo in order to cut down on hijackings.[25] Plans should be updated periodically, emergency contingencies should be well defined, and the role of security personnel should be clearly delineated. Guards should check all packages coming in and out of the company premises, locks should be used freely, and vehicles should be spot-checked. Suspicious vehicles should be brought to the attention of law enforcement personnel immediately.

Security strategists detail the manner in which guards should be employed and trained, as well as ways to maintain high morale. Minimum qualifications are outlined for the guard force, and training in the use of weapons and force are suggested. In addition, these experts recommend a course in tactics employed by cargo thieves. Monitoring devices should be used in conjunction with the guard services. Guards themselves should be rotated at irregular intervals, and they should be assigned identification badges.

Cargo theft has given rise to a multimillion-dollar security industry that attempts to deal with the problem. New electronic devices have been developed to spot-check potential thieves. New alarm systems are being employed to minimize theft. Millions of dollars are spent annually on lighting to hamper thieves. Organized crime has a vast network of contacts that may reach well into the upper echelon of a company's management. Some key company officials can be won over through bribes and blackmail; others may cooperate to stave off labor difficulties. Law enforcement agencies may be corrupt, and thus prosecutions are rare. The best security measure is powerless to stop organized crime and its vast distribution system, as long as management is willing to look away. As long as firms are willing to purchase stolen cargo, security measures may succeed in hampering the activities of the lone thief, but not of well-organized criminal groups.

Security measures have the potential for violating the privacy of employees. The Fair Credit Reporting Act regulates the methods an employer may use to obtain information from an applicant. The credit bureau must tell the applicant in writing what information the potential employer is seeking. If an applicant is denied employment solely on the basis of the credit bureau report, he can request additional information from the credit bureau. The Privacy Act of 1974 prohibits the federal government from collecting and disseminating information about individuals. Numerous other laws, both federal and state, prohibit the invasion of an individual's privacy and open the employer to potential lawsuits. Consequently security measures have only a limited impact on organized crime.

Legal Tools to Combat Cargo Theft

At the state level a number of statutes address the problem of cargo theft and can be employed to combat criminals. The unlawful taking and carrying away of the personal property (cargo) of another with intent to deprive the owner (the company) of it permanently constitutes larceny. Most jurisdictions differentiate between grand and petit larceny and establish the cutoff point between petit and grand larceny as $100. The theft of property exceeding $100 in value is considered grand larceny (a felony) and carries a substantially heavier sentence than petit larceny (a misdemeanor).

One who has lawful possession of another's cargo and converts it to his own use is guilty of embezzlement. These statutes apply to employees of firms who are involved in cargo thefts. The prosecution must demonstrate that the employee enjoyed a relationship of trust with the owner of the cargo. In addition most states have statutes that deal with receiving stolen property; in cargo theft, these apply to a fence or other receiver of the stolen goods.[26] The knowing receipt of stolen property with intent to deprive the owner of it permanently is a crime under these statutes.

If force or threat is employed, to permanently deprive the rightful owner of his personal property (cargo) (as in a hijacking), the robbery statutes can be employed. Many of these statutes state that the theft must occur in the presence of the owner or one of his employees. The victim must be present at the time of the theft. If an employee agrees with outsiders to commit an unlawful act (cargo theft), the agreement is a violation of the conspiracy statutes. That the objective was never accomplished is no defense. Breaking and entering the dwelling of another with intent to commit a felony is a violation of the burglary statutes. Many of the old statutes require that the break-in take place at night; however, modern statutes have modified this to encompass all hours. Further modern statutes include all buildings in the definition of "dwelling." Thus burglary statutes can be applied to cargo thefts.

A number of federal statutes address the problem of cargo theft, since this crime uses interstate and foreign commerce. The theft or embezzlement of goods moving in interstate or foreign commerce is a crime under Section 659 of Title 18 of the federal criminal code. This statute covers motor trucks, ships, railroad cars, aircraft, and the stations, platforms, and depots used by these vehicles. In addition the statute covers receivers of stolen cargo who knew that the goods were stolen. If the value of the stolen goods exceeds $100, the statute provides for penalties of up to ten years of imprisonment and up to $5,000 in fines.[27] Section 660 of the federal criminal code covers officers, directors, managers, and other employees of a firm or association, including corporations, who willfully convert to their own use or that of another property belonging to the employer.[28] It covers insiders in cargo theft cases provided that the cargo is carried by a common carrier moving in interstate or foreign commerce. If the latter requirement is not met, state statutes must be applied.

Stealing cargo or trading in stolen cargo within a federal enclave is also a violation of federal law and carries both prison terms and fines.[29] Entering a military reservation or post to commit an illegal act is also a federal crime.[30] Theft of cargo on a military base is thus covered. Interference with interstate or foreign commerce by robbery or extortion (use of force or threats of force) is a violation of federal law, punishable by imprisonment and a fine.[31]

Whoever breaks the seal or lock of any railroad car, vessel, aircraft, motortruck, wagon, or other vehicle or any pipeline system containing property moving in interstate or foreign commerce, with intent to commit a larceny, may be fined up to $5,000 and imprisoned up to ten years.[32] Whoever enters or breaks into any vessel within the maritime jurisdiction of the United States with intent to commit a felony, is in violation of federal law and can be fined up to $1,000 and imprisoned up to five years.[33] Theft of cargo from such a vessel is covered by this statute.

Section 2314 of the federal criminal code makes it a crime, punishable by a fine of up to $10,000 and imprisonment of up to ten years, for anyone to transport stolen goods, securities, or money in interstate or foreign commerce.[34] The transport of stolen cargo (goods or securities) from one state to another or to a foreign country is covered by this statute. The sale or receipt of these goods is covered by Section 2315 and is punishable by fines of up to $10,000 and imprisonment of up to ten years. This statute covers fences and other receivers of stolen cargo.

Policing Cargo Theft

Policing the theft of cargo is the responsibility of a number of state and federal law enforcement agencies. At the state level a number of city, county, and state police forces become involved. At the federal level primary investigatory jurisdiction falls on the Interstate Commerce Commission (ICC), the Civil Aeronautics Board (CAB), the Federal Maritime Commission (FMC), the Department of Transportation (DOT), and the Bureau of Customs (BC). These federal agencies have no criminal prosecutorial powers; all criminal investigations are turned over to the U.S. Justice Department for prosecution. The Federal Bureau of Investigation (FBI) also becomes involved when cargo thefts occur on federal enclaves or affect federal property.

The war against cargo theft has been marred by bureaucratic red tape, rivalries between the agencies, and a lack of coordination of efforts and strategy. The BC has no jurisdiction in matters involving transport of stolen property from one state to another. The FBI has traditionally shown a reluctance to cooperate with the BC and other federal agencies. The ICC is bogged down by red tape, and its investigators lack training in criminal cases. The CAB has no criminal investigatory jurisdiction. Its investigations are civil in nature; few are ever referred to the Justice Department for prosecution. The FMC has proved receptive to outside political pressures and has a dismal record in cargo thefts involving shipping.

Cargo theft is a serious problem. Although new security measures have been devised, only the lone thieves have been curtailed. The power and influence of organized criminal groups continues in more subtle forms. The present global environment is conducive to the theft of valuable cargo. Terrorist groups and their patrons, as well as the energy crisis, have increased the probability that valuable cargo such as nuclear material may become the target of sophisticated criminal groups. Desperate groups and energy-hungry nations have given rise to new markets for stolen cargo.

Notes

1. Law enforcement sources believe that the Thomas Lucchese Mafia family was behind the attempted theft.

2. Thomas O'Toole, "Magazine Says Israelis Hijacked A-Bomb Fuel," *Washington Post*, October 25, 1977, p. A-3.

3. "U.S. Can't Account for Major Amounts of Nuclear Material," *Wall Street Journal*, August 5, 1977, p. 2.

4. U.S., Congress, Senate, Select Committee on Small Business, *The Impact of Crime on Small Business, Part 6* (Washington, D.C.: U.S. Government Printing Office, 1974), pp. 12-13.

5. Ibid., p. 3.

6. U.S., Department of Transportation, Office of the Secretary, *Cargo Theft and Organized Crime: A Deskbook for Management and Law Enforcement* (Washington, D.C.: U.S. Government Printing Office, 1972), p. 9.

7. For a review of the problem of terrorism, see Jeffrey A. Tannenbaum, "For World's Alienated, Violence Often Reaps Political Recognition," *Wall Street Journal*, January 4, 1977, p. 1.

8. U.S., Department of Commerce, Domestic and International Business Administration, *Crime in Service Industries* (Washington, D.C., 1977), pp. 4, 5.

9. Vincent Teresa, with Thomas C. Renner, *My Life in the Mafia* (Garden City, N.Y.: Doubleday & Co., 1973), p. 135.

10. Ibid., p. 138.

11. Department of Commerce, *Crime in Service Industries*, p. 13.

12. Teresa, with Renner, *My Life in the Mafia*, p. 139.

13. Department of Transportation, *Cargo Theft and Organized Crime*, p. 35.

14. For a review of computer crime see August Bequai, *Computer Crime* (Lexington, Mass.: Lexington Books, D.C. Heath & Co., 1978), p. 14.

15. Department of Transportation, *Cargo Theft and Organized Crime*, p. 5.

16. Ibid., p. 26.

17. Ibid., p. 25.

18. Chamber of Commerce of the United States, *Deskbook on Organized Crime* (Washington, D.C., 1972), p. 12.

19. Nicholas Cage, "Dock Payoffs Reported Found in Undercover Inquiry by FBI," *New York Times*, September 1, 1977, p. A-1.

20. Marcia Kramer, "Accuse a Top Banana in ILA of 100 G Bribe," *Daily News*, December 11, 1976, p. 7.

21. See Walter A. Lucas, "Protection of High Value Cargo," *Security Management*, November 1977, pp. 9, 10; John E. Hurley, "Cutting Cargo Losses in Port," *Security Management*, January 1978, p. 6.

22. U.S., Department of Transportation, Office of the Secretary, *Cargo Security Handbook for Shippers and Receivers* (Washington, D.C.: U.S. Government Printing Office, 1972), pp. 25-26.

23. U.S., Department of Transportation, Office of the Secretary, *Guidelines for the Physical Security of Cargo* (Washington, D.C.: U.S. Government Printing Office, 1972), pp. 11-12.

24. Department of Transportation, *Cargo Theft and Organized Crime*, p. 49.

25. U.S., Department of Transportation, Office of Transportation Security, *St. Louis Helicopter Project: A Cooperative Effort among Fourteen Railroad Police* (Washington, D.C.: U.S. Government Printing Office, 1973), pp. 23-31.

26. The drawbacks of these statutes are discussed in chapter 6.

27. 18 U.S.C. 659.

28. 18 U.S.C. 660.

29. 18 U.S.C. 661, 662.

30. 18 U.S.C. 1382, 1383.

31. 18 U.S.C. 1951.

32. 18 U.S.C. 2117.

33. 18 U.S.C. 2276.

34. 18 U.S.C. 2314.

6 Fencing

A fifteen-month investigation involving local and federal law enforcement agencies resulted in the arrest of more than twenty individuals in a large eastern city.[1] The authorities had penetrated a complex and sophisticated fencing operation. Among those arrested were a prominent attorney, a local politician, and an assistant district attorney. The investigators also recovered more than $500,000 in stolen goods including jewelry, diamonds, even a Rembrandt. The ring that operated this fencing system was said to have ties with criminal syndicates in cities throughout the United States.

A three-month undercover investigation in the nation's capital resulted in several arrests; among those arrested, were several policemen.[2] The ring operated a well-financed interstate fencing system with contacts in several states. In a large southwestern state prosecutors brought indictments against more than sixty individuals for operating a large interstate fencing network.[3] The authorities also recovered more than $2 million worth of stolen property, including a 250-pound pet lion.

In the last several years, under public pressure to deal a blow to a national fencing system, law enforcement agencies have conducted numerous undercover operations (referred to as stings). Operations in ten cities have recovered more than $30 million in stolen goods.[4] However, law enforcement agencies concede that this is only the tip of the iceberg. Fencing in this country is a well-organized, multibillion-dollar business. The annual figures range from a low of $9 billion to a high or more than $20 billion.[5] The problem, although not new, is growing. In the United States there are two markets: a legal one and an illegal one. The latter is not regulated or taxed; it not only defrauds the government of millions of dollars in taxes but also undermines the legitimate business sector.

Defining Fencing

Fences are not a new phenomenon. The Barbary pirates sold their ill-gotten goods to a series of fences, many of whom then sold the goods to a series of smaller fences. Fencing became a sophisticated business in sixteenth-century England, largely as a result of an intermediary system of fencing developed by Moll Cutpurse (1584-1659). Both thief and victim came to her, and she negotiated the return of the goods for a fair price to the thieves and received a commission for her services.

81

Jonathan Wild (1683-1725) was the thief-taker of London. England at that time had no public police forces; law enforcement was still in the hands of private individuals. The thief-taker had the power to make arrests; he could also arrange for thieves to sell their stolen goods to the owner, in return for which Wild received a commission. The thief-taker relied on a system of informers who were paid when the goods were returned to the true owner.

Wild soon came to rule London's underworld. Thieves sold their wares to his agents, who in turn sold them to the real owners. This system flourished and eventually took the shape of a market with agents and buyers in many cities. Thieves who ventured to sell their wares on their own were arrested by Wild and his agents and sent to the gallows. Through sheer force and business intellect, Jonathan Wild estasblished an efficient fencing system.

The cities that sprang up in America adopted the system that Jonathan Wild had developed in London. Private police forces often negotiated with criminals for the return of the stolen goods and received a commission from the owner of the property. Well after the turn of the century detectives were still supplementing their incomes by negotiating with fences for the return of stolen property. The practice was accepted and in some cases appreciated. Insurance companies even today often negotiate with fences for the return of stolen valuables.

The fence is a middleman; he reconciles the needs of the marketplace and those of the seller. He serves as a conduit between the seller (thief) and the buying public.[6] He is a receiver who knowingly traffics in stolen property.[7] His buying and selling habits, like those of the legitimate businessman, depend on the whims of the consuming public. His behavior is dictated by the needs of the marketplace.

Fencing is a multibillion-dollar annual business that dwarfs many legitimate businesses.[8] It provides criminals (both organized and nonorganized) with a meeting place to sell their illegal wares. Buyers from all strata of society come to the fence to find bargains.

Fencing is a nonviolent crime; it is a commercial crime.[9] It consists of a network of receivers; some specialize, while others handle all sorts of stolen property. The fence may help initiate and plan a theft. A fence in one large eastern city assisted thieves in the hijacking of a large truck carrying coffee.[10] Forty-five minutes later the coffee was being sold at a local supermarket. Without a vast network of fences thieves would find it nearly impossible to dispose of their gains. One former thief told a U.S. Senate committee investigating fencing the following:

Senator: How important were these organized crime-connected fences to your operation? In other words, if you did not have them to fence stolen goods for you and take them off your hands and pay you something for them, could your operation have been successful?

Witness: No, not without a fence.

Senator: You would have to have a fence?

Witness: Yes, sir.

Senator: And you found that requirement fulfilled in the ranks of the syndicate or organized crime?

Witness: Yes, sir.

Categorizing Fences

The fence buys and sells stolen goods. Fences may store, deliver, and even market goods sold to them by thieves. They may finance a hijacking or the theft of valuable property. In a few situations thieves deal directly with the buyer. However, since thieves want to minimize the risks of detection and maximize their profits, they generally prefer to deal with the fence rather than the buyer. In cases involving perishable goods and bulky materials, fences serve the thief well. The thief knows that when he deals with the fence he is safe from police intrusion.

Buyers generally seek two types of goods: those that have been stolen and are thus available at a low price and those that are controlled (such as drugs) and thus not readily available. Fences can usually provide both types. Buyers usually fall into one of two categories: those who are aware that the goods are stolen and those who believe that the transaction is legitimate.[11] Buyers in the latter category may easily believe that transactions involving securities and artifacts are legitimate, a buyer who is arrested with the fence usually pleads ignorance, thus making it difficult for both investigators and prosecutors to bring this illegal market under control.

A fence's clients come from all strata of society.[12] Many are simply individual consumers who buy for their own personal use. For example, X buys a carton of stolen cigarettes or a color television from a fence. Legitimate businesses and foreign countries may buy from a fence because the goods can be obtained at a lower price or because the goods are not available in the legal marketplace. Corporations may turn to a fence to buy large quantities of poultry or produce at a price lower than that found in the legitimate marketplace. Foreign countries unable to purchase arms in the legitimate market because of embargoes and so forth may turn to a fence. The fence not only brings the buyer and seller together but also insulates the two. They never meet, and both retain their anonymity.

Fences differ in size, services offered, and markets served. Not all fences can meet the needs of a small country in search of arms. Some fences would not be interested in selling a color television to a local resident. The needs of the marketplace have resulted in specialization and adaptation. There are four types of fences: the local fence, the specialist, the outlet,[13] and the ethnic.[14] This last fence, unique to certain ethnic groups, is prevalent in small communities where kinship ties are important.

The local fence usually operates within a small geographic area. His clients tend to be individuals from the neighborhood. The thieves also tend to come from the same geographic area. A local fence can be compared to the owner of a small store who caters to a localized market. He may operate from a tavern, a garage, a parking lot, a pawn shop, or a small grocery store. He may have ties with organized crime, but he tends to be an independent who pays his dues to the organized criminal elements that control his neighborhood. He can be compared to a franchisee; he works independently but could not survive without cooperating with the organized criminal world. He is a subordinate within the criminal hierarchy.

The quantity and quality of goods handled by the local fence depend on the economic standing of his clients. What he sells and how he sells it ultimately depend on his customers. Local fences are visible in the poor neighborhoods of large urban centers. They may also be found in business districts where they function in a more affluent manner. Local fences provide myriad goods from auto parts to radios and cigarettes. They also supply organized crime with numerous small outlets for its goods. Local fences are at the bottom of the distribution chain.

Law enforcement has traditionally concentrated its efforts against small local fences. The federally funded sting operations have also concentrated on these localized networks. These sting operations appear impressive; they have resulted in more than one thousand arrests and in the recovery of more than $40 million of stolen property.[15] However, for every small fence arrested or small group of thieves apprehended, ten others are ready to take its place. Localized fencing is highly decentralized. Local fences are too numerous and fragmented to be brought under legal control. The thrust of law enforcement should be against the upper echelon of the fencing world, with prosecutions directed at those who finance the multimillion-dollar fencing operations.

The specialized fence represents the upper crust of his profession. Unlike the local fence, he specializes in high-quality goods. He enjoys prestige and is insulated from law enforcement by a group of select clients who value his services as well as their own anonymity. He may trade in diamonds, gold, artifacts, industrial secrets, even nuclear material. The growing demand for nuclear weapons increase specialization in this area.

The specialist poses a problem for investigators because, unlike the local fence, the specialist deals with a small select group of clients. He personally knows his sellers and his buyers, making it difficult for the police to penetrate this specialized network. Further, unlike the local fence, the specialist handles high-quality goods. A sting operation aimed at the specialist fencing network would prove expensive. As one prosecutor noted, "You can't buy artifacts with $50,000." The specialist may also operate internationally. His transactions may take place abroad, buyer and seller meeting with him in another country. The network is highly insulated by agents who act as buffers between the seller, the fence, and the buyer.

Specialized fences may work directly with organized crime, or they may enjoy some autonomy. Even if they are not members of organized criminal cartels, however, they are forced to work with the latter. One fence who was not a member of any organized criminal syndicate but worked closely with those groups was said to have an annual income of more than $1 million from his operations in stolen securities, jewelry, and works of art.[16] He enjoyed a mutually beneficial working relationship with organized criminal groups. Because of his specialized background he was once asked to find a buyer for a diamond weighing 100 carats and valued at more than $500,000 in the illegal market.

Valuable works of art have recently become targets of specialist fences. American buyers are paying more than $50 million annually for these stolen artifacts. Four paintings said to be worth more than $1 million were recently stolen from a New England museum. In a separate incident an English gallery was burglarized, and thieves took more than $5 million in paintings. In Italy more than $10 million of artifacts are stolen yearly; many find their way into this country. A valuable painting stolen from a Spanish museum in the 1930s was only recently recovered; the buyer had been a wealthy American businessman. Fences play a key role in this highly specialized and lucrative illegal market. They bring thief and buyer together.[17]

Artifacts from Asia, Latin America, and the Middle East have also captured the attention of specialist fences. One such fence sold a valuable Italian painting to a wealthy midwestern art collector. Fences have hired vacationing college students to smuggle Aztec artifacts out of Mexico. Some of these relics were sold to a Belgian middleman operating within the United States.[18]

Valuable art works are in great demand by businessmen the world over, and specialist fences cater to this international illegal art market. The growth of this illegal market is largely a result of the sharp increase in the price of artifacts in the last several years. Many wealthy investors consider art a good investment even if the artifacts have been stolen. It is easy to steal and sell these art objects; the risks are few. A specialist fence deals with an extremely small market. His buyers are wealthy individuals who have little to gain by going to the police. In many cases the market spans several countries and continents. A Belgian fence may sell his goods to a wealthy American businessman, and American fences have been known to buy works of art in Ethiopia. The market is too international and sophisticated for the law enforcement officials of any one country to handle successfully. International cooperation is presently lacking.

Federal authorities recently admitted that they did not know what happened to more than two tons of uranium and plutonium used in the last twenty-five years to make nuclear weapons.[19] More than 50 percent of the missing nuclear material was high-grade uranium; the rest was plutonium. It takes less than twenty pounds of the plutonium to build a small nuclear weapon. Federal authorities could not explain how the material was removed from closely guarded plants. Authorities indicate that terrorism is on a global increase.[20] Leaders of small radical nations have indicated a desire to acquire nuclear weaponry; terrorists also want to gain control over nuclear devices. Given the willingness of many small nations and terrorist groups to expend large sums of money for material to build a nuclear weapon, it should come as no shock that specialized fences may soon be able to meet this need.

Some specialist fences have already armed small groups and countries with light weapons. The Third World, with its turmoil and conflicts, provides a ready-made market for the middlemen in arms. Illegal arms have been shipped to numerous small countries and terrorist groups. Sophisticated and highly specialized fences play a key role. One federal investigator stated that thousands of American-made military weapons stolen from military arsenals have already made their way into Latin America.

The specialist fence, even more than his local counterpart, poses problems for law enforcement. His clients are usually men and women from well-respected sectors of our economy: businessmen, professionals, foreign political leaders. The specialist fence operates nationally and internationally. The highly specialized and personalized nature of his work make investigations and prosecutions difficult. His victims are reluctant to testify against him. Few businessmen want the public to know that their firm's industrial secrets were sold to a competitor. Modern technology is increasing the specialist's role, making the job of law enforcement even more difficult.

A third fencing system involves mass distribution of large quantities of stolen goods. This distribution is handled by the outlet fence, who can dispose of large quantities of stolen goods within a short period of time. Outlet fences can easily dispose of several trucks of stolen poultry in a few hours. The outlet fence gears his efforts and operation to the large market.

The outlet fence may be a legitimate business, with national and international contacts. It may be a large national supermarket with stores throughout many cities and states. It can easily dispose of large quantities of stolen property. An organized criminal group may bribe an official of the corporation to purchase the goods from one of its front businesses. Or an official high in management may suspect that the goods are stolen, but the low price makes them attractive, so he pretends to know nothing. During the gasoline shortage of 1973-1974, many garage chains were buying stolen gasoline, pretending ignorance of its true source.

Organized crime owns many businesses that can act as outlet fences. Organized crime members control one of the largest hotel chains in the United States.[21] It would be a simple matter for them to funnel large quantities of stolen goods through this national corporation. One recent study noted that organized crime members own as many as fifteen thousand corporations in this country. They are also said to control at least thirty thousand other firms. In one state organized crime figures own more than five hundred major businesses. In a large city members of organized crime controlled businesses with total assets exceeding $800 million and annual receipts of more than $900 million.[22] Control over such vast corporate empires gives organized crime an outlet for large quantities of stolen goods. For example, hijacked liquor can easily be disposed of through a chain of restaurants and bars owned by organized crime. These activities are not only national in nature; organized crime figures have been known to fence hundreds of automobiles to buyers in the Middle East, Africa, and Asia.[23]

Outlet fences handle goods from scams or bustouts as well as stolen property. Bustouts are planned bankruptcies, in which organized crime is heavily involved.[24] They account for more than $80 million in annual losses to the economy and affect every facet of it.[25] Organized criminal elements may take any one of three initial steps to a bankruptcy fraud: they may establish a new firm; they may form one with a name identical to a well-known and established firm; or they may take over an old, well-established firm.[26]

After organized crime members obtain control of a corporation, they proceed to establish credit. Moderate sums of money are deposited in banks, income statements are doctored, and modest orders are placed. Gradually orders are increased and payments to creditors decreased. In one case organized crime gained control of a meat and poultry supplier.[27] Within a brief period of time they bought more than $1 million of supplies on credit. The poultry was then disposed of, and the creditors were left with the unpaid bills.

Prosecuting outlet fences can prove to be difficult. The outlet fence charged with selling stolen goods usually pleads innocence. One large auto repair firm was charged with serving as an outlet fence for stolen auto parts.[28] The officers of the company pleaded innocent and argued that they did not know the parts had been stolen. The court agreed.

The outlet fence plays a key role in the national fencing network. Without the outlet fence, large quantities of stolen property could not be funneled into the marketplace. Local fences are not capable of handling such marketing needs. Outlet fences operate nationally and internationally. Multinational firms, some controlled by members of organized crime, provide criminals with ready-made markets in this country and abroad. The growing use of computerized records hinders investigators and makes it difficult to detect large fencing schemes. Computerized data can be altered and manipulated to meet the needs of the fence and, at the press of a button, erased. With the growing technology and internationalization of the business community, the outlet fence poses a serious challenge to investigators and prosecutors.

The ethnic fence, although similar to the local fence, displays some unique characteristics.[29] Whereas the local fence trades with neighborhood people who are not necessarily related to him, the ethnic fence usually deals only with a small circle of friends and relatives. The ethnic fence usually handles a more specialized trade. He operates from the comfort of his home and is insulated from prosecution by a code of conduct that demands confidentiality.

The ethnic fence is usually found in small groups of Balkan extraction. Within these small, isolated communities, the fence acts as a link with the outside world. Small Balkan groups in large eastern cities have a propensity to trade in firearms. Guns carry a symbolic value in these communities; they are signs of power. They assure the community security from the outside hostile world. Fences within the community play a key role in supplying its members with guns. A member of this group never contemplates buying weapons from an outsider; instead he approaches his community fence, who in turn contacts the outside world.

The ethnic fence is unique, usually found in small groups with strong kinship ties. There are historical reasons for this. In Balkan societies the fence is considered an important member of the community. His activity is viewed as a service to his friends and relatives. He supplies their needs and receives some monetary compensation and considerable prestige in return. The monetary motive plays a secondary role; one fence told me that he views his role as one of service to his community. In turn he is assured insulation from prosecution. It is unheard of for a client to inform the authorities. As one elderly client confided, "You do not turn in a man who did you a favor." With the gradual Americanization of the younger generation, this may change; at present, the ethnic fence plays a key role within his small community.

Traditional Approach to Fencing

Historically law enforcement efforts have concentrated on stopping fencing by putting the thief out of circulation. This strategy has been a failure; the present backlog in the court systems dooms this policy to failure. For each thief arrested, there are dozens to take his place. With the drug problem in large cities and with addicts responsible for large numbers of thefts, it is unlikely that this strategy will curtail the problem.

The fence is a middleman. Even though he violates the law, he nevertheless fulfills an economic function. Buyers flock to him because he offers goods at a lower price. He may even view himself as a businessman. Many businesses serve on occasion as outlet fences. Many specialized fences are respected in their small worlds. The Belgian fence who sells a valuable artifact to a wealthy American businessman travels in the best circles and is certainly not viewed as a criminal by his client. The ethnic fence is viewed as a vital member of his community.

The courts have concentrated their efforts on the thief rather than the fence, who is usually shown leniency.[30] Judges are reluctant to send fences to prison because their activity is nonviolent. Theirs is a white-collar crime. With prisons filled to capacity, this attitude is not likely to change. And there are no complaints with such treatment. Clients are usually grateful, and few will admit their involvement in open court. Few corporations are willing to admit to the public and their stockholders that they were part of the fencing system.

Receiving stolen property is a crime. Fences sell stolen property; they do not steal property, nor do they keep it for their personal use. There are four key elements to the crime of receiving stolen property: (1) the fence must receive the property; (2) the property must be stolen; (3) the fence must know that it was stolen; and (4) the fence must intend to permanently deprive the owner of his property.[31] The problem for law enforcement is proving that the fence knew the property was stolen. Fences usually have legitimate business fronts, and since many have no prior history of involvement with the law, the thief is not likely to testify against them. Showing intent to permanently deprive the true owner of his property is often difficult to prove. The more sophisticated fences are usually insulated from their clients and the sellers of the stolen goods. It is difficult, even when the buyer testifies, to show that intent was present.

Fencing is an economic crime that has grown and flourished because it offers the consuming public an edge against inflation. With little risk the buyer is assured a lower price. The large business firm is assured goods at a cheaper price and thus gains an advantage over its competitors. The wealthy businessman who buys art is assured possession, if not public display, of these valuable works. Fencing is a serious problem. It offers thieves a ready market and makes it possible for them to sell their goods at a profit. If fencing is to be curtailed, it must be analyzed and dealt with as an economic phenomenon. We know too little about its impact on our economy and about the forces that guide it to deal with it effectively. A new strategy is needed.

1. "Fifteen Month Buffalo Anti-Fencing Operation Closed,"
Organized Crime Bulletin, July 1977, p. 3.

2. Alfred E. Lewis and Martin Weil, "Three Policemen, Former
Officer Arrested after Fencing Probe," *Washington Post*, December 21,
1977, p. B-1.

3. "Sting Operations Shut Down in Indiana and Texas," *Organized
Crime Bulletin*, August 1977, p. 6.

4. "Buffalo Anti-Fencing Operation," p. 4.

5. U.S., Department of Commerce, *Crime in Service Industries*
(Washington, D.C., 1977), pp. 3-6.

6. U.S., Department of Justice, Law Enforcement Assistance Administration, *Strategies for Combatting the Criminal Receiver of Stolen
Goods* (Washington, D.C.: U.S. Government Printing Office, 1976), pp. 7,
8.

7. Chamber of Commerce of the United States, *White Collar Crime*
(Washington, D.C., 1974), pp. 45, 46.

8. G. Robert Blakey and Michael Goldsmith, "Criminal Redistribution of Stolen Property: The Need for Law Reform," *Michigan Law
Review*, August 1976, pp. 1517-1518.

9. U.S., Congress, Senate, Select Committee on Small Business, *The
Impact of Crime on Small Business, Part 4* (Washington, D.C.: U.S.
Government Printing Office, 1974), p. 28.

10. U.S., Department of Transportation, *Cargo Theft and Organized
Crime: A Deskbook for Management and Law Enforcement* (Washington,
D.C.: U.S. Government Printing Office, 1972), pp. 38-39.

11. Bruce H. Jones, "A System's Perspective on Fencing," *Organized
Crime Bulletin*, August 1977, p. 5.

12. Blakey and Goldsmith, "Criminal Redistribution of Stolen Property," pp. 1529-1538; Department of Justice, *Strategies*, pp. 14-21.

13. Based on studies by this author of Balkan communities in the city of
New York. Many of the fences in these communities displayed unique
characteristics; for example, they dealt only with friends and relatives.
Their market was a small one based on ties of kinship and family friendships. They were openly viewed as serving a community need; many of their
fencing operations centered around stolen guns.

14. Ted Roselius and Douglas Benton, *Marketing Theory and Fencing
of Stolen Goods*, report to the Law Enforcement Assistance Administration
(Washington, D.C.: U.S. Department of Justice, 1971), p. 36.

15. "Recap of Police Fencing Operations," *Organized Crime Bulletin*,
August 1977, p. 6.

16. Department of Transportation, *Cargo Theft and Organized Crime*,
p. 40.

17. "Why Art Treasures Are Growing Targets of Thieves," *U.S. News & World Report*, June 6, 1972, pp. 58-60; also Ann-Byrd Platt, "It Takes More Than a Thief to Catch Art Thieves," *Wall Street Journal*, February 16, 1978, p. 1; Andre Emmerich, "Importing Antiquities: A Moral Issue?" *Washington Post*, February 6, 1978, p. A-23.

18. Based on interviews with law enforcement sources at both federal and local levels.

19. Thomas O'Toole, "Four Tons of A-Metal Missing," *Washington Post*, July 5, 1977, pp. A-1, A-11.

20. Jeffrey A. Tannenbaum, "The Terrorists: For World's Alienated, Violence Often Reaps Political Recognition," *Wall Street Journal*, January 4, 1977, p. 1.

21. Chamber of Commerce of the United States, *Deskbook on Organized Crime* (Washington, D.C., 1972), p. 11.

22. Department of Transportation, *Cargo Theft and Organized Crime*, pp. 28, 29.

23. Senate Select Committee on Small Business, *The Impact of Crime*, p. 20.

24. "Anatomy of a Scam," *Economic Crime Project Newsletter of the National District Attorneys Association*, May-June-July 1974, pp. 195-198.

25. U.S. Chamber of Commerce, *Handbook on White Collar Crime*, p. 6.

26. Chamber of Commerce of the United States, *Deskbook on Organized Crime* (Washington, D.C., 1972), pp. 27-30; see also New York State Commission of Investigation, *Racketeer Infiltration into Legitimate Business* (New York, 1970), pp. 98-109.

27. U.S., Department of Justice, Law Enforcement Assistance Administration, *Anatomy of a Scam: A Case Study of a Planned Bankruptcy by Organized Crime* (Washington, D.C., 1973), p. 15.

28. Bernard Rabin and Arthur Mulligan, "Fort Lee Myles, Judge Repairs All the Knocks," *Daily News*, October 2, 1974, p. 14.

29. Based on author's research into Balkan groups in New York.

30. Waverly Yates, executive director of Bonabond of Washington, D.C., in a study of felons sentenced in the District of Columbia and surrounding jurisdictions found that fences and other felons convicted of white-collar crimes received lenient sentences. A study by John Jenkins, a noted journalist in the area of white-collar crime (John A. Jenkins and Robert H. Rhode, "White Collar Justice," *Bureau of National Affairs*, April 13, 1976, pp. 10, 11), confirmed that white-collar felons receive lenient sentences. See also Blakey and Goldsmith, "Criminal Redistribution of Stolen Property," p. 1598.

31. Wayne R. LaFave and Austin W. Scott, Jr., *Criminal Law* (St. Paul, Minn.: West Publishing Co., 1972), pp. 681-691.

7 Gambling

Raids by New York and New Jersey law enforcement agencies resulted in the arrests of a dozen members of the Vito Genovese crime family and the confiscation of more than $300,000 in Super Bowl bets.[1] The police later disclosed that the operation netted the Genovese crime family more than $100 million annually. In a separate case a large Harlem numbers operator, known to his associates as Pappy, was convicted in a federal court on charges of income tax evasion.[2] Prosecutors charged that he had earned more than $90,000 annually from his Harlem operation. Outside the court house a group calling itself the New York Numbers Bankers and Controllers Association picketed in support for Pappy. In Washington, D.C., an internationally known gambling figure was said to be involved in a proposal to build a gambling casino in New Jersey with two prominent Washingtonians; the latter were said to have connections to the Carter administration.[3]

It is estimated that more than 80 million Americans gamble annually. Of these, more than 60 million are said to engage in some form of legal or illegal gambling, while the rest wager only with friends.[4] Experts estimate that at least $4 billion is bet legally at race tracks each year, while $7 billion to $50 billion is bet illegally each year.[5] Gambling in America is big business, bigger than the auto industry, and it undoubtedly has a promising future. Gambling affects almost every facet of society; it corrupts police and politicians alike. In some cities gambling establishments pay as much as $3,500 weekly to local police officials for protection.[6] Gambling is a source of great wealth and power for criminal syndicates. It is a problem that has no simple answers and sharply divides public opinion.

The Problem of Gambling

A study of gamblers concluded that more than ten million Americans are hooked on gambling. The gambler continues to bet "because the action has come to be a refuge from thoughts of the outside world. His anxieties associated with his wife, family, debts, or job disappear when he concentrates on money and action."[7] Theologians and civic leaders regard gambling as a form of moral erosion. They consider it the ultimate form of debauchery. Yet gambling survives and grows in America. Law enforcement sources estimate that more than 1 million New York City residents gamble an average of $500 each in numbers alone.[8] Few public issues cause as much division and emotion as gambling. To organized crime it represents a major source of revenue; it has been used to expand into other ventures.

At the turn of the century one of New York City's police commissioners described gambling establishments as "the headquarters of the most dangerous criminals." Many law enforcement officials and civic leaders still hold this view, at least on the surface. However, gamblers have enjoyed mixed acceptance in past societies. The ancient Greeks encouraged gambling on holidays and elevated it to a religious ritual. The Romans viewed it as a waste of manpower but tolerated it during the holiday of Saturnalia. The Persians were addicted to chess, and card playing became the sport of the upper classes in medieval Europe. Early taboos aimed at discouraging gambling were less inspired by religious reasons than by economic need. The ancient philosophers saw gambling as a needless waste of energy and labor. The rulers of medieval Europe, although they allowed the upper classes to gamble, discouraged the poor for fear that they might become public charges. Thus when the aristocratic classes indulged in gambling, it was tolerated; when the poor partook, it was regulated. This double standard still prevails.

In this country more than thirty states have statutory provisions for some form of legalized gambling. Even during the colonial period many of the colonies tolerated some forms of gambling. Lotteries were viewed as important revenue sources. Gambling itself is ill defined. Most statutes and courts refer to it as gaming,[9] which has been defined by at least one court as "a contract between two or more persons, by which they agree to play by certain rules at cards, dice, or other contrivances, and that one shall be the loser and the other the winner."[10] Some statutes provide that "play at any game for any sum of money or other property of any value" is gambling.[11] In all statutes and court decisions the basic test for gaming is the element of chance.[12] It includes some bets and wagers.[13]

In the case of *Lewis* v. *United States* the U.S. Supreme Court held that an individual does not have a constitutional right to gamble.[14] State legislative attempts to regulate gambling are said to constitute a valid exercise of the police powers of the states,[15] provided that these restraints are not unreasonable.[16] The federal government has also enacted legislation concerning gaming. If a gambling transaction involves interstate commerce, it falls under federal statutes. Both the states and federal government can regulate gambling, provided they do not interfere with any of the inherent rights associated with citizenship.[17] The issue, in enforcing gaming statutes, is whether the activity is a game of chance rather than skill. Games of chance may call for some skill; games of skill may also call for some luck. For the majority of courts, however, the test of gaming is whether chance rather than skill is the controlling factor.[18] For others, the test is whether the activity encourages the gambling instinct.[19]

Gambling takes on numerous forms, some legal and others illegal. Legalized gambling may become illegal if the activity violates a state's gambling regulations. These regulations vary from state to state, and it is these differences that have undermined the enforcment of gaming statutes. Courts themselves differ in their definitions of games of chance and games of skill. In addition, the average citizen, when told that he can gamble in Nevada but not in his home state, tend to believe the argument that gambling laws are aimed at the poor, not the wealthy. This cynicism has resulted in an environment in which the enforcement of gambling laws in the majority of states is a failure.

Categories of Gambling

In Washington, D.C. raids by local police resulted in the arrest of more than twenty individuals, among them several businessmen and a lawyer.[20] The arrests were in connection with an illegal gambling operation that generated over $500,000 a week. Gambling operations fall into several categories. One of the more common is card playing, which falls under the gaming statutes that prohibit gambling whenever money, property, or other things of value are won or lost.[21] Many jurisdictions prohibit merely playing cards in a public place, even if only for recreation or amusement. Poker, baccarat, blackjack, and jackpot, when played for things of value, are considered games of chance and are therefore illegal.[22] Gambling devices are also illegal. A poker table may be considered a gambling device.[23] Cards used for gambling purposes are also considered gambling devices.[24]

Card games are well suited to syndicate-controlled gambling houses. Card games are easy and inexpensive to set up and bring in large returns. They may be played in a social club, an apartment, or the back room of a store. The local police are usually paid off. If the game is played in an apartment, the doorman may also be given a gratuity. Card dealers are hired for the game, and syndicate men provide protection. Local mob figures usually have an interest in these games and receive an agreed percentage of the take. In some cases authorization is given either as a friendly gesture or in return for a debt owed. The games may be run directly by syndicate men or by affiliates of organized crime. The gambling house usually recieves 5 percent of every pot. Good card dealers can easily run eight to ten pots per hour in a poker game.[25]

There are variations in the way that different ethnic criminal groups run card games. Balkan groups in the New York-New Jersey area run their card games in social clubs.[26] The syndicate exerts little control over many of these Balkan groups. Their working relationship is one of mutual convenience more than anything else. The clientele consists of friends and relatives of the house operators. These clubs are not dependent on the syndicate for clients and funding. The syndicate sometimes provides police protection and receives a small percentage of the house profits in return.

Poker games are the most popular form of card game at these Balkan clubs. The games usually start early in the evening (when clients leave their places of work) and continue late into the night. The clubs operate seven days a week, usually twenty-four hours a day. Card players can usually find a game at any time of the day. The clubs also provide the players physical protection from threats of holdups; most clubs keep one or two bodyguards on their payroll. Good club clients are usually extended interest-free credit for several days. The understanding is that the client will continue patronizing the club and recommend it to friends and relatives. The clubs may rent some of their space to syndicate members, who use it for their own card games. The clubs also provide twenty-four-hour food service.

The Balkan gambling clubs cater to a predominantly Balkan clientele. Their ties with the syndicate are based on mutual need and respect. The aggressive nature of the Balkan makes him a tough adversary. His close family ties and clanish life-style ensure his independence from the syndicate. Their working relationship is one of convenience.

Shooting craps is regarded as a game of chance and is thus illegal.[27] A crap table is said to be a gaming device and thus illegal. Dice games come in various forms, for example, craps, poker dice, and barbudi.[28] Craps is one of the more popular dice games in this country. It is a fast-paced game in which the shooter may bet as much as he likes, and his bets are covered by other bettors. Syndicate-controlled crap games are common and are usually played in numerous locations. Crap games played in bars violate state liquor laws as well as state gambling laws. Poker dice games are also common and popular; the dice are rolled out of a cup and the regular rules of poker applied. A popular dice game in Balkan communities is barbudi, usually played by two individuals against each other. These games are quite popular in Balkan social clubs, and the house usually receives a percentage of the winnings. Dice games were also popular in antiquity; archeologists have uncovered dice in Egyptian tombs and in Roman burial vaults.

Bingo, lotto, and keno games also violate gambling statutes, unless specially licensed by the state or locality. They are said to be games of chance. Although these games have not proven attractive to the syndicate in some states, in many other localities the mob has become heavily involved in them. Mob-owned bingo parlors usually bring in large sums of money; they are also used to launder other illegal funds. In Dade County, for example, syndicate-controlled bingo parlors are a lucrative business for the mob.[29]

Pool and billiard games are lawful amusements in most jurisdictions, but betting money or property on these games is illegal.[30] Games of pool and billiards have proved lucrative and attractive to the syndicate. Unfortunately prosecution is often difficult. For example, police have to show that the owner of the pool table knew that the table was used for gambling. However, if prosecutors can prove that money or property was bet on the outcome of the game, then they can argue that the table is a gambling device and that its owner, as well as the players and bettors, was in violation of the gambling laws.

Many jurisdictions make it a misdemeanor to possess slot or pinball machines. Several federal statutes prohibit the interstate transportation of slot machines.[31] In some states it is a felony to possess a slot machine. The take for the house on a slot machine ranges from 5 to 50 percent.[32] A slot machine is not a gaming device if it is played merely for amusement and if no money or property exchanges hands.[33] Some state statutes do not define a slot machine; their concern is not the machine but the way it is used. Statutes prohibiting the possession or operation of slot or pinball machines are usually applicable only when those machines are employed for gaming, not amusement.[34] States, under their police powers, can outlaw gaming involving the use of slot and pinball machines.

The Italian National Lottery was started in the early sixteenth century and is still played. Lotteries were also common in eighteenth-century England and in the American colonies. The lottery usually appealed to the poorer classes; for a small sum of money, a bettor could buy a few tickets in the hope that the winning number would appear on his tickets. Lotteries were popular in nineteenth-century America, but by the turn of the century numerous lottery-connected frauds brought the game into disrepute. During the 1930s the lottery regained its popularity, this time in black neighborhoods. Organized crime was quick to seize the opportunity. With Prohibition at an end, the syndicate was ready to invest its money and energy in new areas. The lottery, or numbers game as it was called in the latter nineteenth century, appeared attractive.

Several states now have legalized state-run lotteries. However, many jurisdictions outlaw lotteries (or numbers games). Federal legislation prohibits the use of the U.S. Postal Service to send any offer, ticket, or money connected with a lottery.[35] Federal laws also prohibit the transportation of lottery tickets in either interstate or foreign commerce.[36] Lotteries are also covered by numerous state nuisance statutes.[37] Despite legislation to outlaw lotteries, organized crime, with its national contacts, has been able to carve out a vast domain in this area. The numbers game is a multimillion-dollar annual industry.

The numbers game is a five-tiered system. At the bottom of the system is the bettor. The player selects three digits from 000 to 999; one of these three-digit numbers will win. The game can be played in various forms: straight, combination, bolita, or single action.[38] The bolita is a favorite in Cuban neighborhoods. The chances of winning for a player are one in a thousand, and the odds in favor of the operators are 999 to 1. Bets range from $1 to $10.

To place a bet, players approach the collector (also known as a runner or policy writer), who represents the second tier in a numbers operation. This individual may work at the numbers game full-time, in which case he may be employed by a large bank; or he may work at it only part-time, from a bar, a store, even a garage. The collectors are the sales team of a numbers operation. They usually come from the same neighborhood in which they take their bets and usually know their clients well. Above the collectors are the controllers (also known as route men). They are the third tier of the system, acting as middle-level managers who hire and supervise the collectors. They also maintain records of bets taken by the collectors, collect the money from the latter, and arrange for payments to winning bettors from the bank. A controller may operate out of an apartment or other private location. His place of business is referred to as the drop or the big drop.

Above the controllers are the bankers; they constitute the fourth tier in the system. They pay all the winning bettors, provide for police protection in their area of operation, and settle all disputes involving their employees. The banker is the direct line to the syndicate, and the bank is the banker's headquarters. Daily receipts from controllers are taken to the bank and recorded. The banker is the overall manager of a numbers operation. As the syndicate's key figure, he reports directly to an affiliate or member of organized crime. In large cities bankers are often members of minority groups. Some even operate in a quasi-independent fashion, working with the syndicate only when doing so is in their interest. The syndicate, in turn, provides the banker with both political and police protection, as well as funds to cover large losses.[39] In return the syndicate receives a percentage of the bank's profits. Independent bankers may pay the syndicate tribute for allowing them to operate in one of its territories. The mob constitutes the fifth tier in the system.

A numbers network also employs lawyers, accountants, bookkeepers, and numerous other professionals. It is said that the numbers games in New York employ between ten thousand and a hundred thousand individuals.[40] A numbers operation is held together by a network of pickup men, who act as messengers between collectors and controllers and between controllers and the bank. The pickup man, usually a salaried employee, transports money and betting records between the different tiers of the system. The system also employs lookout men who warn the collector of an oncoming police raid; they are the eyes of the system.

If a player wins, he is paid at odds of 600 to 1. The collector keeps 10 percent of the winning bet as his commission. Thus a winning player who bet $10 on a number would receive $5,400, and the collector would receive $600 as his commission. Collectors also usually make a commission of 25 percent of all bets they bring in; they give the controller 75 cents of every dollar they take in as bets. The controller also receives a 10 percent commission on all bets the collector brings to him. The bank usually receives the remaining 65 percent, which is split with the syndicate and used to pay legal fees, police protection, and so forth. The numbers game is so lucrative for the syndicate that one well-known crime boss was said to be drawing between $1 million and $2 million annually from his investment. Profits from a numbers operation usually find their way into narcotics, other modes of gambling, and investments in legitimate business.

Betting on sports is big business in America. Billions of dollars are bet each year on everything from horse racing to baseball games. Many Americans bet only among themeselves, but many others bet with a local bookmaker. The latter acts as a middleman between bettors and takes a commission in return for his services. In New York City bookmakers take in more than $1 billion annually in bets.[41] Unlike a collector's clients, those of a bookmaker tend to be more affluent and sometimes come from respected sectors of our society. Even Washington has been racked by scandals involving employees of the U.S. Congress and well-known bookmakers with syndicate contacts.

The bookmaker is the contact point for the public, the salesman. All bettors come to him; he takes the bets and records them. These records are sent with the money to a business office. Some bookmakers operate independently, while others work on the syndicate's payroll. The business office is run by an office manager, who is either a member of organized crime or an independent with ties to the mob. Bookmakers usually operate from bars, pool halls, grocery stores, and corporate plants. Others may operate from a street corner or a parking garage. The more sophisticated may operate from a wire room. This is a location with a telephone; it may be a room in an office or even an apartment. Telephones are installed; the number is given to select clients, often with a code, and clients call in their bets. The phones are never registered in the bookmaker's real name and are thus difficult to trace by law enforcement agencies.

A player betting with a bookmaker is actually betting against fellow bettors; he is not betting against the bookmaker. The latter acts like a middleman. He equalizes the amount bet on each team or horse, or whatever else his clients have bet on, through a system of betting odds or point spread, depending on the sport in question. The odds or point system is dictated by a team's past performance, injured players, the weather, and so forth. For example, in a football or basketball game, if the favorite team is given a five-point spread over the weaker team, the favorite team must win by more than five points if the player who bet on the latter is to win. The odds and point spread are ultimately dictated by the laws of supply and demand. To insure themselves against losses, bookmakers can also lay off their bets with other bookmakers.[42]

The syndicate, through force and national contacts, has been able to gain control over much of the bookmaking activity in this country. The control may be either direct, as when bookmakers work directly for a mob-connected operation, or indirect, as when bookmakers rely on the mob for protection, contacts, and sources of funds. The syndicate's ownership of its own wire service enables the mob to exert great powers even over independent bookmakers.[43] The bookmaker gains distinct advantages by working for the syndicate. The syndicate backs all the bets taken by a bookmaker, thus enabling the bookmaker to take on more clients. In addition, the syndicate provides the bookmaker with a ready-made market of bettors. The bookmaker has no need to establish a clientele; he only has to collect bets.[44] Differences between bookmakers are settled by the syndicate, thus minimizing the likelihood of open violence. Police protection and legal expenses are handled by syndicate sources, freeing the bookmaker to concentrate on taking bets.

Bookmaking is big business. It permeates every facet of the sporting world. Americans currently bet more than $15 billion annually on college and professional football games alone.[45] However, horse racing, boxing, tennis tournaments, carnival games, bowling games, and numerous other sporting events have attracted the attention of organized crime. The syndicate has willing accomplices. The orthopedic surgeon for a nationally known football team was indicted along with two members of organized crime in connection with a $26 million annual sports gambling operation.[46] This was an unusual case, for prosecutions involving high-level members of the syndicate for illegal gambling activity are rare.

Government Regulation

Numerous states have enacted antigambling legislation since the turn of the century. Municipalities have followed suit with their own antigambling legislation. States can do so under their police powers. Municipalities also have power to do so, provided their enactments do not conflict with state and federal law. As a result, there are many antigambling laws at the state and local levels that can be employed against organized crime.

Under the common law numerous forms of gaming were viewed as a public nuisance. Several local antigambling statutes consider some forms of gambling, among them the lottery, a public nuisance and thus illegal. However, to pass a constitutional challenge, a local statute must be clear, reasonable, and within the scope of the powers conferred on the state or municipality. Most local antigambling legislation has withstood this constitutional test.

At the federal level there are also laws to combat organized crime. A series of statutes make it a crime to travel or use any facility in interstate or foreign commerce to assist any business involved in illegal gambling.[47] These statutes cover not only the physical transportation of materials in interstate and foreign commerce, but also use of telephone, radio, and telegraph wires in interstate or foreign commerce. Travel includes more than just intent; there must also be an act in furtherance of the intent. A business enterprise, according to these statutes, is usually an entrenched operation rather than sporadic gaming. There must be proof of a continual enterprise for the federal statutes to come into play.[48] Federal prosecutors are reluctant to prosecute sporadic gaming activities.

Whoever aids and abets the commission of an offense against the United States is punishable under federal law as a principal.[49] Causing a gambling victim to travel in interstate commerce for purposes of extortion could be prosecuted under federal law.[50] The federal conspiracy statutes have also proved valuable in the prosecuting of interstate gambling activity.[51] Conviction for conspiracy to commit a gambling-related offense, however, requires proof of knowledge. Further each conspirator is responsible for the acts of others in relation to the conspiracy.[52] Making or financing extortionate extension of credit to gamblers is also a federal crime,[53] as is collection of extensions of credit by extortionate means.[54] Thus loansharking operations, tied to gambling, can be prosecuted under the federal loanshark statutes. In *United States* v. *Burke,* the defendants were convicted for loansharking activities tied to an interstate gambling ring.[55]

Federal law also provides for fines of up to $10,000 and imprisonment of up to two years for anyone who sets up or operates a gambling establishment in interstate or foreign commerce.[56] Using an American vessel primarily for gambling purposes, either on the high seas or within the jurisdiction of the United States, is also a prosecutable federal offense.[57] A gambling establishment is defined as any gaming establishment operated for the purposes of gambling, including accepting, recording, or registering bets, carrying a lottery, or playing any game of chance for money or other thing of value.[58] It is also unlawful to operate a vessel for the purpose of transporting passengers between a place within the United States and a gambling ship. The objective of these federal gambling establishment statutes is to prohibit the evasion of federal antigambling laws simply by using an American vessel as a gambling establishment. The transmission of wagering information in interstate or foreign commerce is also a federal crime. Information used for news reporting of sporting events or contests is exempted, and news from a state where gambling is legal can be transmitted in interstate or foreign commerce.

Whoever brings or carries lottery tickets in interstate or foreign commerce is in violation of federal law.[59] Use of the U.S. mails to send or deliver lottery tickets or related matter is also a federal crime. Broadcasting

by radio any information or advertisement concerning a lottery is also a
federal offense, and each day's broadcasting is a seperate offense. The use
of interstate and foreign commerce to promote racketeering is a federal
crime.[60] Illegal gambling activities, according to federal law, fall within the
scope of the racketeering statute.[61] Whoever transports in interstate or
foreign commerce wagering paraphernalia is in violation of federal law.[62]
However, common carriers engaged in the usual course of their business are
exempt under the statute. The federal tax laws also lend themselves to prosecutions involving gambling activity in interstate and foreign commerce.
Other federal statutes can also be employed. The United States immigration
and naturalization laws have been employed, with some success, to revoke
the U.S. citizenship of criminals engaged in illegal gambling activities.[63]
Several proposed reforms of the federal criminal code provide heavy
penalties and large fines for illegal gambling activities in interstate and
foreign commerce.[64]

The present federal and state criminal codes are sufficient for the prosecution of individuals engaged in illegal gambling activity. The problem
continues to be the lax approach of prosecutors and judges to gambling activities. For example, a gambling kingpin in Washington, D.C., with a long
history of illegal gambling activity recently received a suspended five-year
sentence and a fine of $10,000.[65] Among his many clients were some of
Washington's better-known professionals, politicians, businessmen, and
journalists. Gambling is a nonviolent crime; the public is not perturbed by
it. Prosecutors, judges, and politicians do not view it as a threat. In fact, the
present gambling model has failed not for lack of legal muscle but for lack
of support by many members of the public and the government. An alternative model is needed.

A New Model Is Needed

Great Britain, Sweden, Australia, and France all have government-operated
gambling. The 1968 Gambling Act in England provided for the licensing of
public betting parlors. France has had a system of legalized off-track betting since the 1950s; it brings the French treasury more than $100 million
annually. Players place their bets with off-track, government-operated parimutuel booths. In 1913 Puerto Rico legalized off-track betting; casino
gambling and weekly lotteries are also legal on the island commonwealth.
New York City's Off-Track Betting Corporation (OTB) first opened its betting parlors in 1970; players are currently betting more than $1 million daily
at OTB parlors.

A growing number of political and law enforcement sources are critical
of the gambling model now found in the majority of states. Antigambling

statutes have given rise to widespread corruption at both the local and federal level. In some cities payoffs by gamblers to the police (the "pad") have become a cost of doing business; these payoffs range from $400 to $1,500 per month.[66] In return the police provide protection from street criminals and de facto immunity from prosecution. One gambler summarized it as follows:

R: When you pay protection, you expected to be tipped?

G: Yeah, you expect to be tipped and everything. And well they will tip you to protect their interest. Yeah, see, they got an interest in the joint.

R: The interest is just the monthly.

G: Monthly payment. See, they're your partners.

The present gambling model has not only undermined effective law enforcement but also reinforced a sense of cynicism in the minds of many members of the public. Why, they ask, can I gamble in Nevada and not in my home state? A model that is questioned by a sizable minority and does not enjoy the support of a large majority of the public is doomed to failure in a democracy.

A debate is now raging within law enforcement on the merits and disadvantages of legalized gambling. Critics charge that legalized gambling is no assurance that organized crime will be driven out, that legalization would only encourage gambling, and lead many who otherwise would not gamble to do so. Opponents also charge that legalized gambling is doomed to failure because the syndicate cannot be undersold. These are all valid criticisms. Critics charge that gambling operations take many forms and that a legalized model cannot possibly serve them all. For example, sports betting and poolselling lend themselves easily to a legalized model, but bookmaking is inappropriate. Nevertheless the debate rages on. Several jurisdictions have legalized some forms of gambling, while others wait on the sidelines.

The Commission on the Review of the National Policy toward Gambling in 1976 submitted its final report to the Congress and the president. Among its recommendations were the removal of statutory prohibition against public social gambling. In addition, the commission recommended that law enforcement shift its attention from low-level gambling offenders to the upper reaches of gambling. The commission also noted that almost 80 percent of those it sampled called for some form of legalized gambling.

Regardless of one's views on gambling, there can be little doubt that the present model has failed. It is indeed doubtful whether the government of a country in which a sizable portion of the population engages in a prohibited activity can curtail that activity without the use of some undemocratic tools.

The threat of the present model comes not only from organized crime but also from zealots whose attempts to enforce the antigambling statutes may curtail our freedoms. A new model is badly needed.

Notes

1. "One Hundred Million Dollar Gambling Operation Raided in New York, New Jersey," *Washington Post,* January 16, 1978, p. A-4.

2. "Numbers Banker Guilty in Tax Case," *New York Daily News,* October 1, 1974, p. 21.

3. Maxine Cheshire, "D.C. Gambling Kingpin Is Linked to Prominent Investors' Casino Deal," *Washington Post,* January 26, 1978, pp. A-1, A-16.

4. Dean R. Phillips, "Gambling Is Inevitable," *Police Chief,* September 1977, pp. 58-59.

5. Donald R. Cressey, *Theft of the Nation* (New York: Harper & Row, 1969), p. 74.

6. Knapp Commission, "Police Corruption in New York City," in *Theft of the City,* ed. John A. Gardiner and David J. Olson (Bloomington, Ind.: Indiana University Press, 1974), p. 175.

7. Jay Livingston, "A Culture Of Losers," *Psychology Today,* March 1974, p. 55.

8. Fund for the City of New York, "Legal Gambling in New York," in *Crime Society,* ed. Francis A.J. Ianni and Elizabeth Reuss-Ianni (New York: New American Library, 1976), p. 259.

9. Maine State Raceways v. La Fleur, 87 A 2d 674 (1952).

10. Shaw v. Clark, 13 NW 786 (1882).

11. Westerhaus Company v. Cincinnati, 135 NE 2d 318 (1956).

12. First National Bank v. Carroll, 45 NW 304 (1890).

13. State v. Stripling, 21 So 409 (1889).

14. 348 U.S. 419 (1954).

15. People v. Monroe, 182 NE 439 (1962).

16. Ah Sin v. Wittman, 198 U.S. 500 (1904).

17. Marvin v. Trout, 199 U.S. 212 (1905).

18. State v. Wiley, 3 NW 2d 620 (1942).

19. Baedaro v. Caldwell, 56 NW 2d 706 (1953).

20. Vernon C. Thompson, "Big-Time Gambling Probe," *Washington Post,* November 2, 1977, pp. C-1, C-3.

21. D'Ario v. Startup Candy Company, 266 P 1037 (1928).

22. Ford v. State, 38 So 229 (1905).

23. Lyle v. Texas, 16 SW 765 (1891).

24. Jacobs v. Chariton, 65 NW 2d 561 (1954).

25. Joey and Dave Fisher, *Killer* (Chicago: Playboy Press, 1973), pp. 177-178.

26. Based on author's study of Balkan groups in the New York-New Jersey area.

27. Long v. State, 2 SW 541 (1886).

28. Denny F. Pace and Jimmie C. Styles, *Organized Crime: Concepts and Control* (Englewood Cliffs, N.J.: Prentice-Hall, 1975), pp. 122-123.

29. Based on interviews with law enforcement sources.

30. State v. Stroupe, 76 SE 2d 313 (1953).

31. 15 U.S.C. 1172.

32. Pace and Styles, *Organized Crime,* p. 125.

33. Hightower v. State, 156 SW 2d 327 (1941).

34. Rousse v. Sisson, 199 So 777 (1941).

35. See 18 U.S.C. 1301-1304 and 18 U.S.C. 1341-1342.

36. 18 U.S.C. 1084.

37. Valdez v. State, 194 So 388 (1940).

38. Frederick W. Egen, *Plainclothesman* (New York: Greenberg Press, 1952), pp. 66-75.

39. Fund for the City of New York, "Legal Gambling in New York," p. 260.

40. D. Wakefield, "Harlem's Magic Numbers," *Reporter,* February 4, 1960, p. 25.

41. John McDonald, "How the Horseplayers Got Involved with the Urban Crisis," in *An Economic Analysis of Crime,* ed. Lawrence J. Kaplan and Dennis Kessler (Springfield, Ill.: Charles C. Thomas, 1976), p. 88.

42. Ibid., pp. 92-93.

43. Pace and Styles, *Organized Crime,* p. 113.

44. Thomas C. Schelling, "What Is the Business of Organized Crime," *Emory Law School Journal of Public Law* 20, no. 1 (1971):74-81.

45. Pace and Styles, *Organized Crime,* p. 119.

46. Neil Andur, "Giant's Ex-Doctor Linked to Bookies," *New York Times,* August 21, 1974, pp. 1, 47.

47. 18 U.S.C. 1952.

48. United States v. Teemer, 214 F. Supp. 952, 953 (1963).

49. 18 U.S.C. 2.

50. United States v. Cavalcante, 440 F 2d 1264 (1971).

51. 18 U.S.C. 371-372.

52. United States v. Roselli, 432 F 2d 879, 880 (1970).

53. 18 U.S.C. 892-893.

54. 18 U.S.C. 894.

55. 495 F 2d 1226 (1974).

56. 18 U.S.C. 1082.

57. 18 U.S.C. 1081-1082.

58. 18 U.S.C. 1081, 1083, 1084.

59. 18 U.S.C. 1301, 1032, 1304.

60. 18 U.S.C. 1952.

61. United States v. Pauldino, 443 F 2d 1108 (1971).

62. 18 U.S.C. 1593.

63. United States v. Montablano, 236 F 2d 757 (1956).

64. See proposed Federal Criminal Code Reform Act of 1977 (S. 1437), Sect. 1841.

65. Laura A. Kierman, "Luck Fails Gambling King," *Washington Post,* December 29, 1977, pp. A-1, A-6.

66. Knapp Commission, "Police Corruption in New York City," p. 181.

8 Loansharking

A documentary filmmaker, faced with declining finances, approaches members of one of New York's major crime families and asks for a short-term loan.[1] The contact tells him to meet with his "business associate" who finances businessmen with similar problems. A garment manufacturer, pressured by creditors, contacts a known member of the underworld, who in turn puts him in contact with a loanshark. The businessman needs $80,000 that same day. In return for the loan the businessman will pay $4,000 in weekly interest until the loan is repaid. Two weeks later he pays the amount of the loan plus $8,000 in interest. In another city an individual who cheated a loanshark meets a violent death.[2]

An auto dealer who had borrowed a large sum of money from a loanshark repaid it by putting the latter on his payroll. The loanshark supplied no labor, and the paycheck was the autodealer's payment for the loan.[3] In New York a Mr. Jones borrowed $8,715 from a local loanshark.[4] When he fell behind on his payments, he was beaten and forced to work in a local gas station. His salary went toward repaying his loan. New York City police smashed a large loansharking operation, said to have more than $70 million in street loans and charging more than 20 percent weekly interest.[5]

Loansharking (also known as shylocking) is big business. Experts note that it is a multibillion-dollar industry.[6] It is ranked as the second largest source of income for organized criminal syndicates;[7] the benefits that organized crime derives from loansharking run into the billions of dollars annually. In addition, it enables organized crime to infiltrate the legitimate business sector and bring respectability to its members. The loanshark, unlike the narcotics dealer, is looked on as a businessman. Many of his clients come from respectable segments of society, and in many instances he serves a legitimate need. However, this business poses a serious threat to our society not only because loansharks often use violence to collect their loans, but because it corrupts every facet of society. It lends respectability to criminals who prey on society, and it enables them to "launder" funds from their illegal activities.

Understanding Loansharking

Loansharking is the lending of money at an extortionate rate of interest.[8] The rates charged by the loanshark are higher than those legally prescribed

107

by law.[9] As collateral, the borrower gives his body and that of his family.[10] Although legal interest rates range from 6 percent to 30 percent annually in most states, interest rates charged by shylocks usually range from 200 percent to 2,000 percent per year. High-risk borrowers pay interest rates of more than 20 percent weekly.[11] The profits for the loanshark can be enormous. A $1 million investment is said to have produced a $2.6 million profit within a year for one such operator.[12] Another such operator made more than $6 million in profits over a four-year period.[13] The enormous interest rates charged on a loan by a loanshark are known as "vigorish" in the trade.[14]

Moneylending is an ancient trade. In antiquity charging interest on a loan was known as usury, and antiusury laws were not unknown in the ancient world. The Old Testament spoke against charging interest on loans. In ancient Athens the rate of interest was kept low by legislation. The legislators of republican Rome prohibited charging interest on loans. During the Middle Ages in Europe usury was declared a sin against the Lord, and those found guilty of usury were often excommunicated from the church. Medieval scholars debated whether usury, under certain circumstances, was consistent with Christian dogma.[15] Another point of debate was the "just price" that a merchant should be permitted to charge on a loan.

With the growth of commerce and international trade, merchants often found themselves in need of large loans. During the Renaissance large banking houses began to appear in Europe. The Medicis of Florence were some of the better known; they became so powerful that they were able to elect one of their family members to the papal seat. Inevitably usury laws began to come under attack. Protestantism had an impact on the usury laws, and the church of Rome was no longer supreme. Protestant churches and states arose in many parts of Europe. Amsterdam became a great center of commerce; the Catholic states had to adapt to the needs of this modern financial system. Scholars such as Jeremy Bentham defended usury. By the eighteenth century the opposition of the Catholic church to usury had been seriously undermined.[16]

During the nineteenth century the growth of industry and commerce led European governments to repeal antiquated usury laws. By 1867 the majority of the European states had repealed their usury laws. In America state usury laws limited interest to 10 percent on a true annual rate. At the turn of the century, starting with Massachusetts in 1911, states relaxed their small-loan laws. Licensed financial institutions that made small loans to the public were exempted from state usury laws. Interest rates were fixed by a sliding scale, ranging from 18 percent and upward a year on any unpaid principal.[17] Until 1928 the large financial institutions had stayed out of the small-loan business. The National City Bank of New York was the first to enter the field. Initially it came under serious attack from both newspapers and small financial institutions, but other large financial institutions eventually followed.

Neither the repeal of usury laws nor the relaxation of small loan laws kept organized crime out of the moneylending business. The large fortunes made during the Prohibition era, as well as the fortunes made afterward from gambling and narcotics, gave the criminal overlords much capital to invest. Loansharking proved a natural outlet, and they had a ready-made market. Many of their clients came willingly; loansharks do not need to twist arms. The demand for their money is great. Financially pressed individuals and businessmen unable to secure loans through the legitimate sector come to them. Gamblers and the ignorant also flock to them. Criminals in need of large sums of money for a narcotics transaction or other criminal scheme also make their way to the loanshark. The loanshark meets an economic need. Violence is the loanshark's last resort; even the Gallo mob paid their loans. They knew that if they failed to do so, loansharks would never make any other loans to them.[18]

Loansharking has grown because it has a ready-made clientele and because it is simple and economical to run. Few trained personnel are needed; there is no need for an army of runners, electronic experts, or the hundreds of other individuals that are needed by many of organized crime's operations. Present laws have proven ineffective against loansharking, so prosecutions are few.[19] Shylocking is founded on three basic principles understood by all the participants. The borrower accepts high interest rates because no other resources are open to him. The loan shark knows that the borrower is a poor risk and usually has no collateral other than his body. Both sides understand that a breach of contract will result in violence and that the loanshark, even when operating as an independent, is often supported by well-organized criminal syndicates. Only when these basic tenets are violated does the borrower become a victim. In most cases the borrower pays his interest, and the loanshark is ready to grant him credit on other occasions.

Loansharking as a Business

More than anything else, loansharking's appeal to organized crime is its simplicity. The profits are enormous, and the bosses of organized crime find themselves insulated from prosecution by layers of underlings who need no training. There are three key ingredients for a successful operation: borrowers, capital, and the ability to ensure that borrowers honor their obligations.[20] The finder has the task of getting customers for the loanshark. He approaches friends and relatives, brings them to a loanshark, and in return receives a commission. The finder may himself be a borrower who repays his loan by bringing clients to the loanshark. The collector ensures that borrowers meet their obligations; violence is employed when all else fails. Capital, in turn, is provided by the banker, who may be either a member of organized crime or a legitimate businessman who has money to invest.[21]

At the top of any loansharking operation is the boss, who usually finances most of these operations. With their billions of dollars of annual profits from numerous enterprises, legal and illegal, national criminal syndicates can make large sums of money available to loanshark systems. As a reward, the boss usually makes large sums of money available to his captains, who pay the boss about 1 percent weekly interest for use of these funds. These captains in turn lend a large part of their funds to large borrowers, such as businesses in need of immediate capital. The remaining funds are usually made available to their subordinates, the third level of the loanshark operation.[22] The latter are charged weekly interest rates ranging from 1.5 percent to 2.5 percent. These low-level subordinates then make loans to the public at weekly interest rates of 5 percent or more. The loanshark system is a simple three-layer operation.

Loansharks meet different needs. At the lowest level is the local or neighborhood loanshark who operates out of a tavern, a restaurant, a factory, or even the piers. His clients tend to come from the lower economic strata of our society. Some of these local shylocks may be independents who fall back on the support of organized crime only for obtaining funds and collecting debts, but most have direct ties to organized crime. Some loansharks specialize. They may limit their dealings to professionals and businessmen, to the financial centers of large cities, or even to politicians. The specialist deals with a more affluent clientele; he is usually an underboss or captain of the crime syndicate. He makes money for his group and develops key links with the business and political world, which can serve his criminal associates well. The specialist is more insulated from discovery and prosecution than the neighborhood shylock, because his clients often stand to lose much more than those of the neighborhood loanshark.

The borrower gives his body as collateral. If he fails to honor his obligations, violence may be used to ensure that others repay their loans. When the borrower is a member of organized crime or an independent member of the underworld, differences may be mediated. The arbitration process often employed to settle disputes between borrower and lender is known as the sitdown.[23] Each presents his story to a mediator; this informal hearing may be held in a restaurant, a place of work, or some other secluded spot. The objective of this mediation procedure is to avoid bloodshed. It is a simple matter to employ violence against members of the public, but violence against other criminals, who may have their own power bases, can result in uncontrolled violence. At the end of the hearing the mediator hands down his decision. Both sides are expected to abide by it. Since mediators tend to be powerful members of the syndicate, their decisions carry great weight and are rarely flouted.

Funds for loanshark operations come from both legal and illegal sources. A study of one criminal family, with a strong power base in New York City, found that much of the funding for their shylock operations came from their legitimate businesses. In fact, the flow of money between the legitimate and illegitimate sectors appears common. The rise of this group and its eventual influx into the legitimate business world were largely the results of shylock operations.[24] Gambling, burglaries, narcotics, pornography, and skimming operations are major souces of funds. Legitimate businesses, banks, lending agencies, and union pension funds are also sources of funds for shylock operations. Businessmen and professionals provide additional sources. In fact, many fall victim to phony shylock schemes. Criminals dupe them into believing that their funds will be invested in loansharking, bringing them large returns. Once the criminal receives the money, his victim never sees it again. If he asks for his money back, he is told to go to the police. One criminal described it this way: "I took Bill for . . . sixty-five grand and John for fifty grand. . . . They sure as hell couldn't go to the police and tell them they'd been taken while investing in the loanshark business."[25]

Loansharking is said to be an invisible crime. However, it has symptoms that both law enforcement and concerned citizens should recognize. Big lenders with no connection to legitimate financial institutions are often shylocks. Individuals who gamble and use narcotics are usually prime targets of loansharks, as are businessmen who have overextended themselves. A firm with financial difficulties that takes on a consultant known to have criminal ties may actually be paying for its loan through the consultation fees. Lenders who charge excessive interest rates, sometimes more than 260 percent per year, are usually shylocks. Employee thefts and embezzlement may be an indication of loansharking. Borrowers are often forced to steal when they have exhausted all other sources of funding to repay their shylock. Beatings and acts of violence are also indications of a loanshark operation in the area. But loansharks often work through a legitimate lending institution, requiring more sophisticated detection techniques. Unfortunately most law enforcement agencies are ill trained to investigate sophisticated shylock operations.

Ethnics and Loansharking

Loansharking operations tend to be somewhat different within isolated ethnic environments. For example, a study of Balkan groups in New York

City showed that culture and group perception of the environment played a key role in how money was lent.[26] The present loanshark system in this country is largely an outgrowth of the history and experience of many of the criminal syndicates and their members. It is also a response to the needs of the American economy. The inability of many members of society to obtain loans, either because of their credit ratings or the governmental regulation that prevents lending institutions from making funds available to them, leads many of these individuals and businesses to the loanshark. In some ethnic communities similar forces lead to an outcome somewhat different from traditional loansharking.

Group X, in New York City, is Balkan. It numbers about fifty thousand men, women, and children and leads an isolated life-style ruled by tradition. Marriages within the community are common and encouraged. A sense of honor and machismo pervades the community. The individual's word is sacred; there is no greater sin within this community than to violate one's word. To do so brings disgrace on the individual and his family. The life of the community centers around social clubs noted for their gambling. Gambling is a popular recreation for the average male in Group X. Most of the gambling takes the form of card playing in the social clubs. Violence, although pervasive, is controlled by cultural norms and values.

The social clubs are owned by powerful families of the community. Although gambling is illegal, the community does not view it as such. Narcotics, prostitution, and many of the traditional forms of crime are viewed with disdain. The illegal activites of Group X are usually limited to gambling and gunrunning. The demand for unregistered guns is enormous. The growing fear of crime has led most males over thirteen to arm themselves. Vendettas are a chronic problem for this small community.

Loansharking in this community takes on a form somewhat different from that found in the rest of society. Moneylending is not alien to this community. Unlike Catholic Europe, which considered usury a sin for many centuries, this community has a historical development that has led to different attitudes toward moneylending. Controlled by the Ottoman Turks in the sixteenth century, this community developed internal moneylending mechanisms that still function in the streets of New York City. One's family and friends are key sources for funds, and except in rare instances, funds are lent interest-free. A member of this community who needs money for business purposes or to repay a gambling debt (a more common need) turns to friends and relatives. The loanshark, as known in the outside world, is not found in this community. A card player who loses large sums at a social club can usually borrow money interest-free from the owners of the club. The only requirement is that the borrower repay it as soon as possible, and that he continue to patronize the club. Even when interest is charged, it is extremely low, comparable with that charged by a local bank. Loansharking is virtually nonexistent. The historical experience of this community and its sense of isolation have reinforced its members' reliance on one another for assistance. Moneylending is viewed not as a business but as an obligation to one's friends and relatives. Although many ethnic criminals made their initial fortunes through loansharking operations within their own communities, criminal elements within this community usually make interest-free loans. Loans are occasionally made to gamblers as an inducement for more gambling. However, tradition reigns, and a loan is viewed as an obligation rather than an avenue for profit.

The Impact of Loansharking

In 1968 New York City's former commissioner of water supply, gas, and electricity pleaded guilty to bribery.[27] The defendant, a politically influential individual in local politics, had run into financial difficulties. A series of bad investments had brought him to the verge of bankruptcy. A business associate suggested that the defendant contact Antonio Corallo, described by law enforcement agencies as a member of organized crime. Corallo made a series of loans to the defendant, and the defendant in turn granted an $835,000 city contract to a firm Corallo had suggested. The defendant had become a tool of criminal elements.

A well-known hairdresser, who operated one of New York City's more fashionable salons, ran into financial difficulties and approached a loanshark for assistance.[28] In return for the loanshark's help the borrower acted as a fingerman for syndicate-run burglary operations. The hairdresser supplied the loanshark with information on his wealthy clients. He told the loanshark which clients kept valuable jewelry at home and when they would be out of town. The loanshark gave this information to the burglary ring. After each successful theft the hairdresser's share was given to the loanshark as part of the hairdresser's payments on his loan. The latter had been forced into a life of crime. A nightclub owner who refused similar overtures was gunned down.[29]

Loansharking is a business. Most borrowers have no trouble with their loanshark, but those who do usually work out some mutually beneficial arrangement. Some borrowers steer clients to the loanshark and in return receive a commission, which then goes to the loanshark as a loan payment. Others may conspire with the loanshark and his associates in burglary operations, as the hairdresser did. Some borrowers have been forced to steer friends into fixed gambling games. A New York Crime Commission was told that a prominent sports figure had steered some of his associates into a mob-controlled dice game. The players never suspected that the game had been fixed, and the borrower received a percentage of the proceeds for his efforts. The vice-president of a large sportswear firm who had fallen behind on his payments to the loanshark was forced to embezzle more than $200,000 to pay off his loan.[30]

Loansharking is often employed as a tool to gain control of legitimate businesses. The business owner who falls behind in his payments may find that the loanshark demands part or all of the business in return for money owed. A well-known racketeer used his loanshark operations to expand his illegal operations into the legitimate business sector.[31] Once the syndicate has acquired a legitimate business, it may allow the previous owners to operate it as before, with syndicate members paid salaries for nonexistent work. Such apparent employment gives members of organized crime the aura of respectability as well as a cover for tax purposes. The salaries paid to syndicate members may actually be loan payments.

Sometimes the new owners have other plans for the business. Bankruptcy frauds now account for more than $80 million in annual losses.[32] Scam operations are a favorite of organized crime.[33] Once criminals gain control of a legitimate business, they initiate the necessary foundations for a successful bankruptcy fraud. The creditors believe that the old owners are still in charge. If the firm had financial difficulties, then the new owners may infuse some additional capital, leading creditors to believe that the firm has overcome many of its financial difficulties. Large bank deposits may be made to establish credit; small orders are placed and are usually paid in full. After credit has been established and the fears of creditors allayed, very large orders are placed, usually for items easily converted into cash with the assistance of local, specialized, or outlet fences.[34] Payments to creditors now become smaller and less frequent. Once the new owners have converted the merchandise into cash, the firm is put into bankruptcy and the criminals disappear. The previous owners, who are technically the legal owners since no legal transfer has taken place, are left holding the bag. In one such case a loanshark who lent just a few thousand dollars to a legitimate businessman was able to gain control of a multimillion-dollar business and, with the assistance of his associates, perpetrate a successful scam that cost creditors more than $1 million.[35]

Loansharks have even been able to take over small Wall Street brokerage firms.[36] Stockbrokers who fall behind in their gambling debts or small brokerage houses that may need capital to overcome their financial difficulties may turn to loansharks. Stolen, counterfeit, and missing securities presently account for billions of dollars in annual losses.[37] These brokerage firms become avenues for multimillion-dollar stock frauds and serve as vehicles for the laundering of stolen securities. The brokerage firms may unwittingly pass stolen securities to other brokers, banks, and unsuspecting clients.

Loansharks have been able to develop an alarming number of ties to the

banking community. Bank funds have been directly employed by loansharks in their operations. One well-known loanshark used more than
$500,000 of a bank's money as his own capital.[38] Much of the money was
never recovered by the bank. The scheme is a simple one. Bank officers who
find themselves in financial difficulties may go to the loanshark, who soon
arranged a loan to the bank official in return for bank loans to clients of the
loanshark. The client, who normally would not qualify for a bank loan, is
sent to the loanshark's bank contact. The bank officer approves a $10,000
loan, for example, and the loanshark receives $3,000 as his share while the
borrower keeps the remaining $7,000. The bank official, in return for his
cooperation, also receives a percentage of the proceeds which goes toward
payment of his loan. The borrower is liable for the loan to the bank. Most
such borrowers tend to be poor risks, so there is a strong likelihood that the
borrower will renege on the bank loan. The loser is the bank. Within a
three-year period, one loanshark arranged for more than $1 million in such
loans.[39] A bank officer may also be pressured into approving loans to firms
controlled by organized crime. These firms may later go into bankruptcy,
and the bank loses large sums of money. It has been estimated that bank-
related frauds have caused the closing of dozens of such institutions in the
last twenty years.[40]

Criminal syndicates have been able to gain control over a number of
financial lending institutions and banks, and they have been able to
establish their own legitimate fronts.[41] These financial institutions serve as
legitimate fronts for loansharking operations. One such financial front was
the First National Service and Discount Corporation with offices on New
York's fashionable Fifth Avenue.[42] The clientele of First National were affluent doctors, lawyers, and businessmen. One government witness described
the interest charged on these loans as follows:

A. They were paying him five percent on tremendous sums of money. . . .

Q. Is that five percent a week?

A. That is five percent a week.

The key sources for much of the money laundered through First
National were investors such as Ruby Stein, Thomas Eboli, Mike Genovese,
and Joe Ross,[43] who are alleged to have had ties to the Vito Genovese crime
family. Thomas Eboli is said to have acted as an underboss in the Genovese
crime family, while Michael Genovese was a brother of the late Vito
Genovese.

Loansharks are also heavily involved in the hijacking of cargo and
cargo thefts on the docks. Many pier guards, hiring agents, carriers, and
longshoremen find their way to the shylock. Some local loansharks work

solely on the piers; many are part-time shylocks who work full-time on the docks and thus have access to other dock employees. Because of their key role in commerce, docks provide the loanshark with access to numerous valuables. Many pilfered goods find their way to the loanshark and his associates. Commerce, obviously, can be threatened because losses are passed on to consumers.

Combating Loansharking

At present, much of the burden of combating loansharking falls on the federal investigatory and prosecutorial apparatus. Much loansharking is interstate, and many localities lack statutes to address this problem. Consequently many local prosecutors deal only with acts associated with loansharking—for example, assault and homicide—rather than with loansharking itself. Prosecutors can rely on assault and homicide statutes; larceny and conspiracy statutes may also be of assistance to local prosecutors. However, if a borrower subjected to violence does not complain, the prosecutor is handicapped. In addition, few courts and juries take a strong stand against loansharking. Some loansharks, such as those who took over First National, appear to be legitimate businessmen. Unless violence is employed (and this is rare, since the loanshark is more interested in making money than paying it to enforcers), the prosecution of loansharking at the local level can be difficult.

At the federal level the Internal Revenue Code provides prosecutors with three key statutes. Section 7201 of the code makes it a felony for anyone to attempt to evade or defeat payment of federal taxes. Section 7206 of the code makes it a felony for an individual to file a false tax return. Loansharks who attempt to evade tax payments or who file false tax returns, by not fully disclosing all their income, can be prosecuted under these two federal tax statues. Similar state tax statutes can also be employed by state prosecutors. Section 7203 of the code makes it a misdemeanor for a willful failure to file a tax return as required by law. State counterparts to this section can also be employed where the loanshark fails to file a tax return.

Several other federal statutes can also be employed against loansharks. For example, the extortionate extension of credit and a conspiracy to extend such credit are felonies under federal law, punishable by up to twenty years of imprisonment and up to $10,000 in fines.[44] Interest rates that exceed an annual rate of 45 percent are dealt with under this statute. Since most shylocks charge rates up to 1,000 percent per year, their activity is covered. Anyone who advances property or money to an individual knowing that this individual will use that property or money to make extortionate extensions of credit can be convicted of a felony and can receive up to twenty years of imprisonment and to $10,000 in fines.[45] Advances disguised as gifts are also covered. The statute can easily be used against the first and second layers of a loansharking operation (the boss and his captains). It can also be applied to noncriminal elements who advance funds to loansharks with the objective of making large profits. Professionals and businessmen who become willing partners with shylocks can be prosecuted under this statute.

The collection or attempt to collect any extension of credit through extortionate means is also a felony under a federal statute.[46] This statute is aimed at the enforcers and the loansharks who resort to violence. Federal prosecutors who are investigating loansharking can grant witnesses immunity from prosecution after obtaining the approval of the U.S. attorney general, or his designated representative, and after petitioning the local federal court to order the witness to testify and produce any records he may have.[47] The witness cannot be prosecuted or subjected to any penalty in relation to his testimony after claiming his privilege against self-incrimination. The statute, at least in theory, provides federal prosecutors with a potent arm to induce witnesses to testify against loansharks.

Loansharking is a serious and growing problem. It is largely an outgrowth of the economic needs of private citizens and businesses. Attempts to reform the present federal criminal code have not been derelict in the area of loansharking. The extortionate extensions of credit will continue to be a crime under proposed federal criminal code reforms,[48] but the problem is more subtle than first meets the eye. Borrowers are not innocent bystanders, drawn into the evil clutches of the shylock through deceit and trickery. The borrower is a willing victim; many continue to borrow over a period of time. Few borrowers, in fact, pose any problem for the loanshark. The great majority pay their debts and go about their business.

Many individuals and businesses turn to the loanshark as a last resort. The banks and other legitimate financial sources have turned them down, but the loanshark may be willing to take a chance where the legitimate financial institutions are not. Shylocks, too, turn down potential clients, but the loanshark can afford to take a chance. The borrower gives his own body as collateral; few are willing to risk the consequences of failing to repay. Arbitration procedures are available to both borrower and shylock. These procedures have been institutionalized in the sitdown. Shylocking is undoubtedly big business. It is a multibillion-dollar annual industry that employs thousands of individuals and serves many sectors of society. Future attempts to curtail it must recognize the economic realities of the borrower, or they will fare no better than past attempts.[49] As long as a large number of individuals and firms are unable to find financial institutions to serve their economic needs, they will turn to criminal moneylenders. Loansharking is one of society's oldest professions. Although despised and prosecuted by many societies, it has continued to survive. Attempts to curtail it must address themselves primarily to the roots of the problem; law enforcement can play only a limited role in this strategy. Grandiose plans to curtail it solely through prosecution are doomed to waste the taxpayer's money.

Notes

1. Francis A.J. Ianni and Elizabeth Reuss-Ianni, *A Family Business* (New York: New American Library, 1973), p. 114.

2. Joey and Dave Fisher, *Killer* (Chicago: Playboy Press, 1973), pp. 108-109.

3. New York State Commission on Investigation, "The Loanshark Racket," in *The Crime Society*, ed. Francis A.J. Ianni and Elizabeth Reuss-Ianni (New York: New American Library, 1976), p. 207.

4. "Claim Loanshark Trio Forced Man into Job," *New York Daily News*, October 2, 1974, p. B-7.

5. Fisher and Fisher, *Killer*, p. 105.

6. Denny F. Pace and Jimmy C. Styles, *Organized Crime: Concepts and Control* (Englewood Cliffs, N.J.: Prentice-Hall, 1975), pp. 192, 194.

7. Lawrence J. Kaplan and Salvatore Matteis, "The Economics of Loansharking," in *An Economic Analysis of Crime*, ed. Lawrence J. Kaplan and Dennis Kessler (Springfield, Ill.: Charles C. Thomas, 1976), p. 177.

8. Pace and Styles, *Organized Crime*, p. 192.

9. Donald R. Cressey, *Theft of the Nation* (New York: Harper & Row, 1969), p. 77.

10. N.Y. Commission on Investigation, "The Loanshark Racket," in *Crime Society*, p. 216.

11. Kaplan and Matteis, "The Economics of Loansharking," in *Economic Analysis of Crime*, pp. 177, 179.

12. N.Y. Commission on Investigation, "The Loanshark Racket," in *Crime Society*, p. 206.

13. Cressey, *Theft of the Nation*, p. 77; see also Jonathan Rubinstein, *City Police* (New York: Ballantine Books, 1973), pp. 50, 51.

14. N.Y. Commission on Investigation, "The Loanshark Racket," in *Crime Society*, p. 203.

15. Norman F. Cantor, *Medieval History* (New York: Macmillan, 1969), pp. 395, 468.

16. Kaplan and Matteis, "The Economics of Loansharking," in *Economic Analysis of Crime*, p. 180.

17. Ibid., pp. 181, 182.

18. Richard B. Miller, "The Impingement of Loansharking on the Banking Industry," *Bankers Magazine*, Winter 1966, pp. 89-91.

19. Ibid., pp. 90-91.

20. Cressey, *Theft of the Nation*, p. 77.

21. Vincent Teresa, with Thomas C. Renner, *My Life in the Mafia* (Garden City, N.Y.: Doubleday, 1973), p. 240.

22. Kaplan and Matteis, "The Economics of Loansharking," pp. 185-187.

23. N.Y. Commission on Investigation, "The Loanshark Racket," in *Crime Society*, p. 205.

24. Ianni and Reuss-Ianni, *A Family Business*, pp. 71, 74, 107-110.

25. Teresa, with Renner, *My Life in the Mafia*, p. 234.

26. Based on interviews with Balkan groups involved in gambling operations in the New York-New Jersey area.

27. Cressey, *Theft of the Nation*, pp. 78-79.

28. N.Y. Commission on Investigation, "The Loanshark Racket," in *Crime Society*, p. 217.

29. "Loan Shark Threats Laid to Six by FBI," *New York Daily News*, October 3, 1974, p. 5.

30. N.Y. Commission on Investigation, "The Loanshark Racket," in *Crime Society*, pp. 217-218.

31. Ianni and Reuss-Ianni, *A Family Business*, pp. 71, 74.

32. Chamber of Commerce of the United States, *White Collar Crime* (Washington, D.C.: 1974), p. 6.

33. Edward J. DeFranco, *Anatomy of a Scam: A Case Study of a Planned Bankruptcy by Organized Crime* (Washington, D.C.: U.S. Department of Justice, 1973), pp. 4-5.

34. U.S., Department of Justice, Law Enforcement Assistance Administration, *Strategies for Combating the Criminal Receiver of Stolen Goods* (Washington, D.C.: U.S. Government Printing Office, 1976), pp. 18-21.

35. "Anatomy of a Scam," *National District Attorneys Association Economic Crime Project Newsletter,* May-June-July 1974, p. 196.

36. Based on author's observations while employed with the U.S. Securities and Exchange Commission.

37. U.S. Chamber of Commerce, *White Collar Crime*, p. 6.

38. N.Y. Commission on Investigation, "The Loanshark Racket, in *Crime Society*, p. 223.

39. Ibid., p. 224.

40. U.S. Chamber of Commerce, *White Collar Crime*, p. 4.

41. Miller, "The Impingement of Loansharking," pp. 89-91.

42. N.Y. Commission on Investigation, "The Loanshark Racket," in *Crime Society*, p. 209.

42. N.Y. Commission on Investigation, "The Loanshark Racket," in *Crime Society*, p. 209.

43. Ibid., p. 211.

44. 18 U.S.C. 892.

45. 18 U.S.C. 893.

46. 18 U.S.C. 894.

47. 18 U.S.C. 895.

48. See Section 1804, of the proposed Federal Criminal Code Reform Act of 1977.

49. Lawrence J. Kaplan and James M. Maher, "The Economics of the Numbers Game," in *Economic Analysis of Crime*, pp. 119-133.

9 The Drug Trade

The ambassador of a Latin American country is arrested for smuggling 100 kilograms of heroin on a Paris-New York flight. American and Canadian law enforcement agents arrest two other ambassadors and confiscate 138 pounds of pure heroin.[1] In a separate incident the United States Coast Guard seizes three ships carrying more than 100 tons of marijuana.[2] At Washington's Dulles International Airport, federal agents seize a sixty-seven-crate shipment of brass doorknockers; forty-six contain hashish.[3]

The trade in drugs is big business; it costs the nation more than $10 billion annually.[4] In New York City addicts steal an average of $4 million daily to support their habits. It is one of the fastest expanding industries in America, with an annual growth rate exceeding 10 percent and profits between 15 percent and 1,000 percent.[5] Its clientele runs into the millions and extends over dozens of countries. In the United States the number of addicts exceeds five hundred thousand. In one year law enforcement agencies spent more than $250 million just in the arrest stage. This does not include the billions of dollars spent annually to investigate, intercept, and prosecute drug-related offenses. In one year more than 250,000 Americans were arrested for drug-related incidents.[6]

For more than fifty years America has wrestled with the problem of narcotics. There are no simple solutions. It is a problem that has grown proportionately with the population and has dissipated the resources of this country's law enforcement agencies. Some call it the Viet Nam of our police agencies. Domestic and international criminal cartels have entered this lucrative industry. The intelligence services of several countries have also found their way into it. Organized crime has played and continues to play a dominant role, with no end in sight.

The History of U.S. Drug Legislation

The opium poppy was known in Europe more than four thousand years ago; poppy capsules have been found in the Swiss lake dwellings of the Neolithic Age. The psychological effects of opium were known to the ancient Sumerians, who referred to it as the plant of joy (hul). Homer refers to the opium poppy in his *Iliad,* and Arab physicians used its medicinal qualities for the treatment of dysentery. The Arabs introduced the opium poppy to the Chinese, and by the eighteenth century opium smoking had grown to epidemic proportions in the Far East and China.

Opium eating was common in eighteenth-century Europe, but it was not until 1803 that the German pharmacist Sertuner isolated an opium alkaloid that he named morphine. In 1832 scientists isolated codeine, also an opium alkaloid. By the midnineteenth century morphine and codeine were widely used in this country and abroad. The discovery of the hypodermic needle, combined with the expansion of the world trade in narcotics, gave rise to serious abuses in the industrialized West. During the American Civil War period morphine was widely employed as a painkiller. So much of it was used that thousands of Civil War veterans found themselves addicted to morphine. Narcotic addicts were said to suffer from the soldier's disease.

In the late 1870s the German pharmaceutical firm Bayer and Company produced a new miracle drug to cure morphine addiction. The new drug was a morphine derivative called heroin. By the turn of this century it became apparent that heroin was much more dangerous than morphine. In fact, it was more addictive. During this same period great reformist movements took hold; this was the era of the great movements against slavery and prostitution and for temperance. China had attracted the attention of Western missionaries. With 10 million opium addicts, the Chinese government was anxious to take some action.[7] For the missionaries opium came to symbolize a social vice that had to be outlawed. The reformist groups in this country and in Great Britain turned their attention to the drug problem. They came to view it in moral and religious terms; for them this was a crusade against evil. The medical establishment was not consulted, nor did it offer any solutions to the problem of addiction.

On February 9, 1909, under pressure from the Women's Christian Temperance Union, the Anti-Saloon League, the Endeavor Society, and the numerous American Christian missionary societies in the Far East, the U.S. Congress passed the Opium Exclusion Act.[8] The act made it unlawful to import opium or any of its derivatives into the United States, except for medicinal purposes, and then only in accordance with rules and regulations prescribed by the secretary of the Treasury. The act also provided for fines of up to $5,000 and prison terms of up to two years for anyone receiving, concealing, buying, or selling opium or facilitating its transportation.[9] The act was the precursor of the Narcotic Drugs Import and Export Act of 1922.[10]

Much of the impetus for legislation banning the import of opium for nonmedicinal uses came from the missionary societies in the United States. Missionaries to China were alarmed at existing British-Chinese treaties requiring China to allow imports of British-shipped opium from India. The International Reform Bureau, which represented over thirty missionary societies within the United States, called on the secretary of state and on foreign governments to hold an international conference on opium. Missionaries were concerned that the Philippines, then under United States jurisdiction, would increase its use of opium, as China had. The Philippines Opium Commission, heavily influenced by the missionaries, called for the prohibition of opium save for medicinal purposes. The commission also called for prison terms for those who violated opium regulations. In 1909, under the initiative of the American government, an International Opium Commission met in Shanghai. One of the delegates to the Shanghai Convention was Bishop Brent, a strong proponent of antiopium legislation. The delegates to the Shanghai Convention passed resolutions calling for an end to the smuggling of opium and for international controls over the manufacture of narcotics.[11]

In 1912 a narcotics convention was held in The Hague. The conferees agreed on the need for international control of the opium trade and the need to suppress the abuses of opium. They called for the control of the manufacture, sale, and use of narcotics, specifically morphine and cocaine. They were to be used strictly as medicine. In large part the convention's measures were later adopted by a number of nations, including the United States. Under pressure from a small but well-organized and powerful coalition of antiopium groups, the U.S. Congress passed the Harrison Anti-Narcotic Act in 1914. Narcotics were not then a problem for law enforcement. Of more then two hundred thousand arrests made by the New York City Police Department in that year, fewer than two hundred were drug connected.[12] Many of the drug users were women of middle-class background. The addict class, although sizable, was not a problem for law enforcement. Yet some reformers ranked drug addiction with prostitution, gambling, and alcohol. The Harrison Act was an attempt to impose on a large segment of the population a law that was neither understood nor supported. Many law enforcement agencies were quick to see this act as a basis for requesting increases in manpower and funds. Unlike the alcohol industry, the pharmaceutical industry and the medical profession suffered no economic loss from passage of the act; thus they offered no organized opposition to its passage.

The Harrison Act was a revenue-raising measure, a regulatory statute in the guise of a tax measure. The act provided that every individual who "produces, manufactures, compounds, deals in, dispenses, sells, distributes or gives away opium or any compound, salt, derivative, or preparation thereof" must register with the internal revenue district collector and pay a special tax of one dollar annually. The act covered importers, wholesalers, retailers, and doctors. Congress next passed a series of drug-related acts aimed at curbing the use of drugs. The policy and strategy legislated by the Congress had three purposes: (1) To stop the flow of illicit drugs into this country. (2) To punish those engaged in this illegal importation and distribution. (3) To punish those who use these illegal drugs. The Harrison Act was soon followed by other federal statutes, among them the Narcotic Drug Import and Export Act of 1922, the Marijuana Tax Act of 1937, the Narcotic Transportation Act of 1939, the Opium Poppy Control Act of 1942, the Narcotic Control Act of 1956, and additional acts and amendments passed in the 1960s and 1970s.

These domestic statutes were reinforced by a series of international treaties and conventions. The Geneva Convention of 1925 called on governments to submit annual reports concerning the production and consumption of narcotic drugs to the League of Nations. The league itself was called on to play a greater role in the regulation of narcotics. The 1931 Convention for Limiting the Manufacture and Regulating and Distribution of Narcotic Drugs called on each country to limit its manufacture of narcotics to the amount needed for medicinal purposes. Each government was to submit to the Drug Supervisory Body estimates of narcotics needed for legitimate medical purposes. The convention of 1936 attempted to encourage all signing parties to impose strong penal sanctions on opium traffickers. After World War II the United Nations took over where the League of Nations left off, and a series of additional agreements was established. In 1946 the Commission on Narcotic Drugs was established. The Paris Protocol of 1948 and the Opium Protocol of 1953 followed. Once again the contracting nations attempted to limit the production and distribution of narcotics to the legitimate sectors. Additional conventions followed, and other organizations were established to assist in the international control and regulation of the drug trade among nations.[13] However, the international political climate and conflicting economic needs of many nations (especially those in less developed areas), as well as the inability of many countries to curtail the trade in drugs, made many of these protocols meaningless.

The states soon followed the federal example and enacted their own legislation to curb trafficking in drugs. Until 1930 the war against narcotics was waged solely by the federal government, with occasional assistance from local police forces. The federal government, along with the antiopium groups, had urged the states to enact their own statutes. Many states adopted the Uniform Narcotics Act model, which had been developed by the National Conference of Commissioners on Uniform State Laws. The act was patterned after federal legislation and had the blessing of the American Bar Association. The act outlawed the manufacture or distribution of narcotics without a license and possession except for medicinal purposes. The act also provided for exchanges of data between local and federal law enforcement agencies, as well as for uniform recordkeeping. The majority of the states adopted the act, with some modification, and imposed penalties ranging from six months for a first sale or transfer offense to twenty-five years of imprisonment.[14]

Federal and state statutes were challenged in the courts. In 1918 the case of *Webb* v. *United States* was heard by the United States Supreme Court.[15] The Harrison Act did not make addiction itself a crime; rather it sought to regulate the dispensing of narcotics by making it illegal for an addict to secure drugs from sources not licensed under law. In the *Webb* case a physician had prescribed morphine to an addict to keep him comfortable by maintaining his customary use. The Court held that the physician had violated the Harrison Act because the morphine had not been issued in the course of treating the addict and was thus not covered by the act's exemption for the physician-patient situation.

The Narcotics Division of the Treasury Department came to view addiction as a criminal problem.[16] The *Webb* case was one of several Supreme Court decisions that left a deep imprint on this country's handling of drug addiction. The next important test for the Harrison Act came in the case of *Jin Fuey Moy* v. *United States.*[17] In this case a doctor had prescribed morphine to several patients in quantities of eight to ten grains at a time. The Court held that a doctor did not enjoy immunity under the act when he prescribed drugs to cater to the cravings of addicts.

In the next test case a New York doctor was arrested for prescribing to a known addict 150 grains of heroin, 360 grams of morphine, and 210 grams of cocaine to use as the patient saw fit. The case, *United States* v. *Behrman,* attracted national attention.[18] The question to be answered by the United States Supreme Court was whether this doctor had acted within the "course of his professional practice." The prosecutors did not charge the defendant with acting in bad faith or in a manner not in accord with proper therapeutic treatment. Rather the government charged that the defendant had violated the law by simply prescribing narcotics to a known addict. The Court sustained the government's position. Henceforth any doctor who prescribed drugs to an addict could face prosecution.

In *Linder* v. *United States* the United States Supreme Court was once again faced with a challenge to the Harrison Act.[19] An informer for the Narcotics Division had gone to the defendant's offices, complaining of stomach pains. The defendant had prescribed three tablets of cocaine and one of morphine. He was later arrested and prosecuted, but the court held that addicts could be proper patients for dispensing drugs. The Court went on to note that

> we cannot possibly conclude that a physician acted improperly or unwisely or for other than medical purpose solely because he had dispensed to one of them, in the ordinary course and in good faith, four small tablets of morphine or cocaine for relief of conditions incident to addiction.[20]

The Court thus softened the impact of the *Behrman* decision. However, the aggressive posture of the Narcotics Division and the reluctance of many physicians to jeopardize themselves left many addicts to find illegal sources of drugs. The addict became more dependent on the illegal market.

After 1925 the addict came to be viewed as a criminal even by many members of the medical profession. Physicians who ventured to assist him did so at their own risk; some were prosecuted. Not until 1962, in the now classic case of *Robinson* v. *California,* was the addict's legal medical status restored.[21] The *Robinson* case involved a California statute that made addiction itself a crime. The Court held that making it a crime to be diseased (addicted) is cruel and unusual punishment and therefore unconstitutional under the Eighth and Fourteenth Amendments. The *Robinson* case, although hailed as a landmark decision, did not invalidate more than forty years of drug regulation at federal and state levels.[22] The addict remains dependent on criminal distributors and suppliers.

The Present Drug Model

Between 1912 and 1923 more than forty cities established clinics to legally dispense narcotics to addicts. Two of the better-known clinics were in New Orleans and Shreveport.[23] The objectives of these early clinics were to relieve the addict's suffering and to keep him out of the clutches of criminals. Some clinics dispensed drugs only to addicts who were registered with them; others demanded that the addict also find employment. Drugs were dispensed directly, thus avoiding the abuses connected with prescriptions. The clinics were able to compete successfully with the criminal market by underselling it. At the same time local police forces were ordered to crack down on criminal rings who peddled drugs to addicts.

Although the clinics proved somewhat successful in keeping the addict from criminals, they met criticism from the public and open opposition from the federal enforcement apparatus. Addicts often bribed hospital attendants to sell them drugs, fueling the criticism of the clinics. Critics charged that they were perpetuating the narcotic craving of the addict and spreading addiction by making cheap drugs available. By 1924 the last of the local clinics was closed. No new attempts were made to assist the addict until 1935, when the federal government established the Public Health Service hospital at Lexington. A second federal facility was opened in 1938 at Forth Worth.

These two federal facilities treated federal prisoners and individuals who voluntarily committed themselves. Once admitted, federal prisoners could not be released through parole or commutation of their sentences until the surgeon general deemed their treatment completed. Until passage of the Narcotic Addict Rehabilitation Act of 1966, patients who voluntarily committed themselves could leave at will. More than 90 percent of those who went through these federal hospitals returned to drugs within the first year of their discharge.[24] Treatment at these facilities consisted of withdrawal, psychiatric care, and vocational rehabilitation. These hospitals treated several thousand patients per year, hardly sufficient to meet the needs of a large addict population. The federal model, unlike the early clinics, stigmatized the addict as a criminal and left it to the courts and the federal apparatus to determine when and under what conditions he should be released.

In 1966 Congress passed the Narcotic Addict Rehabilitation Act which provides that convicted felons who are addicted to narcotics can in lieu of sentencing be committed by a civil proceeding for treatment.[25] The key test is that they must be deemed capable of rehabilitation. Persons convicted for violations of federal law can also enter this program, if they are addicted to narcotics. They are committed for treatment that may last as long as forty-two months. More than thirty states have similar civil commitment proceedings. New York's Metcalf-Volker Act allows addicts convicted to state courts to volunteer for a civil commitment program.[26] The addict's charges are dropped within three years after completion of the program. Many addicts choose the criminal route and risk prosecution, since conviction often means a shorter confinement. In California a court can order the commitment of an addict convicted of a crime; the addict himself can also commit himself voluntarily.[27] Commitment consists of confinement and a closely supervised conditional release. The released addict has to abstain from the use of narcotics for at least three years before he is eligible for permanent discharge.

These federal and state models have been complemented by other models, including halfway houses, methadone clinics, and the use of narcotic antagonists. But these programs have generally been unable to stem the drug trade. Groups like Synanon tend to be run by ex-addicts, and therapy consists of intense interaction among members. Entrance is usually voluntary, and the addict can leave at will. Such groups shy away from use of any kind of drugs. Halfway houses have been used extensively. In some, addicts can find assistance in withdrawal; in others, addicts discharged from a hospital may enter them. The halfway house provides, at least in theory, assistance in the form of psychotherapy, vocational guidance, and assistance in finding a job. The success of halfway houses is questionable, and many addicts enter them as a way of escaping prosecution and prison.

Since 1965 methadone maintenance programs have grown rapidly. Millions of dollars have been allocated yearly by the federal government for these programs. Their success rate, however, has proven dubious. Methadone is a narcotic derivative. A number of addicts have died from methadone overdoses, and a lucrative black market in methadone has developed. Those maintained on methadone become dependent on it and experience withdrawal symptoms if the drug is taken away. Withdrawal from methadone only brings back the craving for heroin. It is not a cure, only a substitute drug of questionable merit.

Narcotic antagonists have been used in the last several years to combat the drug problem. The antagonists most often used are cyclazocine, nalorphine, and naloxone. Like methadone, they do not alleviate the craving for heroin; instead they occupy the morphine receptor sites in the central nervous system, thus preventing the narcotic from producing any effects. They must be taken daily and have negative side effects such as dizziness, constipation, and depression. Whether these antagonists will provide a solution to the problem of narcotic addiction remains to be seen.

The Foreign Drug Markets

In the mountainous regions of Burma, Thailand, and Laos (the Golden Triangle), an army of five thousand local tribesmen and veterans of Chiang Kai-Shek's old Kuomintang 93rd Independent Division escort huge caravans of opium through the jungles of Southeast Asia.[28] In Paraguay so-called Mau Mau pilots fly narcotics to the Americas in their Cessna 500s. In Panama's Tocumen International Airport police are on the lookout for the dozens of aircraft that stop there monthly, carrying large quantities of narcotics for delivery to various international locations.[29] In Bulgaria customs agents seize two tons of hashish from trucks crossing its borders.[30]

Drug addiction is an international problem, in large part magnified by modern technology. At the flick of a television switch the youth of the West can have a glimpse at the opium dens of the East. A drug trafficker can board an airplane in Ankara and be in Paris that same day to close a major transaction. Technology has brought buyer and seller together by bridging continents and cultures. The problem is neither uniquely Western nor exclusively American; the East also suffers from it. Egypt has had a drug problem for several centuries. Until World War I it had a population of some one million addicts, many from the upper strata of Egyptian society.[31] By the 1920s heroin and cocaine had replaced hashish as the drug of choice among Egypt's addict population. A series of tough laws enacted between 1925 and 1928 failed to stem the tide. A well-organized network soon took hold and reigned supreme for many years in Egypt's underworld. Laws alone, Egypt soon found, were not enough.

India, the world's largest producer of licit opium, has a drug problem. Farmers in Uttar Pradesh and the Punjab are licensed by the government to grow opium. Some four thousand villages are involved in India's licit opium production. Government agents purchase the opium after it has been dried to a moisture content of 30 percent. The opium is then sent to processing plants in Madhya Pradesh and Uttar Pradesh. Russia and the United States are India's chief licit opium markets; more than 50 percent of India's crop is exported. However, some finds its way into the illicit market.

India has had an addict population for several centuries. In 1857 the British-controlled government enacted the India Opium Act. Another act followed in 1878, and the Dangerous Drugs Act was passed in 1930. Illegal possession, transportation, import, export, and sale of opium are punishable under these acts. The cultivation or manufacture of opium or its derivatives without a government license is prohibited. Contravention of these provisions carries a prison term and a fine. Still an estimated one hundred tons of opium finds its way each year into the illicit Indian market and into neighboring countries.[32] India's registration system allows the more than two hundred thousand known addicts to obtain licit opium from dentists, veterinarians, and medical doctors. But this limited legalized market has not stopped the growth of a lucrative black market in cities such as New Delhi and Bombay, where prices range from $7 to $107 per kilogram. Regulation and enforcement are lax and have strained India's limited resources. India is opposed to any international restrictions on the production and export of opium, since exports supply the country with badly needed foreign exchanges. A global shortage in the illicit opium market can easily be replenished from India's large poppy fields.

Pakistan is also a major grower of opium. Cultivation takes place in the Northwest Frontier Province and produces at least thirty-two tons. Licensed farmers are paid an average of $8 per kilogram, three times the price paid for one hectare of wheat. Pakistan has a large addict population; exact figures are not known, but the number is said to exceed twenty thousand. The opium is purchased by the government and sold to pharmacists and medical personnel. However, much of it finds its way to the illicit market; especially in the tribal areas where the central government has little control. Pushtun-speaking tribesmen play a key role in this illegal market; the opium then finds its way into neighboring countries.[33]

Opium production in Afghanistan is said to exceed eighty tons annually, a conservative estimate according to experts. The major growing areas are Helmand and Quandarhar. Low-priced morphine, codeine, and cocaine are readily available. Since growing opium is more lucrative than growing wheat, many farmers do so and sell their harvest to narcotics traffickers. The traditionally weak central government has been unable to control the tribal groups in the countryside. The Pushtun tribes are instrumental in the smuggling of illicit drugs into Iran, which has a large addict population.

Opium in Iran has been grown and used for centuries. Prior to World War II Iran produced more than a thousand tons annually.[34] An attempt to control the use of opium was first made in 1910, but it was unsuccessful. Complete prohibition against the illegal use of any narcotics came in 1959.

Iran is said to have more than a million addicts; over a hundred thousand are registered with the government and receive supplies from government-licensed pharmacies and physicians. In 1969 Iran imposed the death penalty for drug traffickers, but the illicit trade continues and the market survives. Much of the illicit supply comes from Turkey and Afghanistan. Dubai, in the Persian Gulf, is a center of the Iranian drug trade.

The Golden Triangle accounts for half the world's supply of illicit opium. The central governments of Burma, Thailand, and Laos (although the situation may have changed in Laos since the Communist takeover) have traditionally exerted little control. Some of the opium finds its way to Hong Kong, which has an addict population of more than a hundred thousand. The Ch'ao-chou organizations are said to control the drug trade in Hong Kong.[35] Law enforcement has made little headway against these criminal syndicates, and the situation appears to be deteriorating. Some of the opium from the Golden Triangle goes to Singapore and Malaysia. There is an open tolerance of drug use in both countries, and shooting galleries are common in Singapore.

For many years Turkey has been the primary supplier of the raw material from which the illicit heroin for the American market is produced. For more than a thousand years Turkish fields have produced opium that has a high morphine content and is preferred by both addicts and traffickers. A small number of provinces have been licensed to grow the opium poppy. However, the government has been criticized by both nationalist groups and the far Left, who have charged it with capitulating to American pressure. Some of the Turkish opium finds its way into Iran, but Syria and Lebanon are also lucrative markets. In the late 1960s the Turkish underworld began to process its own morphine and sell it directly to European buyers, circumventing Middle Eastern agents.

Western Europe is known to have a growing drug addiction problem. The number of known narcotic addicts is placed at more than fifty thousand and is rapidly increasing.[36] France may have as many as thirty thousand addicts, and the United Kingdom some forty-five hundred (three thousand of these are registered with the government).[37] France grows a low-yield European opium poppy in the Loire Valley, which satisfies some of France's medicinal needs. The illegal narcotics come from the Middle East and the Far East. Marseille, with its long history of a criminal underworld, plays a key role not only in the American but also in the French illicit drug market. The Marseille heroin laboratories enjoy a reputation as producers of the best grades of heroin, sometimes reaching 98 percent purity.

Although Italy has a growing drug problem, this country is primarily a transit point for shipments of morphine base from the Middle East en route to France. Shipments of heroin also stop there en route to the American market. International smuggling groups, made up of Corsican, Sicilian, and

Sardinian gangsters, as well as Turkish, Lebanese, and Far Eastern groups, make their way through Italy. Lax law enforcement and an unstable political environment marked by serious acts of terrorism have consistently undermined the capability of Italian law enforcement in this area.

The Federal Republic of Germany has no serious narcotic problem, but it is a routing point for narcotics that make their way from the Middle East through the Balkans. The large number of alien workers, many Turkish, who come to Germany in search of employment makes it difficult for law enforcement to curtail the flow of narcotics through the country. Munich and West Berlin, with large alien-worker populations, have become key centers in the European narcotics trade. The East Europeans, especially the East Germans, who could easily halt the flow of narcotics through East Europe, tend to be somewhat lax, since they see this as an opportunity to undermine the West.

In the past Norway did not have a serious narcotics problem. However, since 1965 the abuse of drugs by the younger generation has become a real concern. Although first confined to the city of Oslo and its surrounding suburbs, the use of drugs has spread to other areas of the country. In 1969 the Office of Director General of Health Services was charged with coordinating attempts to curtail the illegal use of drugs. Sweden, has had drug problems since the early 1920s.[38] Heroin and cocaine addiction were known before World War II, and although cocaine has decreased in use, heroin has not. There are some ten thousand known addicts in this country; at least half are known to live in the Stockholm area. A national survey found that at least 16 percent of all those surveyed had used illegal drugs at least once.[39] As a result the Swedes have tightened their narcotics control laws. Penalties for illegal use of drugs can range from small fines for minor violations to two years' imprisonment for average offenses and up to ten years' imprisonment for the more serious ones. Treatment of addicts ranges from psychiatric assistance to the prescribing of methadone. Sweden, with a small and homogeneous population, has shown some success in curtailing the abuse of narcotics.

The United Kingdom, like the United States, first became concerned with the problem of opiates at the turn of the century. Opium derivatives had been used in Britain for several centuries; Chaucer mentions them in his works. Throughout the nineteenth century opium was freely supplied for the treatment of colds, hay fever, and nervous conditions. During the First World War pressure from antiopium groups led to legislation banning the use of cocaine. In 1920 the first Dangerous Drugs Act was passed; a series of other acts soon followed. The use and possession of opium derivatives was restricted to people designated by the home secretary and to patients who used it solely for medical purposes. In 1926 the Rollerston Report observed that drug addiction was not a serious problem in Britain and that addiction should be regarded as an illness rather than a form of over-indulgence.[40] The report outlined a range of medical alternatives to handle the problem of addiction. The Rollerston Report became the cornerstone of Britain's narcotic legislation and marked a divergence from the American model, which continued to view drug addiction as moral decadence.

In 1958 the Brian Committee was set up to study the problem of drug addiction in Britain. Its 1961 report concluded that the addict population was very small and that the illicit market was almost negligible. In 1965 the committee's second report revealed the number of known addicts had increased from 454 to 753. Many came from the professional classes, whereas the number of addicts from the lower classes was small. Most addicts were located in the London area, and the pushers were primarily local doctors who had been authorized to supply heroin and cocaine to addicts. The committee recommended a number of changes in the country's drug laws.

Since the late 1920s Britain had allowed doctors to prescribe narcotics to patients who were undergoing gradual withdrawal. If every effort to cure the addict had failed, the patient could continue on drugs, provided the doctor concluded that depriving the patient of drugs would disrupt his normal life. Although doctors had abused these provisions, the Brian Committee concluded that taking drugs from the addict was no answer. Instead it recommended tightening regulations and restructuring the heroin maintenance model. The Dangerous Drugs Act of 1967 included regulations to curtail past abuses in Britain's medical approach to drug addiction. Under the new law physicians could not supply addicts with heroin or cocaine except to relieve pain due to organic disease or injury. Licenses to prescribe drugs were to be granted only to physicians who worked in hospitals or similar institutions, and a physician treating a patient addicted to drugs was to notify the authorities. The medical maintenance of addicts was taken out of the hands of the general practitioner and placed into the hands of the British Hospital Service.

Under the present British model the addict first checks in with one of the licensed treatment clinics. He must be certified by a clinic physician as addicted to such a degree that drugs must be prescribed as a prelude to withdrawal or maintenance. The severity of the patient's addiction is tested. The treatment center then checks the central index of known drug addicts to determine whether the patient is already obtaining drugs from another clinic. Once an addict is accepted for treatment, the clinic usually sends prescriptions for drugs directly to the pharmacy, thereby curtailing drug-related frauds by addicts. The addict goes to the pharmacy daily to pick up his dose, thus addicts cannot hold large quantities of drugs in their possession. Although abuses may still be found, the British model has served that country well. The addict is viewed as suffering from an illness. This is not to say that Britain tolerates the sale and possession of illicit drugs. The Misuse of Drugs Act of 1971 provides for up to fourteen years in prison and fines for anyone trafficking in illegal drugs. The addict is treated medically, while the trafficker is punished severely.

The narcotics problem is an international one. Most Western countries suffer from it, as do many Third World nations. Criminal syndicates play a key role in the marketing and distribution of drugs. Many syndicates have international contacts and often work with similar groups in other countries. For example, Afghani traffickers work with their counterparts in Iran. Save for the totalitarian systems of Asia, Eastern Europe, and Russia, the buying and selling of narcotics is big business throughout the world. However, the United States is unique in the size and sophistication of its illegal drug market, an industry that brings in billions of dollars annually for criminal syndicates.

The Domestic Drug Market

Off the Florida coast federal agents intercept a shipment of drugs said to have a street value of $100 million.[41] In New York City a narcotics gang is said to be responsible for at least a dozen killings.[42] Law enforcement officials are concerned with this group's enormous capacity for violence. In one large city alone more than nine hundred men, women, and children died of narcotics-related deaths.[43] More than forty of these victims were young children. Narcotics is big business in the United States. Numerous criminal groups are active in this trade. The Mafia families and the Cuban criminal underworld are known to be major traffickers.

To better understand why narcotics is big business, it is first necessary to understand the opium-processing phase. Opium and its derivatives are sold in seven forms. In raw form the morphine content varies from the 14 percent level of Turkish opium to the 5 percent levels of Far Eastern opium. Raw opium may be eaten, sniffed, or smoked. Cooked opium, opium from which moisture has been removed, also finds its way into the illicit drug market. This form is usually ingested in the same fashion as raw opium. A third opium derivative is morphine-base opium. Once the organic impurities are chemically removed from the opium, the morphine content can be as high as 70 percent. This form of opium is usually an intermediate form not readily absorbed by the human body. It is usually converted into either morphine salt compounds or heroin.

Morphine salts are used principally for legitimate medical needs. They are soluble in water and can be injected. Morphine salts are often stolen from hospitals and pharmacies. Although not in great demand in this country, addicts in the Far East use morphine salts. A fifth form of opium derivative is crude heroin, known as number 2 heroin. It usually has a content of 75 percent pure heroin. In Asian countries crude heroin is often converted into number 3 heroin and smoked.

Number 3 heroin (also known as purple heroin) is brownish or purplish in color and is found in the Far East. Addicts in Hong Kong, Thailand, Singapore, the Golden Triangle, and Malaysia, tend to favor number 3 heroin. It is often smoked and sometimes mixed with caffeine to facilitate its absorption into the body. A seventh opium derivative is number 4 heroin (also known as white heroin). This opium derivative resembles flour and is usually 95 percent pure heroin. On the American market number 4 heroin is often adulterated as it moves down the chain of distribution. When it finally reaches the street its heroin content may run less than 5 percent. Brownish, high-purity heroin often comes from Mexico. Pure white heroin usually orginates in the Anatolian farmlands of Turkey.

The conversion of opium into heroin is a simple process requiring only a rudimentary understanding of basic chemistry. The famed laboratories are usually makeshift operations run by amateur chemists who have generally learned their trade by working for other heroin chemists. The equipment needed for these laboratories is simple and inexpensive: copper vats, filters, pans, and trays and a simple source of heat. A laboratory that produces an average of one hundred kilograms of heroin can be equipped for as little as $5,000. The laboratories themselves are usually located in small villas, village huts, even basements. The raw opium is converted into a morphine base and then into a crude heroin. Numbers 3 and 4 (or pure heroin) are derivatives of the crude heroin base. For every kilogram of heroin the chemist needs a kilogram of acetic anhydride. Since this last chemical is relatively cheap and easily purchased in the legitimate market, law enforcement agencies have a difficult time tracing such purchases to heroin chemists.

There are three key stages in every narcotics-smuggling operation: (1) a foreign country, from which the drugs are shipped into the United States; (2) an entry point into this country, where the drugs enter the American market for distribution; and (3) the first stage of the domestic distribution phase.[44] The actors in the domestic smuggling operation are many. Five key levels can usually be identified, but the sublevels within these complicate investigation by law enforcement agencies. At the top of the domestic chain is the importer. He arranges for the purchase abroad and usually pays 50 percent of the price in advance and the remainder on delivery.[45] The importer usually purchases large amounts of heroin (about one hundred kilograms at a time) and pays an average of $5,000 to $6,000 per kilo. The importer's foreign sellers may be Corsican gangsters, who may have purchased the morphine base from Middle Eastern gangsters at a price of $1,000 to $2,000 per kilogram. The cost of converting the morphine base into pure heroin is about $400 per kilogram in a European laboratory, even less in a Latin

American laboratory. The profits for the seller of pure heroin may be as high as 150 percent on his investment. An investment of $100,000 to $300,000 in one hundred kilograms of heroin can gross the seller as much as $1 million. The prices vary with the available supply and demand.

After the heroin is brought into this country, the importer sells the heroin to one or more wholesalers. There may be one to five of these first-level wholesalers, and each may buy five to twenty kilograms of heroin at a price of $10,000 to $30,000 per kilogram (the prices fluctuate with current supply and demand). The first-level wholesaler in turn sells his supply to ten or more second-level wholesalers. Each second-level wholesaler may buy one to three kilograms of heroin at a price ranging from $20,000 to $30,000 per kilogram.

Below the second-level wholesaler are the cutters who run the small local factories found in many slum areas. These individuals package the heroin for street distribution. The factories are crude operations that employ six or more individuals (packers) who dilute the heroin with quinine or milk sugar and then package it in small glassine bags. These packers are usually part-time workers. As the price of the heroin increases, the purity decreases. Each glassine bag contains about one hundred milligrams of heroin. One ounce of heroin, 10 percent to 15 percent pure, can bring the cutter $600 to $1,000 on the street. At the bottom of the chain is an army of dealers and pushers. The dealers buy the glassine bags in bundles of twenty-five bags each. Dealers are usually addicts who sell the glassine bags to pushers, who in turn sell them on the street. Bags usually sell for $5 each, depending on their heroin content. The pusher, like the dealer, is a user who sells primarily to support his habit. The pusher is the victim of his own addiction; he is at the bottom of the domestic narcotic chain.

A frequently asked question is, at which level does organized crime enter the market? Narcotics transactions usually begin outside the United States. Seller and buyer rarely meet; they conduct their transactions through a series of agents who act as buffers and thus insulating the principals from prosecution. Sellers are usually foreign criminal syndicates that operate internationally in the narcotics distribution chain. The American Mafia has worked closely with its Italian counterpart and with Corsican gangsters in arranging these initial transactions. In the early 1960s the American Mafia was said to have authorized the Corsican syndicate to deal directly with Hispanic gangsters in return for a share of the profits. The American Mafia and its associates usually bank most of the profits from foreign heroin transactions; they are said to indirectly control as much as 85 percent of the heroin that finds its way into the U.S. market. Since large sums of capital are needed to initiate these transactions, and since international contacts are crucial to any such transaction, the importer and first-level wholesalers tend to be tied directly to organized crime. High-level syndicate officers are usually assigned the task of acting as importers by their criminal chieftains.[46] First-level wholesalers are usually soldiers of Mafia families.

It is no accident that the elite of America's organized crime controls the foreign departure and domestic entry points of the narcotics distribution chain. Their vast capital, international experience and contacts with foreign criminal groups have enabled them to do so. Through a series of international agreements these criminal syndicates have divided the lucrative narcotics trade into territories and allocated franchises to allies and associates. The upper levels of the narcotics trade are in the hands of the Mafia and Corsican gangster families. The second-level wholesalers are usually associates or allies who are not directly tied to the Mafia families. Black and Latin gangsters are usually heavily involved as cutters, dealers, and pushers; some have made their way into the second-level wholesaler group. Cuban gangsters, because of their international contacts in Latin America have developed their own cocain-smuggling networks, independent of the Mafia and its associates.

The growing diversity of the drug market has meant that many criminal groups independent of Mafia control have entered the market. The Cubans have developed a sizable, independent cocaine operation. Other ethnic groups have made their way into the hashish, mescaline, methedrine, morphine, and methadone markets. Chicano crime groups on the West Coast control much of the illegal methadone market and are playing an increasingly important role in the smuggling of Mexican heroin into the United States. The growing market in amphetamines, codeine, LSD, and demerol has enabled many independents to enter the drug market. Because the drug market is becoming more diversified, the Mafia and its associates can no longer control every facet of this complex domestic market. America's overindulgence in drugs has opened opportunities for numerous criminal groups.

Foreign criminal syndicates, many with the assistance of their intelligence services, have also made their way into the American drug market. The intelligence agencies see the American narcotics market as a source of additional funds for their intelligence operations; some see it as lucrative market for personal gain. Mexican officials have been known to work with other corrupt Latin American government officials and with criminal elements in servicing the lucrative U.S. drug market.[47] The elite of America's criminal underworld has not lost its control of the drug market; they have come to play a greater role through indirect means. They now exert control from afar and share an ever-growing market with others. One law enforcement official said there is enough business for all. In 1958 Vito Genovese, Natale Evola, Rocco Mazzie, and Carmine Galente were charged with conspiring to smuggle narcotics into this country. Vito Genovese was sentenced to fifteen years in prison.[48] That lesson has never escaped the criminal establishment. They now buffer their activities through a series of agents.

Establishment of the Drug Routes

Asian heroin smugglers are said to be using shaving cream cans to smuggle number 4 heroin into the United States.[49] Smugglers have also hidden drugs inside fire extinguishers, wire coat hangers, even book covers. Off the Florida coast federal officials intercept a Latin American cargo vessel loaded with more than $10 million worth of drugs.[50] In late December 1977 at a meeting in Plains, President Carter is told by a visiting delegation of U.S. farmers that drugs are being smuggled from Mexico into this country inside crates of vegetables and fruits.[51]

The illegal drug trade is big business, well organized, well financed, and international. Much of the "credit" for its size and scope must go to the American and Sicilian Mafia families. These groups laid the foundations and, with the assistance of Corsican gansters, developed a sophisticated trade in drugs. The Corsican involvement in the drug trade goes back to the early 1930s. However, the trade in narcotics did not assume major proportions until the post-World War II period. Contrary to popular opinion in law enforcement circles, a large quantity of drugs that made its way into the illegal U.S. market from 1946 to 1952 came from Italian pharmaceutical firms such as Schiapparelli, the pharmaceutical firms headed by Dr. Gugliemo Bonamo, and firms in Milan and Genoa. During the late 1940s Italy, rather than Turkey, was the major source for the illicit U.S. drug market. Nice and Marseille, and San Remo, Genoa, and Milan were key cities where drug transactions were conducted and couriers came to make their pickups.[52]

On February 8, 1949, Francesco Paolo Saverino, from Salemi, was arrested by Italian police at the Palermo airport. In his possession he had four pounds of cocaine. Police suspected that Saverino was connected to Francesco Pirico, a member of Palermo's underworld. Pirico had been linked to a transaction involving fourteen pounds of heroin and four pounds of cocaine, seized at Ciampimo airport from Charles Vincent Trupia. The latter was an associate of Joseph Di Palermo, a caporegime with the Gaetano Lucchese Mafia family of New York. The arrest of Saverino confirmed what some law enforcement officials had long suspected—that the Sicilian and American Mafia groups had close ties and were working closely in the burgeoning drug trade. In 1953 an investigation by French police tied Pirico to the growing Turkish narcotics trade. Pirico had developed good connections with the Corsican underworld. Drugs from Marseille were making their way into Italian ports and then into Sicily; their final destination was the United States and Canada. New York City and Montreal had early become key dumping points for the illegal heroin market. With the Italian pharmaceutical companies drying up as sources for narcotics (the Italian government, under international pressure, had begun a crackdown on these firms), gangsters both in Europe and the United States began looking to Turkey and other sources. Thus Pirico, representing Mafia interests, was a key link in the French-Italian connection.

In June 1951 two Italian-American Mafia figures, Frank Callace and Giusseppe Pici, were charged by Italian police in Palermo with possessing thirty-four pounds of heroin. Callace had ties to the Gaetano Lucchese Mafia family of New York. Two key Sicilian Mafiosi were also arrested: Salvatore Vitale of Partinico and Francesco Lo Cicero of Palermo. Vitale and Cicero also had ties with a narcotics network involving a series of Italian pharmaceutical firms. On February 18, 1957, almost six years after their arrest, the two American gangsters were sentenced to two years in prison. The drug trade continued unperturbed.

On May 15, 1952, Italian police seized twelve pounds of illicit heroin at Alcamo, Italy. The police charged several key Sicilian and American Mafiosi with involvement in this transaction. Among those charged were Francesco Paolo Cappola from Partinico, Cappola's son-in-law Giusseppe Corso, Giusseppe and Serafino Mancuso, Salvatore Vitale, Salvatore Greco (also known as Tota the Long One), and Angelo Di Carlo (the Captain) from Corleone. Also charged were Mafia figures from Detroit, including John Priziola, a boss of the Detroit group. The Alcamo arrests confirmed that Sicilian and American Mafia groups were playing an increasingly important role in the international narcotics trade.

In 1952 the Italian police cracked down on the Schiapparelli pharmaceutical firm in Turin and arrested a professor there who had diverted hundreds of pounds of heroin to Frank Callace and Giusseppe Pici. In 1957 the Italian authorities discovered heroin laboratories in Milan; one of these, in operation since 1954, had been linked to Enzo Berti and Constantino Gamba (of the Gamba brothers). The Turkish connection had grown, and the Sicilian Mafia had developed a Swiss route. Morphine-base narcotics were smuggled from Turkey to Switzerland and then found their way into Italian heroin laboratories. The Gamba labs sold the heroin to Pirico, who in turn sold them to Ugo and Salvatore Caneba. The drugs then made their way to the United States, via Genoa.

The Caneba brothers played a key role in the heroin trade from the early 1950s through 1961. The Canebas worked through a series of financial companies, with offices in Rome. The Sarci brothers (Antonio and Pietro), key Siciiian Mafiosi, provided the Canebas with key contacts in the Italian and U.S. underworlds. The Canebas also had contracts with the Marseille group of Antoine Cordoliani. The latter, with Giusseppe Catrone of Reggio Calabria, was connected to a heroin seizure in 1959 in Montreal.

On June 6, 1961, the Italian police charged the Caneba brothers, along with more than thirty Italian, American, French, and Canadian gangsters, with trafficking in heroin. The police also outlined how the Sicilian Mafia, with the assistance of its Canadian and American counterparts and the aid of Corsican gangsters operating out of France, had developed a narcotics network of international dimensions. The Caneba operation first surfaced in October 1960, when New York City police arrested Salvatore Rinaldo and Matteo Palmeri, two American Mafia figures, for possession of twenty pounds of heroin. The drugs had been smuggled in from Palermo aboard the Italian liner the *Saturnia*. From the early 1950s until the Caneba drug network was finally broken, more than seven hundred pounds of pure heroin had been smuggled into the United States; more than three hundred pounds had been shipped directly from Italian ports. The drugs had come by auto from France to Italy, where they were picked up by Sicilian Mafia sources. The Marseille underworld cooperated with Sicilian gangsters in this French-Italian operation. The drugs were then smuggled into the United States. Representing the French underworld in this narcotics traffic were Eduard Giribone, Antoine Gardoliani, Joseph Andre Cesari, and Jean Baptiste Piersanti.

The Caneba brothers were not the only ones involved in the narcotics traffic in the 1950s. They were joined by two other key groups, the Salemi and Casimo gangs. The Canebas and Casimo groups operated from Rome; the Salemi group, from Sicily. Members of the Salemi group included Vincenzo Di Tropani, Francesco Paolo Gileccian, and the Agueci brothers (Alberto and Vito). Much of the heroin for the Salemi operation came from laboratories in France. Between 1951 and 1960 the Salemi group shipped more than one hundred pounds of heroin to the United States. The Salemi ring operated out of Sicily, Toronto, Detroit, and New York. The Agueci brothers lived in Canada; Cristoforo Robino was the ring's New York contact. His cousin, Calogero Robino, operated out of Italy, along with Giusseppe Palmeri and Vincenzo Di Tropani. Additional contacts for the Salemi group included Salvatore Valenti, who worked with the Italian Shipping Company of Palermo, Vincente Mauro, the ring's contact with the Vito Genovese New York Mafia famiy, and Frank Caruso, the contact with the Chicago underworld. John Papalia, Bendetto Zizzo, Settimo Accardi, and the Agueci brothers were the ring's Canadian contacts. The drugs were shipped from Naples and Palermo.

The Angelo Di Casimo group included Alberto Marazziti and, like the Caneba ring, was based in Rome. However, the Casimo ring, like the other two rings, was Sicilian dominated. Giusseppe Provenzano coordinated the ring's operations with the Salemi group and with the French group headed by Eduard Giribone. The Casimo group operated out of France, Italy, and the United States. The Casimo group paid their French contacts an average of $1,500 for a pound of heroin and sold it to American Mafiosi for an average of $10,000; that pound of heroin had a value of $100,000 in the U.S. market.

These three groups provided more than 50 percent of the narcotics for the U.S. drug market from 1951 to 1960. In 1967 members of these groups were sentenced by Italian courts to a total of more than two hundred years in prison. Of the three rings the Canebas were the largest, with contacts in France, the United States, and Canada. Rosario Magavero and Carmine Lo Coscio were the group's New York contacts. Vincenzo Renno, arrested in April 1961, was the group's courier to Canada. Other contacts for the Canebas in Canada and America were Franco Tarabella (arrested in 1971), Salvatore Rinaldo, and Matteo Palmeri. These three groups provide ample evidence of an international network of criminals, dominated by the Sicilian and North American Mafia families. These criminal groups have played a dominant role in the international narcotic traffic since the end of World War II.

The post-World War II domination of the U.S. heroin market by the Mafia was formalized at key meetings of criminal representatives from the U.S. and Sicilian Mafia families: the 1956 Binghamton meeting, the 1957 Palermo meeting, and the 1957 Appalachian meeting. These high-level Mafia meetings established Sicily as a major base in the U.S. drug trade. Cuba, a major distributor in the smuggling of narcotics into the United States, had fallen into political turmoil and could no longer serve the Mafia's needs. A new base was needed, and the three meetings of Mafia chieftains were held to establish such a base. Mafia leaders on both sides of the Atlantic had decided to formulate a common strategy.

On October 17, 1956, the small New York town of Binghamton became the meeting place for Mafia chieftains from Europe and North America. The meeting, held in the Arlington Hotel, was attended by members of various Mafia families. Joe Bonnano, who was to play a key role in all three meetings, was a driving force behind the Binghamton meeting. With him were Giovanni Bonventro, his underboss, and Camillo Galante, his counselor. Joseph Di Palermo represented the Gaetano Lucchese family, and Joseph Barbara the Detroit family of John Prisiola. The meeting was adjourned on October 19, with the understanding that other meetings would follow.

October 12-16, 1957, the Mafia chieftains met at the Hotel Delle Palme, in Palermo. Among those present were Joe Bonanno, Camillo Gallante, Santo Sorce, Lucky Luciano, Vito Vitale (Don Vitale), Giusseppe Genco Russo, Gaspare Magaddino, and John Di Bella, of the Vito Genovese crime family. Di Bella was related to the Sarci brothers and was a close friend of Lucky Luciano. The Palermo meeting dealt with improving the drug trade. Russo and Magaddino represented the Sicilian Mafia's interests, while Luciano represented those of the Genovese crime family of New York. Santo Sorge spoke for the Mafia Commission. The conferees agreed on a series of matters. Bonanno, Galante, and others would coordinate the drug traffic between the United States and Sicily. Luciano and Cappola would ensure discipline on the U.S. side, while Russo would do the same for the Sicilian side. Sorge would act as a liaison officer between Luciano and

Russo. Francesco Garafalo would act as a liaison officer between the Castellammare Mafia families and those of Palermo and the United States. Don Vitale would ensure cooperation from the Detroit Mafia, while Magaddino and Diego Plaia would do the same for the Sicilian underworld.

On November 14, 1957, a third conference was held in New York's Appalachian Mountains at the estate of Joseph Barbera. Present were Joe Bonanno, Camillo Galante, Joseph Di Bella, and others. The conferees discussed the successor to Carlo Gambino's command of the Albert Anastasia crime family. (Gambino had retired temporarily from Mafia activities since the attempt on his life in September 1957; he soon became active again.) The conferees also discussed, at great length, the growing trans-Atlantic narcotics trafficking. On December 18, 1957, Bonanno made a trip to Palermo to inform the Sicilian Mafia bosses of the results of the Appalachian conference. The Bonanno and Detroit Mafia crime families had close ties with the Partinico and Castellammare Mafia families of Sicily. In fact, most of the Appalachian conferees had their roots in the Sicilian provinces of Trapani and Palermo. The ties of kinship and a network of alliances built on need and friendship were a cohesive factor in the Mafia narcotics trade on both sides of the Atlantic.

Three Palermo Mafia families were understood to have played an integral role in the Sicilian side of the drug trade: the Barbera family, the Greco family, and the Torretta family. In June 1963 more than half a dozen Italian policemen were killed in Palermo by Mafia assassins. At the same time a vicious Mafia war broke out among these three groups. The series of indictments that followed in Italy and in the United States diminished the hold of the Mafia over the trans-Atlantic traffic in narcotics but by no means destroyed it. The Mafia still plays a key role in the drug trade. Given its lengthy involvement in this area, it enjoys an acknowledged mastery and monopoly in this area.

The Barbera family dealt with the Sarci brothers and also Giusseppe Pici in the narcotics trade. Rosario Mancino, a chieftain of the Barbera family, also had contacts in Lebanon. Both he and Elio Formi operated drug transactions out of Beirut. Formi was a well-known gangster from Genoa. The Barberas also had ties to Pietro Davi (Jimmy the American), who was a key contact with the American Mafia. In 1960 Mancino and Giovanni Mira traveled to Mexico and Canada to develop alternate drug routes. The Barberas had close ties to Pascal Molinelli and Michel de Val, both French gangsters.

The Greco Mafia group was entrenched in the eastern section of Palermo. In 1963 they were involved in a war with the Barberas and Torrettas, that took more than a dozen lives. The Grecos, like the other Sicilian Mafia families, had extensive experience in the illegal trafficking in tobacco and other goods. Salvatore Greco (U Ciaschiteddin) was boss of the Greco family. He was related to Toto the Long One (the Engineer), a former student at the University of Palermo. The Grecos were well-known tobacco smugglers; it was an easy matter for them to transfer that experience to the smuggling of heroin. The Grecos were also closely connected to the Detroit Mafia groups through Peter Ganino. In 1960 they joined the Salemi group in a heroin smuggling venture that ended in failure. The Grecos also had excellent contacts with the French, Spanish, and Moroccan underworlds.

The Torrettas, headed by Pietro Torretta, operated out of the Uditore section of Palermo. They also had power bases throughout Palermo. In 1962 they were involved in a bloody war that broke the truce between the Palermo Mafia families. The feud began with the death of Calcedonio Di Pisa (also known as Daruccio), who was shot on a Palermo street. Daruccio, a friend of the Grecos, was deeply involved in the U.S. drug traffic. Daruccio was said to have swindled some of the Sicilian Mafia bosses of funds from a U.S. heroin transaction. A Mafia tribunal consisting of Salvatore Greco, Salvatore La Barbera (head of the Barbera Mafia group), and Vincenzo D'Accardi found Daruccio innocent of the charges. The tribunal's decision, however, was not shared by all the Barberas, who killed Daruccio and commenced a bloody war between the Sicilian Mafia groups. The Grecos in turn may have killed Salvatore La Barbera and several Barbera lieutenants. The streets of Palermo became a battleground. Bombings and assassinations spread throughout Italy, as the war became national. The war, in large part a struggle for the control of the narcotics traffic, actually weakened the Sicilian Mafia's control over this trade, paving the way for the Corsicans and other groups to enhance their power and control. From 1963 onward the role of the Sicilian Mafia in the drug trade declined. However, through joint cooperation with the American Mafia, it maintains visible control over this traffic.

The Mafia's role should not be underestimated. Through international contacts it continues to be a dominant force, even though other criminal groups have made their way into this trade and, in some cases, have circumvented the Mafia. The changing drug routes have had an equal impact on the Mafia's loss of monopoly control. Hispanic gangsters, working with Corsicans, can now finance their own drug transactions. The European labor migrations have also played a key role. Turkish migrant workers are found in Germany, France, Italy, and Scandinavia. Middle Eastern gangsters can circumvent the Mafia by using their own kinship ties in numerous European cities; they can sell directly to wholesalers and independent buyers who are willing to risk the dangers of law enforcement and the Mafia in dealing with Turkish traffickers directly. Pressure by law enforcement and large-scale labor migrations have weakened the Mafia's monopoly and forced the rerouting of many drug transactions. However, the Mafia remains dominant. Informers have been killed, and peace has been restored, save for an occasional eruption of violence among Mafia families in Italy and the United States. The Mafia's organizational experience and its long history of involvement in smuggling, from tobacco to drugs, give it an edge over other criminal groups. The strategic locations of Italy and France on the European continent make them important transit points for the Middle Eastern and Far Eastern narcotics trade. The current political chaos in Italy has weakened the police apparatus and has given the Mafia a respite. At present it is the dominant power in the illegal trafficking of heroin.

Kinship and the Narcotics Trade

Ties based on friendship, bloodline, and even geography (as for example, where individuals can trace their roots to the same village or town) have played a major role in the international narcotics trade. Fear of detection and prosecution have led many international narcotics smugglers to limit their activities and contacts to individuals they trust and to whom they have some tie. The success of the Mafia's narcotics trafficking has been due largely to the ties of bloodline, friendship, and geography. Joe Bonanno, a major American Mafia figure, was born in Castellammare in 1905 and is a friend of many Sicilian Mafia figures. Giovanni (John) Bonventre is related to Joe Bonanno and is an underboss in the Bonanno family. He attended the three drug-related Mafia meetings of 1956-1957; in November 1957 he returned to Castellammare. In 1971 he was exiled to a small island off of the coast of Sicily by the Italian government for Mafia-related activity.

Camillo (Carmine) Galante was born in New York in 1910 and is an underboss in the Bonanno family. He attended all three Mafia meetings in 1956-1957. In 1962 a New York court sentenced him to fifteen years in prison for narcotics-related activity. Giovanne Priziola (John Papa) was born in Parinico, Sicily, in 1893 and is a leading Mafia chieftain in Detroit. He was a friend of Joe Bonanno and Frank Cappola, had ties with Vito Vitale, and attended the Palermo meeting of 1957. He also worked closely with Raffaele Quasaramo, Vito Vitale's son-in-law. Quasaramo was born in Detroit in 1910 and was a member of the Detroit Mafia. In 1952 the Italian government charged him with narcotics-related offenses. He was also a close associate of Frank Cappola.

Santo Sorge, born in Mussomeli, Sicily, in 1908 was a United States citizen. He was known to the authorities in the United States, Italy, France, and Belgium. Sorge was a counselor to the Mafia Commission, although not an official member of a Mafia family. Because of his ties to key Mafia figures, in 1957 he was given the task of coordinating investments between the U.S. and Sicilian underworlds.

Another key figure was Giusseppe Genco Russo, born in Mussomeli, Sicily, in 1893. He attended the Palermo meeting of 1957 and was a close friend of Lucky Luciano, Santo Sorge, and Camillo Galante. Frank (Francesco) Cappola, born in Partinico in 1889 lived in Sicily and was arrested several times in the United States. In 1948 he was deported to Italy, where he continued working closely with the Sicilian Mafia. He was a close friend of Salvatore Greco, Don Vitale, and Angelo Di Carlo. In 1950 he made his way to Mexico, where he was accused of killing Charles Bianaccio of Kansas City, a notorious gangster. Although he did not attend the Palermo meeting of 1957, he sent a representative.

Caspare Magaddino, born in Castellammare in 1908 also attended the Palermo meeting of 1957. A relative of Joe Magaddino, head of the Buffalo Mafia family, he fled from Italy in 1964 to escape prosecution. Caspare Magaddino had long been active in the Catellammare Mafia and was connected to Diego Plaia, another Castellammare Mafia chieftain, through his son's marriage to Plaia's family. Imperiale Gioe, born in Palermo in 1914, was heavily involved in the narcotics trafficking and was connected to the Francesco (Frank) Garafalo group. Garafalo was born in Castellammare and was an officer in the Bonanno family. A number of other Sicilian and American Mafia figures also played a key role in the narcotics traffic, among them Gaetano Russo, Giusseppe Cerrito, Angelo Coffaro, Rosario Vitaliti, and Giusseppe Scandariato. The illicit narcotics trade, at least at the upper levels, remains a closed club whose membership is usually limited to criminals connected to one another, either through blood or friendship. The independent trafficker has proved an easy target for law enforcement. Only the Chinese and Cubans can rival the Sicilian and American Mafia families in the illicit drug trade. Kinship ties have given Mafia groups an advantage over the many independent traffickers who have made their way into the lucrative narcotics trade since the mid 1960s.

The Drug Routes

Four major drug-smuggling networks have been identified in the last thirty years. The complexity and the political nature of the countries involved in these drug networks make it virtually impossible to curtail the flow of narcotics into the United States, especially given that the illicit U.S. market needs only two or three tons of heroin annually. It is, as one law enforcement officer said, like finding a needle in a haystack.

One of the oldest drug networks is the Turkish-French system. The poppy fields of Turkey have for many years supplied the heroin for America's addicts. Drugs make their way from Turkey into Syria and Lebanon and from there by sea and air to Italy, France, or Spain. A second Turkish route makes it way, by auto or railway, through Bulgaria and Yugoslavia into Austria, Germany, Switzerland, and France. Another route is from Yugoslavia to France, the initial dispatch point for the trip to the United States. From France, the heroin makes its way into Canada, Latin America, and Mexico; from any of these three countries it is invariably shipped to the United States. Although not as rich in morphine content as Turkish heroin, Mexican brown heroin is increasingly making its way into the U.S. market as Turkish heroin becomes scarcer.

A second heroin network, which was extremely active during the United States' involvement in the Indochina War, is the Southeast Asia route. Opium grown in the Golden Triangle area is taken to Bangkok; from there the heroin is sent by sea or air to Singapore, Hong Kong, or directly to the U.S. market. With its growing addict population, Europe has also become an increasingly important market for drug traffickers from Southeast Asia.

A third drug network is found in South Asia. Illicit drugs are shipped from India to Iran and other countries in the Middle East, via air or sea. Bombay has become a key shipping port for this trade. Drugs from Pakistan and Afghanistan also make their way across the Iranian frontier into Iran and other countries in the Middle East. The South Asia network has played a minor role in the American illicit drug market, but Latin America has become a major drug network. Drugs from Europe are directed through Argentina, Paraguay, Bolivia, and Panama to Miami. The Caribbean Islands have also become shipping points for the European traffickers. Bolivia has become a major supplier of the U.S. cocaine market. More than $1 billion a year is fed into the Bolivian economy from the U.S. cocaine market. International traffickers have shown themselves able to meet this new demand. Mexico has also become a source of (brown) heroin for the U.S. market. The Mexican drug network has become a multibillion-dollar annual business, with the heroin coming into the United States by both air and land routes. The drug traffickers have shown an ingenuity and sophistication that matches or excels that of law enforcement. With large sums of money and international contacts, the illicit drug traders are winning the war against U.S. law enforcement agencies.

Drug Enforcement in the United States

When the Harrison Act was passed on December 14, 1914, the Treasury Department was made responsible for enforcing it. The Bureau of Internal Revenue, now called the Internal Revenue Service, was given primary responsibility for policing and enforcing the act. The bureau, an arm of the Treasury Department, was charged with the registration and issuance of narcotics order forms, special tax stamps, and commodity tax stamps.[53] In

1930 the newly created Bureau of Narcotics was given the duties of investigating and enforcing the provisions of the Harrison Act. It replaced the Bureau of Prohibition, which had been set up in 1927 to enforce the Harrison Act.

Until 1966 the federal narcotics enforcement effort was handled primarily by the Treasury Department, in large part explaining why the United States, unlike the British, has been slow to view drug addiction as a medical problem. In 1965 Congress passed the Drug Abuse Control Amendments (Public Law 89-74) thus creating a new enforcement arm outside the control of the Treasury Department. The very next year the Bureau of Drug Abuse Control (BDAC) was established, under the supervision of the Food and Drug Administration of the Department of Health, Education, and Welfare (HEW). The BDAC was charged with enforcing federal laws that dealt with the manufacture, distribution, and sale of depressants, stimulants, and hallucinogenic drugs.

In 1968 President Johnson called for a revamping of the entire drug enforcement program and for bringing the policing and enforcement functions within the control of the Justice Department. On July 1, 1973, under executive order (Reorganization Plan No. 2 of 1973), the entire federal narcotics enforcement program was consolidated under the Justice Department's Drug Enforcement Agency (DEA). This new agency combined the functions and enforcement jurisdictions of the BDAC, the Office of Drug Abuse Law Enforcement, the Office of National Narcotics Intelligence, and segments of the roles played by the White House Office of Science and Technology, as well as some enforcement powers exercised by the Customs Service. In 1975 DEA had a staff of more than four thousand; over two thousand were investigators.[54]

The jurisdiction of the DEA is broad. It enforces the criminal and regulatory provisions of Title II (Controlled Substances Act) and Title III (Controlled Substances Import and Export Act) of the Comprehensive Drug Abuse Prevention and Control Act of 1970 (Public Law 91-513).[55] The DEA is empowered to detect and investigate violations of the federal narcotics laws both overseas and domestically. It is also charged with regulating and investigating violations of federal drug laws relating to controlled depressant, stimulant, and hallucinogenic drugs. In its overseas role the DEA has become involved in drug-related operations in Mexico, India, South Asia, Southeast Asia, Europe, and Latin America. Some critics have charged that its zeal to capture drug traffickers may have led the DEA to become involved in the internal political machinations of the host country. DEA training, equipment, and funds can easily be used by the host government to quell internal political opposition. In the last several years, the DEA has also come under increasing attack for failure to police internal corruption and for failure to direct its efforts against top narcotic traffickers. Although the arrest rate has increased, many of those arrested are low-level narcotics dealers. In fact, since the creation of DEA, the narcotics problem has continued to grow.

The U.S. Customs Service (CS) has traditionally played a key role in the investigation and prosecution of narcotics traffickers. The mission of CS is to collect and protect the revenue and enforce customs-related laws. Among its many assigned responsibilities is interdicting and seizing contraband, including narcotics and illegal drugs. The Controlled Substances Import and Export Act provides the CS with special enforcement authority to cope with the smuggling of narcotics and other controlled substances.[56] CS agents are empowered by federal law to work closely with other federal law enforcement agents.[57] There are primarily four categories of CS agents: customs inspectors, who examine incoming cargo, baggage, persons, vehicles, vessels, and aircraft; import specialists, who classify incoming merchandise to insure that proper duties are levied; the customs patrol, who interdict smuggled merchandise and contraband crossing U.S. borders; and special agents, who investigate criminal violations of customs and related laws.

The State Department, the U.S. Coast Guard, the Federal Aviation Administration, and an array of state and local police forces are also involved in the war against narcotics traffickers. But law enforcement, hampered by red tape, a lack of coordinated strategy, and only halfhearted support from the public and politicians, has proven incapable of waging a successful struggle against organized crime's involvement in narcotics. Although billions of dollars have been spent on the war, critics question whether anything has been gained.

An Alternative Model

The public is far from happy with narcotics control. Although numerous attempts have been made to solve the present problems, most have concentrated on law enforcement. A number of nondrug programs, as well as methadone clinics, have sprouted in the last several years to address the needs of the more than five hundred thousand U.S. drug addicts. Billions of dollars have been spent in these programs, yet the situation appears no better. A growing and vocal minority has advocated the development of a heroin maintenance model, while critics of such programs charge that the British drug maintenance model has proven a failure and that such a model would only strain the already overburdened and costly medical delivery system of the United States.

The present U.S. narcotics model is based on one key premise: if the flow of illegal narcotics into this country is curtailed, then the addict will be forced to seek help and will eventually be cured. Attempts over the last fifty years to stop the flow of narcotics into this country have proven a dismal failure. An open and free society, with its many constitutional safeguards, is ill-equipped to curtail the flow of three tons of heroin through its borders. A totalitarian society, with its harsh measures, may be able to succeed. A democratic society that succeeds does so at the expense of its freedom. Whether the addict can be cured is debatable. The present programs, including the British model, may have alleviated some of the addict's suffering, but they have neither cured nor saved him. There are no solutions to the problem of addiction. The present model serves neither the addict nor the public.

It appears that the British do not believe that their model has failed. They appear to be, with some reservations, adjusted to a heroin maintenance model. Their model has spared them the horrors of the U.S. experience, even if it does not fully serve the addict. Can the present medical delivery system of the United States, with its prohibitive inflationary costs, accommodate a heroin maintenance model? Can it absorb a population of more than half a million addicts, with their chronic medical needs, and yet keep costs down? Probably not.

The narcotics problem of the United States differs somewhat from that of Britain and raises questions that go well beyond the medical to the political. Many U.S. addicts come from city slums; a large percentage come from minority groups. The black market in drugs is highly flexible and well organized. To combat it effectively, one must undersell it. Many physicians might be reluctant to partake in a legalized heroin maintenance model for fear of antagonizing their peers or the local community. The stigma of pusher remains sufficiently strong to dissuade many doctors from participating in such a program. A real danger is that such a program may meet opposition from minority groups, which may view it as an attempt to anesthetize demands for social reform.

Any alternative model must take all these factors into consideration. It must be able to cater to the needs of the urban addict at a time when most physicians are reluctant to open offices in inner cities. It must provide twenty-four-hour treatment, since addicts have unique problems. It must also combine many services to assist the addict and must make these services available seven days a week. The model should discourage the use of drugs and medical services, unless really needed. The present medical delivery system encourages the abuse of drugs and medical technology. The economic incentive is still to use rather than to curtail. The alternative model should also make use of various drugs, not just heroin, together with mental treatment programs. A health maintenance organization (HMO) could serve as such an alternative model.[58] It provides varied medical services at a low cost and incorporates a discentive to provide unnecessary drugs and medical services to its subscribers. The HMO, however, has suffered many reverses in the last several years. Present economics may not be fully conducive to using the HMO as an alternative model without an infusion of funds by the government.

The U.S. drug policy of the last half century has failed. Although the intent of the early reformers may have been to preserve the welfare of society, the United States now has a criminal class of addicts that easily numbers more than half a million. Drug-related crimes absorb much of the manpower and funds of law enforcement agencies, as well as the courts. One-third of all U.S. prisoners are there because of some drug-related crime. In passing the Harrison Act, Congress knew that many Americans neither supported it nor understood it. The U.S. narcotics strategy has entangled the country in the domestic affairs of many foreign countries. Thus the United States is supplying helicopters to interdict drugs, but the helicopters are in fact used to quell political opposition. This is a strange quagmire with no simple solutions. As a result of this unfortunate and ineffective process, we have enriched beyond belief the coffers of organized crime.

Notes

1. McClellan Committee, "Organized Crime and Illicit Traffic in Narcotics," in *The Crime Society,* ed. Francis A.J. Ianni and Elizabeth Reuss-Ianni (New York: New American Library, 1976), p. 197.

2. "Coast Guard Stops 3 Ships, Seizes Huge Marijuana Haul," *Washington Post,* December 29, 1977, p. A-3.

3. Lynn Darling, "Hashish Cache Found at Dulles, Eleven Arrested," *Washington Post,* December 7, 1977, p. C-1.

4. U.S. Congress, Senate, Committee on Government Operations, *Federal Narcotics Enforcement* (Washington, D.C.: U.S. Government Printing Office, 1976), p. 1.

5. "There Are People Who Say, 'Well, Business Is Business,' " in *An Economic Analysis of Crime,* ed. Lawrence J. Kaplan and Dennis Kessler (Springfield, Ill.: Charles C. Thomas, 1976), pp. 213, 215.

6. "Over 400,000 Arrested on Pot Charges in '73," *Washington Post,* July 22, 1974, p. A-2.

7. Ian G. Waddell, "International Narcotics Control," *American Journal of International Law* 64 (1970):311-312.

8. Joseph D. McNamara, "The History of U.S. Anti-Opium Policy," *Federal Probation,* June 1973, pp. 15-16.

9. C.G. Hoff, Jr., "Drug Abuse," *Military Law Review* 51 (1971): 162.

10. The 1922 Narcotic Drugs Import and Export Act was an amended version of the 1909 Opium Exclusion Act.

11. McNamara, "The History of U.S. Anti-Opium Policy," pp. 15, 16.

12. Ibid., p. 18.

13. Cabinet Committee on International Narcotics Control, *World Opium Survey* (Washington, D.C.: U.S. State Department, 1972), pp. 38-40.

14. M.I. El-Kayal, "A Comparative Study of Narcotics and the Law in the United Arab Republic and the U.S.," *De Paul Law Review* 21 (1971):889-890.

15. 249 U.S. 96 (1918).

16. Rufus King, *The Drug Hang-Up: America's Fifty-Year Folly* (Springfield, Ill.: Charles C. Thomas, 1974), pp. 23-40.

17. 254 U.S. 189 (1920).

18. 258 U.S. 280 (1922).

19. 268 U.S. 5 (1925).

20. Ibid., p. 18.

21. 370 U.S. 660 (1962).

22. Boyd v. United States, 271 U.S. 104 (1926); also Teller v. United States, 12 F 2d 224 (7th Cir. 1926).

23. Andrew G. Bucaro and Mary W. Cazalas, "Methadone Treatment and Control of Narcotic Addiction," *Tulane Law Review* vol. 44, no. 1 (1969):24.

24. Ibid., p. 25.

25. Ibid., p. 27; see also, 18 U.S.C. Secs. 4251-4255.

26. "Commitment of the Narcotic Addict Convicted of Crime," *Albany Law Review* 32 (1968):360.

27. "Control and Treatment of Narcotic Addicts: Civil Commitment in California," *San Diego Law Review* vol. 6, no. 1 (1969):35-36.

28. "Search and Destroy: The War on Drugs," *Time,* September 4, 1972, pp. 28, 29; see also U.S., Congress, House, Committee on Foreign Affairs, *International Aspects of the Narcotics Problem* (Washington, D.C.: U.S. Government Printing Office, 1971), p. 26.

29. "Search and Destroy," p. 30.

30. Murray Seeger, "Cooperation on Drugs Reflects Closer U.S.-Bulgaria Ties," *Washington Post,* December 26, 1977, p. A-14.

31. El-Kayal, "A Comparative Study of Narcotics," pp. 873-874.

32. Cabinet Committee on International Narcotics Control, *World Opium Survey,* p. A-31.

33. Ibid., pp. A-17, A-18.

34. Ibid., p. A-11.

35. Ibid., p. A-41.

36. "Search and Destroy," p. 30.

37. Cabinet Committee on International Narcotics Control, *World Opium Survey,* p. A-47.

38. Swedish Institute, *Drug Abuse in Sweden* (Washington, D.C.: Swedish Embassy, 1973), pp. 1, 2.

39. Swedish Institute, "Drug Abuse in Sweden: Prophylactic and Therapeutic Measures," *Current Sweden,* November 1973, p. 2.

40. Alfred R. Lindesmith, "The British System of Narcotic Control," *Law and Contemporary Problems* 22 (1957):138.

41. "Coast Guard Stops 3 Ships," p. A-3.

42. "A New Gang," *Washington Post,* December 17, 1977, p. A-4.

43. Joseph Martin, "Pusher Program Draws Praise," *Daily News,* February 19, 1973, p. 5.

44. U.S. Congress, Senate, Committee on Government Operations, *Federal Narcotics Enforcement,* pp. 51-53.

45. "Well, Business Is Business," in *Economic Analysis of Crime*, pp. 216-219.

46. Ibid., pp. 219, 232.

47. Jack Anderson, "Drug Trafficking in Latin Americas," *Washington Post,* January 2, 1978, p. D-11.

48. McClellan Committee, "Organized Crime and Illicit Traffic in Narcotics," in *Crime Society,* p. 200.

49. Jack Anderson, "Carter an Enigma in the Kremlin," *Washington Post,* June 24, 1978, p. E-39.

50. "Marijuana Seizure," *Washington Post,* December 24, 1977, p. A-2.

51. Based on interview with key federal official in late December 1977, in Washington, D.C.

52. The history that follows is based on interviews and research by this author; sources have not been identified at the request of the individuals interviewed.

53. For a history of the narcotics problem, see Senate Committee on Government Operations, *Federal Narcotics Enforcement,* pp. 1-23.

54. U.S., Justice Department, *Annual Report of the Attorney General of the United States for 1975* (Washington, D.C.: U.S. Government Printing Office, 1976), p. 151.

55. Codified in 21 U.S.C. secs. 801-966.

56. See 21 U.S.C. secs. 843, 951-966.

57. 19 U.S.C. sec. 1202 et seq.

58. August Bequai, "Developing a Legal Heroin Maintenance Program," *Police Law Quarterly,* October 1977, pp. 34-46.

10 Political Corruption

A file clerk for the Federal Bureau of Investigation (FBI) and his wife were indicted by a federal grand jury on charges of selling confidential U.S. Justice Department investigatory documents to organized crime figures.[1] In a separate case, federal investigators were looking into allegations of bribes running into the millions of dollars annually, paid by shipping firms to labor unions controlled by organized crime.[2] In the South federal investigators were checking allegations of ties between local prosecutors and the Dixie Mafia.[3]

In Richmond a federal employee incurred debts exceeding $100,000. An associate of organized crime set up a meeting between the distraught bureaucrat and two members of eastern-based criminal syndicates.[4] A deal was soon struck; in return for financial assistance, the bureaucrat agreed to assist firms that were fronts for organized crime to obtain federal loans. Within a brief span of time these firms obtained four federal loans totaling more than $500,000.

Political corruption in the United States goes back to the early colonial era. During the nineteenth century political machines employed criminals to assist them in getting the vote out. By the turn of the century the balance of power began to shift in favor of the gangster. Political corruption now affects every facet of governmental structure. Judges, politicians, police, and even our intelligence agencies have worked hand in hand with criminal syndicates. As a result, the public's confidence and trust in those chosen to govern and lead has diminished substantially. The cost of governmental services has increased, while the quality of those services has decreased. In some cities political bribery has increased the cost of running local government by as much as 20 percent.

Defining Corruption

Political corruption in the United States affects politicians, law enforcement, prosecutors, judges, the bureaucracy, and the intelligence community. In essence it infects the very pillars of law and government.

Numerous theories have been put forth to explain or define political corruption. The lay individual usually defines a corrupt act as one that deviates from the accepted norm; it is a debased act. Even scholars offer differing definitions. Some view it in terms of class: the abuses of power by the wealthy against the weak and poor of society. Others view it as a deviation from the formal duties of public office. Some define it as an intentional misperformance or neglect of a recognized duty for personal gain. Corruption is generally associated with misuse of authority. Some law enforcement sources see it as a mode of neutralizing law enforcement. Still others view it as an outgrowth of the modern corporate world.[5]

Political corruption touches the moral, ethical, and legal fiber of our society. In the strictest legal sense it is behavior made criminal by the legislatures and court interpretation of the laws. Numerous statutes, both local and federal, have been enacted to outlaw various corrupt political practices. To define it in legal terms one need only turn to the criminal codes.

The legendary George W. Plunkitt of Tammany Hall, when asked to define corruption, noted that it was merely "honest graft."[6] He saw his "opportunities and took 'em." Plunkitt lived in an era free of securities-fraud statutes, an age without consumer and environmental legislation. Federal and local legislatures had not addressed themselves to the growing problem of corrupt practices. The post-Civil War era, with its great expansion of industry and commerce, gave rise to new links of corruption between business and politics. Today Plunkitt would find himself indicted under the many statutes that have been enacted to curtail political corruption. The problem in the study of political corruption is not only defining it but also analyzing and understanding the forces that impede its prosecution.

A History of Corruption

Three weeks after the U.S. Constitution was ratified, William Mooney, a New York paperhanger, established the little-known Columbia Order, which also went by the name of the Society of St. Tammany, the patron saint of Pennsylvania. The order had been formed by a small group of American patriots to counter the aristocratic political forces that emerged after the American Revolution. With Alexander Hamilton and his friends entrenched in New York City, then the capital of the new nation, the Society of St. Tammany was formed to ensure that the new republic would not fall under the control of the upper class. Many of its supporters came from the middle and lower classes. The society was, in essence, a political party whose objective was the preservation of the republic.

In 1800 the society used its political muscle to help elect Thomas Jefferson to the presidency. Tammany was incorporated in 1805 as a nonprofit organization to assist the needy. The society established local committees to ensure votes for Tammany-supported candidates. In return supporters received food and other forms of assistance. Thus, by the early nineteenth century, Tammany had established a system for selling votes. Other states and municipalities later followed this model.

In 1806 one of the society's leaders was forced out of office as New York's comptroller for using city property without authorization. Soon after, another Tammany official was asked to resign as New York's food inspector for taking bribes. The society's founder was accused of taking part in payoff schemes. Federal investigators in 1838 unraveled a kickback scheme involving Tammany officials. New York City employees were required to pay 1 percent of their salaries to the society.

To win elections, Tammany recruited gangs of hoodlums to intimidate its opponents. Inmates at the city's prisons were released on the understanding that they vote for society candidates. Tammany officials contacted their allies in other cities and rented voters for $10 each. Gangs such as the Bowery Boys, the True Blue Americans, the American Guards, and the O'Connell Guards sold their muscle to the highest bidders. San Francisco gangs such as the Hounds, the Sydney Ducks, and the Hoodlums sold their support to various political factions. A liaison began to take shape between local political organizations and the criminal underworld. This relationship continued throughout the nineteenth century and took on a more lasting form at the turn of the century. Through the use of corrupt tactics and criminal gangs, groups like Tammany maintained their grip on local politics. National candidates, in need of their support, either condoned or ignored their ways.

During the midnineteenth century a large influx of poor immigrants came from Europe to the United States. Cities grew, and the country's population doubled within a short span of time. In the post-Civil war period the voting population in many large urban centers changed dramatically. In cities such as New York poor immigrants constituted more than 50 percent of all voting adults. The Tammany political machine soon adapted its tactics to this new consituency. Naturalization papers were sold to those who supported Tammany candidates. Tammany-controlled judges naturalized more than a hundred thousand immigrants in one year alone. In return the immigrants gave Tammany candidates their votes. Tammany's corrupt practices soon gained national attention, especially from 1868 to 1874. During this period Tammany leaders bilked New York City of more than $100 million. Tammany leaders such as William ("Boss") Tweed gave the city's business to firms controlled either by them or their friends. City funds were deposited in banks owned by Tammany chieftains.

Tammany leaders such as Tom Foley and "Big Tim" Sullivan commonly employed criminals during election time. Abe Relse was counted on to bring the New York City gangs to Tammany's assistance, and the Mafia was employed to get the Italian vote out. In return the criminal gangs were given protection from the police and occasional payments from Tammany's treasury. The model was emulated in other cities. In Chicago the gangster Michael Cassius McDonald developed ties with the political establishment. By the turn of the century political machines in Cleveland were using gangsters to scare away their opponents. Gangsters such as Alfred Polizzi of Cleveland and Arnold Rothstein of New York not only gave local political groups gangs to get the vote out but also used proceeds from their illegal enterprises to reinforce the criminal-political link that had taken shape in the nineteenth century. After Prohibition the modern gangster, armed with billions of dollars from his illicit operations, rose from being the servant of politics to its equal and, at times, even its master.[7]

While local politics became corrupt, the U.S. Congress fared no better. President Andrew Johnson (1865-1869) was quoted as saying that the legislators "stink in the very nostrils of the nation."[8] In the early nineteenth century Congressmen often represented private interests who had claims against the federal government. Many advertised their services. In the post-Civil War period the growing industrial interests began to turn their attention to Congress and the executive branch of goverment. Washington, D.C., became more important in the life of industrial America. The railroads made it a practice to hire Congressmen. Graft and bribery became everyday affairs. Congressman Oakes Ames from Massachusetts was on the payroll of the Union Pacific Railroad; he advised his employer to give each member of Congress two hundred shares in the company. Collis P. Huntington, an agent for a competing railroad, gave thousands of dollars in bribes to members of Congress.[9] In return Congress gave millions of dollars in government contracts and rights. Congress was likened to a giant auction room.

The executive was not free from corruption either. The Grant administration faced two serious scandals involving key government officials. The president's secretary, General Orville E. Babcock, was involved in the notorious Whiskey Ring scandal.[10] The Babcock affair involved Internal Revenue collectors who had falsified records to defraud the federal government of taxes. Babcock, and even President Grant himself, had attempted to block federal prosecutors from investigating the scandal.

In 1876 the U.S. Senate held impeachment hearings against Secretary of War W.W. Belknap.[11] The secretary had been selling government offices to the highest bidder; when exposed, he resigned from Grant's cabinet. In 1926 the Harding administration became embroiled in a scandal that came to be called the Teapot Dome oil fraud. It involved Secretary of the Interior Albert B. Fall, Attorney General Harry Daugherty, Director of the Veterans Bureau Charles R. Forbes, and a local brothel owner.

Secretary of the Interior Fall was a former U.S. senator from New Mexico. In return for more than $200,000 in bribes, Fall gave government oil rights at Teapot Dome, Wyoming, to oil firms. Attorney General Daugherty in turn had made it a practice to offer immunity from prosecution to criminals for a price; also for sale were pardons and paroles, as well as liquor permits.[12] Forbes sold more than $200 million in federal property to private interests. The Veterans Bureau depot in Maryland became the private warehouse of Forbes and his associates. As Watergate later proved, even the president could become directly involved in corrupt practices.

Corruption of the Political Machinery

Political corruption is found at every level of the political machinery. In large part it is the outcome of corrupt practices that go back to the early days of the country. It is also due to the political machines' lack of ideological commitment. European political parties have traditionally been heavily influenced by the political ideologies of the eighteenth and nineteenth centuries. Political machines arose to implement ideological goals.

In the United States, however, with large immigrant groups and a decentralized political apparatus, ideology gave way to accomodation. Politics, especially in the post-Civil War period, became a vehicle for social mobility. City bosses, with their political machines, became conduits for wealth and position. The nineteenth-century politician cared little for revolution and ideology. His objectives were simple: gain power and stay in power by rewarding friends and punishing opponents. In essence the political apparatus of the nineteenth century had more in common with that of feudal England than a modern and growing industrial state. The fragmented nature of political parties and their sole commitment to gaining power made them easy bedfellows for criminal groups. Decentralized conflict-ridden political structure made it inevitable that organized crime would reach a working relationship with many political figures and groups. Boss Tweed, when questioned by an aldermanic committee investigating his political behavior, noted: "This population is too hopelessly split up into races and factions to govern it under universal suffrage, except by bribery or patronage and corruption."[13]

Organized crime was political corruption to neutralize the forces of the state. It pursues the minimal accomodation necessary to ensure freedom from governmental interference in its illicit activities. In addition, the bribery of political figures ensures that its illicit business ventures will have a significant competitive advantage in government contracts, grants, and licenses. With growing governmental involvement in the daily lives of citizens, the purse of government has grown; government grants and contracts now run into the billions of dollars annually. Government programs, such as welfare and other social service-related expenditures, run into the billions of dollars annually. These are indeed attractive plums for organized criminal syndicates. The key objectives of political corruption, local or national, are to buy immunity from prosecution and to ensure a competitive advantage over legitimate businesses in the governmental service area.[14]

In a large southeastern city the former deputy director of the city's public works department was convicted of misusing his office by fixing bids on demolition contracts. In a western state a federal grand jury was told of a secret meeting between high state political figures and representatives of a large eastern industrial consultant. A former attorney for one of the wealthiest men in America told a court that he had helped distribute more than $1 million to local politicians. A powerful Pennsylvania political figure was charged with more than a hundred counts of racketeering and obstruction of justice. In a large eastern city noted for its political corruption and collusion between local political figures and organized crime a poll found residents so embittered with local corruption that more than 50 percent would leave the city if they could.[15]

Corruption at the local political level is not a thing of the past; it continues and does so with greater impact. Abner ("Longie") Zwillman controlled politics in Newark for more than a decade.[16] Zwillman ruled the city with an iron hand and helped finance state gubernatorial campaigns. When he left the scene Newark fell under the control of other criminal elements.[17] Its mayor and key law enforcement officials became puppets of the Mafia and its associates. In return for protection from prosecutorial harassment and police interference in illicit operations, organized crime syndicates shared the proceeds from their investments with the local political establishment. Similar accommodations have also been worked out at the national level.

A maitre d' in one of Washington's most prestigious restaurants was found murdered near his Washington apartment. In his home police found notes and records that showed a pattern of dealings with senators, congressmen, lobbyists, drug traffickers, call girls, and organized crime. The authorities were looking into ties between members of Capitol Hill and organized crime families operating out of New York, New Jersey, and Miami. In a separate case four large firms admitted giving national political figures more than $5 million in illegal payoffs. The top aide to a congressman once told friends that his job was really "worth $100,000" annually, in payoffs and other gratuities. A well-known former congressman pleaded guilty in federal court to receiving more than $100,000 from a foreign government. Several congressmen were said to be pressuring federal prosecutors not to pursue a nationwide investigation involving shippers and members of organized crime.[18]

The executive branch of government has also been racked by numerous scandals. A former national chairman of the Democratic party was forced during the Truman presidency to resign because of his involvement in a bribery scandal. One of President Truman's former campaign managers admitted that he pressured the U.S. Board of Parole to free several well-known members of organized crime. The links between organized crime and the federal apparatus go back to the early years of this century. During World War II the power of organized crime grew. A large and growing black market provided it with additional sources of income. During the post-World War II era the growth in federal programs and contracts focused syndicate attention on Washington.[19] Organized crime has even been able to elect its own representatives to Congress.[20]

The criminal syndicate of the twentieth century, like their counterparts in the business world, have sought the favor and the assistance of the political establishment. They have sought both protection and advancement form the political machine. The criminal groups initially served the political machines, but by the 1930s, with their great wealth amassed during the Prohibition era, and with the growing vacuum left by the business sector (which now relinquished local politics in favor of the national arena), organized crime found local political machines in need of support. The local politician came to rely on these criminal syndicates for both electoral and monetary support.

With the expansion of government programs and contracts following World War II, national criminal syndicates turned their attention to Washington. The Small Business Administration and the multibillion dollar antipoverty programs, with their minimal safeguards, became targets. In California Chicano criminal syndicates have been preying on these programs for a number of years. In Harlem many antipoverty programs have suffered similar fates.[21] Political corruption now has an additional objective: ensuring criminal cartels access to lucrative and highly vulnerable government programs. The corruption of politicians has made the growth of organized crime possible; it guarantees criminal syndicates not only protection and freedom from police and prosecutorial harrassment but also freedom to pillage the federal treasury. With more than $300 billion spent annually by the federal government on an array of programs and services, criminal syndicates are turning to Washington.

Corruption of Law Enforcement

In one midwestern city the local police force was abolished and its function taken over by the county sheriff's office when it was found that members of the police force engaged in robberies, burglaries, car thefts, and even extortion. In another case Senate investigators have charged that law enforcement agencies failed to act on information supplied by the French police, which incriminated several associates of powerful political figures in the United States. A comprehensive study of one of the largest police departments in this country found that police officers and detectives in all of the city's seventy-three precincts took narcotics payments, passed confidential intelligence data to organized crime figures, ran prostitution rings, engaged in illegal gambling operations, sold drugs, and were involved in thefts of property and in "ripoffs" and robberies of narcotics dealers.[22]

Corruption of law enforcement agencies goes back to the early days of this nation. A National Advisory Committee studying police corruption found that it took six basic forms: agreements to drop investigations prematurely, agreements not to investigate various violations, agreements to alter or fabricate testimony at trial, dropped or reduced charges, influences on licensing recommendations, and agreements to alter or fabricate departmental records.[23] A New York state investigatory committee studying police involvement with criminal groups found that police officers were involved in bribery and extortion schemes, bought and sold drugs, associated with known criminals, aided and abetted criminals, committed perjury, tipped off criminals and retained narcotics money. The commission was informed of many instances of direct police involvement in the narcotics trade.

> *Q.* Are you saying that the police officer, the member of the Narcotics Division who arrested her, was then supplying her with narcotics?
>
> *A.* That is correct.
>
> *Q.* Are we talking about heroin?
>
> *A.* Yes.
>
> *Q.* Did she tell you this?
>
> *A.* Yes, she did.
>
> *Q.* We are talking about Patrolman T?
>
> *A.* That is correct.
>
> *Q.* Did he deny that he was supplying her with heroin?
>
> *A.* No, he freely admitted it.[24]

"Neutralizing local law enforcement," noted the President's Commission on Law Enforcement, "is central to organized crime's operations."[25] What can the public do if there is no one to investigate the corrupt public officials, judges, prosecutors, and bureaucrats? Attempts to control police behavior can be either direct, such as bribing police officers, or indirect, such as selecting the officials who will control and set policy for the department. Examples of the former are by far the most common. For example, the racket squad chief of Pennsylvania's Allegheny County was convicted of receiving protection payoffs.[26] In Kansas City a direct attempt was made to control the local police by placing key officials in leadership positions.[27]

Police corruption is largely the outgrowth of the historical corruption of law enforcement in this country. From the 1850s until the turn of the century it was common for local police agencies to deal with criminal groups and even work out financial accommodations. In the "compromise system" that took form in the 1860s, criminals would approach local police officials and offer to return stolen valuables for an agreed payment. The police, in return for their services as negotiators, often received a fee from the owners of the valuables. On occasion police officers engineered these thefts in order to receive a commission for the return of the stolen valuables.

During the 1890s police corruption was so common in cities such as New York that bribes were generally accepted as a cost of doing business by both criminals and businessmen. A New York state investigation commission concluded that the practice was so common and well regulated that it would be impossible to eradicate it. Each police precinct in New York City appointed one police officer whose sole task was to collect bribes and extortion money. Local politicians shared in the booty; for example, a wardman received 20 percent of all bribes taken by police in his ward. In 1909 the police commissioner for New York City noted that he cold have easily made $1 million in bribes had he wanted to. Police jobs themselves were sold by local political machines to the highest bidder. In New York City a policeman's job sold for approximately $200 to $500. Promotions were also sold, and the prices ran in the thousands of dollars. These corrupt practices were so accepted and established that Tammany Hall's boss Charles F. Murphy used the police as intermediaries with the criminal syndicates of New York City. The police were rewarded by increased shares of the graft and corruption from vice and gambling.

Police corruption has also made its way into government contracts and programs. Many local police agencies have major regulatory powers. In the construction industry local police forces visit construction sites to ensure that the projects comply with local ordinances. If violations are found, the police issue a summons. Weekly and monthly payments to local police precincts have been found to be common in many cities.[28] The advent of federal antipoverty progams has created new opportunities for corrupt policemen. Many of these programs have fallen under the sway of local criminal syndicates. Many criminals have been retained as consultants and salaried employees by these programs.[29] Methadone clinics have been sacked, and drugs have made their way to the black market. The bribing of police officials has assured these criminals immunity from prosecution.

Proposals to curb police corruption have included paying police officers higher wages and providing more benefits, creating offices of special prosecutors insulated from political pressures and thus able to prosecute police corruption, and establishing statewide, permanent investigative crime commissions. Training police officers in the avoidance of techniques to corrupt them, establishing a code of ethics, and setting up training and educational programs that stress an anticorruption philosophy have also been recommended. It has also been suggested that the police should be insulated from political pressure and that merit systems should be established and enforced to ensure that advancement is based on competence and not political connections. These measures would probably help, but the fragmented nature of local police forces makes action difficult. Training programs to battle corruption may not be possible in the more than ten thousand local police agencies that have fewer than ten full-time employees. At the minimum, however, that vigorous prosecution of those who betray the public trust and the development and institutionalization of a code of ethics would be serious attempts to deter corruption.

Prosecutorial Corruption

A study of a midwestern city found that the prosecuting attorney was the key figure in the corruption of the political process. In addition, he was the political boss of the locality and wielded great power over local political affairs. Prostitution, gambling, and other vices were organized; city officials and the prosecuting attorney worked hand in hand with organized crime. In a southern state a county prosecutor and several of his associates were convicted on counts of conspiring to operate a prostitution ring. In some states local prosecutors are permitted to practice law on the side. Some even employ city or county employees to assist them in their private practice.[30]

The prosecutorial machinery at the local level includes county, city, and state prosecutors. Many of these offices are only part-time jobs, many are elective, and others are part of the local political patronage system. The federal prosecutorial umbrella covers dozens of agencies, divisions, and U.S. attorney offices within the U.S. Justice Department. The federal apparatus is no less burdened by political pressure and interests than the local one. President Carter's attempts to depoliticize the federal prosecutorial machinery met with opposition. In December 1976 an understanding was reached between the president and the opposition.[31] The U.S. attorney would continue to be a political appointee.

The very structure of the present prosecutorial machinery lends itself to pressures from organized crime. Some local prosecutors have openly cooperated with criminal groups or overlooked their activities. The Dixie Mafia has been able to reach accommodations with some local prosecutors.[32] Even when a local prosecutor seeks to serve the public, the local political apparatus is brought to bear against his office. For example, Pennsylvania's attorney general found his investigation sabotaged by local police who had bugged the premises where staff investigators questioned witnesses.[33] A special prosecutor who resisted political pressure was disarmed when local legislators refused to allocate any more funds for his office. The prosecutor of one large eastern city, together with the chief of police and the major, cooperated openly with organized criminal elements and received a percentage of the proceeds from prostitution, gambling, and city contract frauds.[34]

The present prosecutorial machinery is outdated and highly fragmented. Many honest county and city prosecutors lack the know-how and resources to investigate and prosecute organized criminal activity. The job is often only a part-time position, and the prosecuting attorney may hesitate to oppose the local political establishment or affluent potential clients, especially if they are members of organized crime. State prosecutors fare no better. The state attorney general is usually an elected official, and few state prosecutors would risk their long-term political objectives on short-term prosecutorial gains. Organized crime has both economic and political clout, and it operates in interstate and foreign commerce, making its prosecution difficult. The federal apparatus has proven vulnerable to political manipulation. For example, under the Nixon administration numerous attempts were made by organized crime figures to buy freedom from prosecution. Several mobsters employed the services of congressional aides to attempt a deal with the Justice Department, pledging a $100,000 contribution to the Nixon campaign fund in return for having their prosecution dropped.

Judicial Indiscretion

In March 1920 "Big Jim" Collisimo, lord of Chicago's prostitution rackets, was murdered by his associates. A large gangland funeral was held for Big Jim, and among those attending were some of that city's judges. New York mobster Frank Costello personally selected Thomas Aurelio as judge for the New York State Supreme Court. In 1952 a former judge told a New York state crime investigatory body that he had known one of the state's most notorious gangsters for more than thirty years and that "there is intermarriage in the family."[35] Investigators who have attempted to prosecute dishonest judges note that the job is a difficult one: "The money never goes to them. It goes to a friend or employee. It's always in cash."[36]

Judicial indiscretion, if not dishonesty, is not new. A former Alabama judge was convicted of sexual "bribery"; he had proposed leniency in return for sexual favors from women defendants appearing before his bench.[37] In one large eastern state there were charges of judges being involved in a massive ticket-fixing ring. One letter that has surfaced noted:

"Personal friend of mine has a clean record. Please reduce."[38] In Cleveland federal agents raided the local courthouse to confiscate potential evidence in a massive bribery investigation.[39] In New Jersey one former judge being tried for obstruction of justice was shot and killed by an unknown assailant.

A study of more than a thousand criminal cases involving members of organized crime in New York State found that the rate of dismissals or acquittals for these defendants was almost five times that of other defendants. More than 40 percent of all indictments brought against organized crime figures were dismissed by local judges; the dismissal rate for others was 11.5 percent. A check-fraud scheme that netted more than $1 million resulted in the arrest and prosecution of about half a dozen individuals, one a member of organized crime. All the defendants eventually pleaded guilty. While his codefendants went to prison, the defendant with links to organized crime received only a suspended sentence.[40] In a case involving a member of the Carlo Gambino Mafia family, the probation department recommended that the defendant receive at least a year in prison, but the judge sentenced him to three months.[41] One judge's secretary put it this way: "If you come in front of him [the judge] and you're a friend of his, he'll bend over backwards to find law to support you."[42]

Many municipalities elect their judges. The local party machinery, in some instances corrupt and laden with organized crime ties, usually selects a "party man" for important political positions. These posts are considered rewards for long years of party loyalty. In the appointment of judges, local or federal, politics plays a major role.[43] Judgeships are viewed as rewards for political debts; thus the selection process is fraught with political pressures and is open to corruption, especially at local levels. Police and prosecutors hesitate to bring dishonest judges before the courts. For example, although "job buying" is common in New York's judicial circles, no judge in that city has ever been prosecuted for buying his seat or charged with fixing cases, although sociologists and criminologists as well as political observers note that these practices go back to the days of Boss Tweed and even earlier. Judges and their selection process must be insulated from political pressures and control by a merit system, especially at the local level. Perhaps, selection should be based on examination as it is in some European countries. Advancement within the judiciary should be based on ability. Prosecution of judges involved in crimes should be swift and certain.

Bureaucratic Corruption

The scandals that erupted at the turn of this century led many reformers to press for the insulation of the bureaucracy from political pressures and corruption. As a result the civil service system was instituted at both the local and federal levels. However, this system gave rise to a new form of corruption—crimes by bureaucrats. In large part this corruption is the result of lax prosecution of corrupt bureaucrats at every government level. Bureaucrats, like other governmental officials, tend to protect one another, producing an understandable reluctance to "blow the whistle." The bureaucracy deals harshly with those who reveal corrupt practices among fellow bureaucrats. For example, one employee with the U.S. General Services Administration (GSA) who informed federal investigators of numerous improprieties between GSA and local construction firms found himself unemployed. An employee with the U.S. Department of Agriculture who revealed improprieties involving the mislabeling of low-grade meats as choice was passed over for promotion.[44]

Corruption of bureaucrats by organized crime is not restricted to the local levels; the very pinnacles of the federal bureaucracy have proven susceptible to such advances. One former high official of the U.S. Department of Housing and Urban Development (HUD) has acknowledged having met with a reputed Mafia boss in a New York restaurant. When asked about the meeting, he said that the Mafia boss wanted to talk to him because "he [the official] had a good reputation at HUD."[45] At the same time a federal grand jury was investigating allegations of links between organized crime figures and high civil servants at the Interstate Commerce Commission (ICC).[46] The Small Business Administration (SBA) has been racked with scandals involving organized crime-controlled firms and employees of the SBA. Corrupt practices by bureaucrats are so common in many cities that criminal syndicates do not need to offer temptations; they find willing victims. In Chicago, for example, frauds involving city workers are common. As one federal investigator recently told me in a confidential interview, "The mob doesn't have to bend over backward to pay these guys off." Chicago liquor inspectors received payments of up to $50; city building inspectors took less, as little as $15.70.[47]

By insulating the bureaucracy and introducing some form of merit system, the early reformers had hoped to curtail many of the abuses that they saw in large urban centers. Although the bureaucracy was being insulated, no steps were taken to instill a sense of accountability. Civil servants who have revealed misconduct have often been treated poorly by both prosecutors and the bureaucracy. Thus government employees who witness abuses hesitate to come forth and give testimony. As one "whistle blower" told me, "There is nothing to be gained. Your fellow employees hate you, and prosecutors distrust you." Civil service rules enacted to protect honest bureaucrats instead often protect the dishonest ones from governmental action. New York's highest tribunal has held that the state's law does not require the firing of state employees who receive bribes.[48] Civil service regulations, and the entire civil service model, at both local and federal levels, need reevaluation and a critical analysis. Insulating the bureaucrat from outside political pressures has also created opportunities for corruption.

Abuses by the Intelligence Community

In the summer of 1975 while I was investigating payoffs and kickbacks to armed forces personnel I received a telephone call from a source within the intelligence community. He asked me whether I had met a Mr. X. I replied I had not. Mr. X, my source noted, was someone I should meet; in fact, he was coming to Washington on his way to the Middle East. I agreed to interview him. When Mr. X came to my office two days later, he related stories of payoffs, Swiss bank accounts, and members of the armed forces being involved in corruption—even murder—in several Asian capitals. He told me of "wild drug" orgies and of couriers passing money back and forth from Asia to Switzerland. After several hours of questioning, I asked Mr. X who his employer was. He said, "The government and the Mob." Mr. X, I later discovered, worked for both the underworld and the intelligence community.

The links between the U.S. intelligence service and the criminal underworld go back at least to the days of "Lucky" Luciano. In 1936 Luciano was sentenced to thirty to fifty years, as the organizer of New York's prostitution rackets. During the war years Luciano and the underworld struck a deal with the U.S. Navy. In return for his assistance, Lucky was released from prison in 1946. This was the beginning of an enduring relationship between organized crime and the intelligence community.

During the Cold War years Castro's Communist regime attracted the attention of U.S. foreign policymakers, who considered Castro a threat to U.S. security. In 1960 John Rosselli, the flamboyant mobster from Chicago's underworld, was selected by the Central Intelligence Agency (CIA) to assist in the assassination of Cuba's Fidel Castro. Rosselli asked for assistance from Sam ("Momo") Giancana, another noted mobster, and from members of Miami's underworld. Organized crime, anxious to regain its Cuban investments, was a willing partner. This alliance may, in fact, have been responsible for the assassination of President John F. Kennedy.[49] Between 1960 and 1965 more than half a dozen attempts were made on Castro's life. When Rosselli was arrested in 1967 for gambling-related activities, he called on his former CIA contact to assist him. In return for their assistance, these criminal elements expected the intelligence community to help stave off domestic prosecution.

In 1975 both Giancana and Rosselli were murdered. Their stories and the CIA's involvement with organized crime may never be completely known. However, additional scandals involving the CIA have surfaced. The agency is said to have obstructed efforts to probe the drug trade in Asia. Foreign narcotics traffickers may have escaped prosecution by cooperating with the agency.[50] Domestically the agency has intervened in at least one case involving a major drug trafficker. A Thai citizen studying in the United States was charged by federal authorities with helping smuggle more than $3 million in narcotics into this country.[51] The defendant was later identified as a CIA operative; the agency refused to assist federal prosecutors, and the case was dropped shortly thereafter. The agency has also been linked to narcotics deals and prostitution rings within this country. Federal investigators have speculated that some CIA employees may have been running their own narcotics operations for personal gain or even to raise funds for the agency's more clandestine operations.

Temporary alliances between powerful criminal syndicates and governmental agencies are not unique to this country. Europe provides many such examples. In 1943, when the Allied armies landed in Sicily, the local landowners struck a deal with Mafia chieftains. The new Italian postwar government was weak, beset by strikes in the north and peasant revolts in the south. By the late 1940s some elements within the ruling Christian Democrats reached an agreement with the Mafia. In return for immunity from prosecution, the Mafia ensured that elections would favor the Christian Democrats. Opposition candidates were scared away, occasionally even murdered. In 1957 Pasquale Almerico, a member of the left wing of the Christian Democratic Party who had openly opposed the party's association with the Mafia, was found murdered.[52] The fear of Communism and the Cold War gave rise to rather curious alliances in the United States and Europe between the intelligence apparatus of the state and the criminal cartels. Corsican gangsters worked hand in hand with French authorities to eliminate members of France's extreme leftist factions.

During the Crusades, the rulers of both Islam and the West employed assassins and criminals to slay each other. The kings of Europe employed criminals to eliminate their opponents both at home and abroad. The ties that evolved between organized crime and the intelligence community after World War II were poorly planned and only of temporary advantage. In the long run they hurt the agencies' image and the public's trust in them. Organized crime is not democracy's ally; it is one of its worst enemies. Aligning with it only lends it legitimacy and immunity from prosecution.

Legal Arsenal to Combat Corruption

In December 1968 a federal grand jury in the Southern District of New York indicted Carmine DeSapio and several associates on charges of traveling in interstate commerce for the purpose of committing bribery.[53] DeSapio had conspired with others to bribe James Marcus, New York City's commissioner of water, gas, and electricity. DeSapio was sent to prison, ending his power as one of the city's most powerful and feared politicians.

Numerous statutes presently on the books can easily be employed to combat political corruption.[54] Bribing public officials is a felony that can result in fines of up to $20,000 and imprisonment of up to fifteen years.[55] Anyone who bribes a member of Congress or any employee, officer, or agent of the federal government can be prosecuted under this statute. Any member of Congress, any official, anyone engaged in matters affecting the government who accepts a bribe can be prosecuted. Conviction carries a fine of up to $10,000 and imprisonment for up to two years.

Conspiracy to commit an offense against the United States is punishable by a fine of up to $10,000 and a prison term of up to five years. Anyone who intimidates voters can be fined up to $1,000 and can receive up to one year of imprisonment. A political candidate who, in order to secure his election, promises to use his influence or support for the appointment of any person to any public or private job can be fined up to $1,000 and imprisoned up to one year; if the violation was willful, the fine can range up to $10,000 and imprisonment can be up to two years.[56] The objective of this statute is to keep the election process free of corrupting influences. However, this law is rarely enforced, and the practices that it is intended to curb are still prevalent.

Blackmail is punishable by fines ranging up to $2,000 and imprisonment of up to one year. Extortion by employees of the federal government can result in fines of up to $5,000 and imprisonment of up to three years. Use of the United States mails for purposes of perpetrating a corrupt act may result in prosecution under the mail fraud statutes. Use of the wires for corrupt purposes can be prosecuted under the wire fraud statute. Willful interference with the civil service examination is punishable by fines of up to $1,000 and imprisonment for up to one year. Several federal statutes deal with the disclosure of confidential information by government employees to individuals outside the government. The purpose of these statutes is to preserve the integrity of the bureaucracy. Concealment, removal, and mutilation of government or court records are felonies.[57]

Many other federal statutes could easily be used to discourage political corruption. The Congress is now considering the Criminal Code Reform Act of 1977. The proposed code would make the obstruction of elections or of political campaigns a felony. Other sections deal with bureaucratic corruption and campaign expenditures. The proposed code would simplify present federal law and give prosecutors a legal arsenal adequate for addressing political corruption by organized crime.

Political corruption is neither new nor unique to U.S. society; it has been found in all societies. But few have fallen under its clutches as ours has. A democracy, unlike a dictatorship, can survive only as long as its citizens trust and respect those it has chosen to serve in government. When that trust fades, then the very pillars of democracy are eroded. That is why political corruption by criminal syndicates is dangerous. It threatens more than our pocketbooks; it also threatens our democratic way of life.

Notes

1. "Ex-FBI File Clerk Indicted," *Washington Post*, March 16, 1978, p. A-37.

2. "Bugging the FBI," *Time*, March 20, 1978, p. 19.

3. Jack Anderson and Les Whitten, "D.A. in Vice Case Flunks Lie Test," *Washington Post*, September 14, 1977, p. B-15.

4. Jack Anderson, "The Shadow of the Mafia over Our Government," *Parade Magazine*, August 7, 1977, p. 9.

5. David M. Gordon, "Class and the Economics of Crime," *Review of Radical Political Economics* 3, no. 3 (Summer 1971):51-55; James C. Scott, *Comparative Political Corruption* (Englewood Cliffs, N.J.: Prentice-Hall, 1972), pp. 3-8; Robert C. Brooks, *Corruption in American Politics and Life* (New York: Dodd, Mead, 1910), pp. 44-50; Arnold J. Heidenheimer, ed., *Political Corruption: Readings in Comparative Analysis* (New York: Holt, Rinehart and Winston, 1970), pp. 3-6; President's Commission on Law Enforcement and Administration of Justice, *Task Force Report: Organized Crime* (Washington, D.C.: U.S. Government Printing Office, 1976), p. 6; Sanford J. Ungar, "Get Away with What You Can," in *In the Name of Profit*, ed. Robert L. Heilbroner et al. (Garden City, N.Y.: Doubleday, 1972), pp. 106-127.

6. William L. Riordan, "Honest Graft," in *Theft of the City*, ed. John A. Gardiner and David J. Olson (Bloomington, Ind.: Indiana University Press, 1974), p. 6.

7. Kefauver Committee, "Official Corruption and Organized Crime," in Gardiner and Olson, ed., *Theft of the City*, pp. 69-71; see also Mike Royko, *Boss: Richard J. Daley of Chicago* (New York: E.P. Dutton, 1971), pp. 64-69.

8. Fred J. Cook, "Who Rules New Jersey," in *Theft of the City*, pp. 75-78.

9. Walter Goodman, "All Honorable Men," in *Official Deviance*, ed. Jack D. Douglas and John M. Johnson (Philadelphia: J.B. Lippincott, 1977), pp. 14, 31.

10. James B. Dickenson, "How the Scandals of History Left . . . Mud on the White House Steps," in *Official Deviance*, p. 38.

11. Ibid., p. 34.

12. Ibid., pp. 38-39.

13. Jack D. Douglas, "Mayor John Lindsay and the Revenge of Boss Tweed," in *Official Deviance*, p. 84; for a review of political corruption in New York City, see Edward R. Ellis, *The Epic of New York City* (New York: Coward, McCann, 1966), pp. 230-247.

14. Knapp Commission, "Corruption in the Construction Industry," in *Theft of the City*, pp. 229-231.

15. "Former Official in Maryland Gets 4 Years," *Washington Post*, December 7, 1977, p. B-4; Wolfgang Saxon, "U.S. Attorney Calls Inquiry Limited," *New York Times*, August 6, 1974, p. 11; "Howard Hughes' Gifts," *Washington Post*, March 17, 1978, p. A-14.; Ray Holton, "Once-Powerful Pennsylvania Politician Is Expected to Plead Guilty," *Washington Post*, December 28, 1977, p. A-3; Neal R. Pierce, "Jersey City: A Saga of Reform Lost," *Washington Post*, August 4, 1977, p. A-19.

16. Mike Royko, *Daley's Machine in Chicago* (New York: E.P. Dutton, 1971), pp. 60-65; see also Cook, "Who Rules New Jersey," in *Theft of the City*, pp. 75-78.

17. Ron Porambo, *No Cause for Indictment: An Autopsy of Newark* (New York: Holt, Rinehart and Winston, 1971), pp. 75-78.

18. Ron Sarro and Jerry Oppenheimer, "Slain Maitre d' Kept Notes on His Influential Friends," *Washington Star*, June 30, 1977, p. A-1; Jack Anderson and Les Whitten, "Four Firms Gave Politicians $8 Million," *Washington Post*, March 22, 1976, p. B-10; Charles R. Babcock, "Elko Said to Value Job at $100,000," *Washington Post*, February 19, 1978, p. A-1; Timothy S. Robinson and Charles R. Babcock, "Ex-Representative Hanna Pleads Guilty in Influence Case," *Washington Post*, March 18, 1978, p. A-1; Larry Kramer, "U.S. Refuses to Delay Ship Probe," *Washington Post*, February 9, 1978, p. D-13.

19. Frank Browning, "Organized Crime in Washington," *Washingtonian*, April 1976, pp. 93-100.

20. Lincoln Steffens, "Los Angeles and the Apple," in *Theft of the City*, pp. 287-289.

21. Based on author's interviews with Waverly Yates, executive director, Bonabond, Washington, D.C., who has studied frauds in the anti-poverty programs.

22. "Police Force Abolished," *Washington Post*, March 8, 1978, p. A-3; Bernard Valery, "Charge Feds Ignored Narco Info," *New York Daily News*, July 5, 1975, p. 8; Carl J. Pelleck, "Study Finds Police Graft in Most Precincts," *New York Post*, December 28, 1973, p. 10.

23. National Advisory Committee on Criminal Justice and Goals, *Report of the Task Force on Organized Crime* (Washington, D.C.: U.S. Government Printing Office, 1976), p. 24.

24. Temporary Commission of Investigation of the State of New York, *Fourteenth Annual Report to the Governor and Legislature of the State of New York* (New York, 1972), pp. 26-27.

25. President's Commission on Law Enforcement and Administration of Justice, *Task Force Report: Organized Crime*, p. 6.

26. National Advisory Committee on Criminal Justice and Goals, *Organized Crime*, p. 25.

27. Kefauver Committee, "Official Corruption and Organized Crime," in *Theft of the City*, p. 71.

28. Knapp Commission, "Corruption in the Construction Industry," in *Theft of the City*, pp. 231-235.

29. Based on author's interviews with various law enforcement sources.

30. For an excellent review of corruption in one city, see William J. Chamblis, "Vice, Corruption, Bureaucracy and Power," *Wisconsin Law Review* no. 4 (1971), pp. 1150-1173; "City Prosecutors; Two Others Convicted in Prostitution," *Washington Post*, December 24, 1977, p. A-2; "Keystone Cops," *Time*, March 27, 1978, p. 84.

31. "Bell 'Only Witnessed' Eastland, Carter Pact," *Miami Herald*, February 3, 1978, p. 14-A.

32. Anderson and Whitten, "D.A. in Vice Case Flunks Lie Test," p. B-15.

33. Jack Anderson and Les Whitten, "Quashing a Probe in Pennsylvania," *Washington Post*, March 17, 1978, p. B-15.

34. John A. Gardiner, "Wincanton: The Politics of Corruption," in the President's Commission on Law Enforcement and Administration of Justice, *Task Force Report: Organized Crime*, pp. 61-79.

35. Ralph Salerno and John S. Tompkins, *The Crime Confederation: Cosa Nostra and Allied Operations in Organized Crime* (Garden City, N.Y.: Doubleday, 1969), pp. 245-252.

36. Based on author's interviews with various law enforcement sources.

37. Morton Mintz, "Review Denied Alabama Ex-Judge Convicted of Sexual Bribery," *Washington Post*, November 15, 1977, p. A-14.

38. Edward Hudson, "Ticket Fixing by Judges Charged in New York," *New York Times*, December 1, 1977, p. 23.

39. Based on author's interviews with federal law enforcement sources.

40. Nicholas Gage, "Organized Crime in Court," in *Theft of the City*, pp. 165-166.

41. Ibid., p. 167.

42. Ibid., p. 173.

43. Susan Ness, "A Sexist Selection Process Keeps Qualified Women off the Bench," *Washington Post*, March 26, 1978, p. C-8.

44. "When Workers Blow Whistle on Federal Waste, Fraud," *U.S. News & World Report*, December 19, 1977, p. 55; see also "The High Cost of Whistling," *Newsweek*, February 14, 1977, p. 75.

45. Jerry Oppenheimer, "Former HUD Aid Quizzed on Mafia Talk," *Washington Star*, June 21, 1977, p. A-1.

46. John M. Goshko and William M. Jones, "Grand Jury Is Probing ICC Moves," *Washington Post*, June 4, 1977, p. A-1.

47. T.R. Reid, "Government by Envelope: Chicago's System Exposed," *Washington Post*, January 15, 1978, p. A-3.

48. "Addenda," *Washington Post*, February 24, 1978, p. A-7.

49. Jack Anderson and Les Whitten, "CIA Plots against Castro Recounted," *Washington Post*, March 10, 1975, p. D-13; Jack Anderson and Les Whitten, "Behind John F. Kennedy's Murder," *Washington Post*, September 7, 1976, p. C-19; see also Ronald Kessler and Laurence Stern, "Slain Mobster Claimed Cuban Link to JFK Death," *Washington Post*, August 22, 1976, pp. A-1, A-8.

50. Harry S. Bradster, "CIA Drug Cover-Up in Vietnam Alleged," *Washington Star*, November 21, 1977, p. A-2.

51. "CIA Mum in Opium Case," *Washington Star*, June 19, 1975, p. A-5.

52. Anton Blok, *The Mafia of a Sicilian Village* (New York: Harper & Row, 1974), pp. 190, 205-206.

53. United States v. DeSapio, 435 F.2d 274 (1970).

54. See United States v. Corallo, 413 F.2d 1306 (1969); United States v. Addonizio, 451 F.2d 49 (1972); United States v. Kahaner, 317 F.2d 459 (1963); People v. Diaguardi, 168 NE 2d 683 (1960); and United States v. Hyde, 448 F.2d 815 (1971).

55. 18 U.S.C. sec. 201, 203, 204-215.

56. Ibid., secs. 371, 599.

57. Ibid., secs. 873, 872, 1341-1343, 1901-1917, 2071.

11 Illegal Trade in Aliens

In an interview with newspapermen the director of the Immigration and Naturalization Service (INS) noted that organized crime had established a national network that specialized in smuggling aliens into this country and providing employers with cheap labor.[1] In return the illegal aliens paid fees ranging from $200 to $1,000; some paid a percentage of their salaries for a period of years. The network is so well organized that the aliens are supplied with false identifications and jobs within a short space of time.

At the San Clemente checkpoint with Mexico, U.S. Border Patrol agents conducting their usual checks stopped two moving vans carrying more than a hundred men and women.[2] By mere chance they had stumbled on an organized smuggling network run by American citizens.

The illegal alien trade is a growing problem for law enforcement; it is also a lucrative market for organized crime. The number of illegal aliens captured while crossing the border has increased by more than 40 percent in the last few years.[3] Many of these aliens, once within the country, become "serfs" for criminal groups. The problem appears to be growing as U.S. businesses search for cheap labor. In many instances the criminal syndicate plays the role of middleman, bringing together job-hungry aliens and businessmen in need of workers willing to perform tasks that the U.S. labor force finds too degrading.

Understanding Immigration Laws

An alien is any individual not a citizen or national of this country. Although a number of states have passed legislation making it illegal for employers to hire illegal aliens, immigration is controlled largely by federal law and is policed by the INS.[4] Every alien entering this country must have a valid entry document; otherwise he is here illegally and can be deported. There are four major categories of entry documents: visas for immigrants and nonimmigrants, reentry permits, alien registration receipt cards, nonresident alien Mexican border cards, and nonresident alien Canadian border cards.

A visa is a formal authorization to enter the United States. To obtain one, an alien is usually required to present a passport at an American consular office in his country. If the alien has a criminal history or is a member of any group that threatens U.S. security, INS officials may turn the alien

173

back at the entry point. Entry with a visa is legal; the rights of this class of aliens have been clearly defined.

The INS usually issues reentry permits to any alien lawfully admitted into this country. The permit makes it possible for the alien to return to this country without formally requesting the reissuance of a visa. It is a time-saving device for aliens who travel between countries on business or pleasure. Lawful permanent residents in this country who are not yet citizens are issued alien registration receipt cards when leaving this country for travel abroad. An alien who has such a card may return to this country as a permanent resident within a period of one year without having to reapply for a visa. However, the holder of a receipt card is prohibited from traveling to certain Communist countries.

Citizens of Mexico who wish to enter the United States must obtain nonresident border-crossing cards. These cards, which are available at the American consulate in Mexico and from the INS, are formal entry documents for pleasure or business within the United States. They are not an authorization for permanent residency. Canadian citizens, as well as British subjects residing in Canada, are also entitled to nonresident border-crossing cards, which are issued at Canadian border offices.

The INS defines an immigrant as any alien applying for admission to this country who is not a nonimmigrant. The latter group consists of aliens in immediate and continuous transit through the United States, foreign officials or diplomats, foreign journalists, employees of international organizations, and aliens visiting for temporary work in the United States are classified as nonimmigrants. The Quota Act of 1924 established a quota system based on national origin; the 1965 amendments fixed the quota at 170,000 immigrants from the Eastern Hemisphere countries and 120,000 for individuals from Western Hemisphere countries. Under the 1965 changes the number of immigrants from any one Eastern Hemisphere country could not exceed 20,000 but no such limit was placed on Western Hemisphere natives. However, in 1977 a new act (Public Law 94-571; 90 Stat. 2703) applied this ceiling for the first time to Western Hemisphere natives. Spouses, children, and parents of American citizens are not included in these limits and can petition the INS for permanent residency.

Many aliens have attempted to enter the United States through sham marriages.[5] Criminal groups have found a lucrative market in arranging for American citizens to marry aliens for a price.[6] The INS now requires that both parties be present at the time of the marriage ceremony and that the marriage be consummated.[7] Criminals who arrange these sham marriages are known as brokers. A broker is contacted either by the alien or by a broker in another country; the U.S. broker, for an advance fee (as high as $5,000), finds an American citizen willing to marry the alien. The American citizen in turn receives a fee; if organized crime is involved, it may be a way of paying back a loan or gambling debt. After the marriage the American citizen petitions the INS for permanent resident status for the alien spouse. After this status has been granted, the two are divorced. Sham marriages are usually difficult to prove, and when organized criminal elements are involved, the task becomes even more difficult.

Nonimmigrants, who can be requested to post bond, or who are expected to leave once the period of authorized stay expires (or when the purpose of the visit has been fulfilled) may attempt to gain permanent residency through sham marriages. Aliens who do not fall within the classes listed by the INS and those who violate the terms of their legal entry can be deported. An alien who engages in criminal activitiy, even one with permanent resident status, can be deported. The INS is responsible for policing immigration; it is a grave responsibility.

Role of the Immigration and Naturalization Service

The INS is the unit of the U.S. Justice Department that enforces and administers the immigration laws. The admission, investigation, and deportation of aliens falls within its jurisdiction. On the average, more than 200 million individuals pass through U.S. ports of entry annually.[8] More than 7 million aliens enter this country annually as tourists, businessmen, foreign officials, foreign journalists, and even foreign espionage agents. Of this number more than 1 million petition the INS annually to remain. In just one year INS agents located over five hundred thousand deportable aliens; 30 percent were working at the time, and at least ten thousand had been involved in crimes. More than six thousand of these apprehended illegal aliens had been involved in smuggling activities, mostly narcotics.[9] Completion of more than twenty thousand INS investigations revealed widespread frauds involving counterfeit passports, visas, and other immigration documents.

The task of the INS is not easy; the number of illegal aliens has been estimated to be in the millions. New York is known to have more than five hundred thousand; Texas has more than three hundred thousand; and California has over 1 million.[10] These are said to be extremely conservative figures.[11] In one three-week period the INS caught more than fifty thousand illegal aliens.[12] Alien-related welfare costs, according to a federal study, run over $60 million annually in just five states.[13] Many aliens, despite apprehension and deportation, return. Not surprisingly the costs of deportation run into the millions. Organized crime acts as a broker between individuals willing to pay any sum to enter this country and employers willing to hire them.

Once an alien is apprehended, the INS begins deportation proceedings. It is up to the alien to prove that he is in this country legally. U.S. courts have held that admission into this country is a privilege rather than a right; the alien enjoys this privilege only if he abides by the laws of this country. Deportation hearings are conducted by an INS administrative law judge. His decisions, either oral or written, can be appealed to the Board of Immigration Appeals. Aliens with enough money have been known to tie up the INS in appeals for months and even years. Although the deportation proceeding is a civil rather than a criminal hearing, many constitutional safeguards, including the right against self-incrimination, apply. The alien must also be informed of all charges and can present evidence on his behalf. Decisions by the administrative law judge must be unbiased and based solely on the evidence presented at the hearing.

The attorney general of the United States is ultimately responsible for the enforcement of all immigration laws, but he has delegated some of his functions to the INS and to the Board of Immigration Appeals. The board, composed of a chairman and four members and assisted by a staff of attorneys, hears all appeals from INS hearings. During the last several years it has heard an average of more than two thousand appeals each year. The board's decisions can be reviewed by local federal appellate courts. Because it has a heavy case load and hears many appeals, the board's decisions are often slow in coming. One INS agent put it this way: "By the time we catch them and the board comes down with a decision, it can take years." If the alien appeals to local federal courts, it can take even longer. Given this large backlog, criminals can manipulate the system to their advantage.

Illegal Aliens and Organized Crime

In 1943 Umberto Anastasio (known publicly as Albert Anastasia), a native of Italy, appeared before a Pennsylvania court and was granted U.S. citizenship.[14] On December 9, 1952, federal prosecutors instituted proceedings under the Nationality Act of 1940 to set aside his naturalization decree on the ground that it was illegally procured. In 1931, when he entered this country, Anastasio had concealed his criminal record from the authorities.

In a similar case federal prosecutors charged that Vito Genovese had procured U.S. citizenship fraudulently and illegally.[15] When interviewed by naturalization examiners, Genovese had hidden his long history of criminal involvement. Prosecutors argued that the law required that each applicant for citizenship be an individual of "good moral character" and that the defendant, in fact, had been involved in numerous crimes ranging from felonious assault to homicide. The court agreed, and his citizenship was revoked.

Immigration laws were used to deport many criminals who had successfully evaded prosecution. The problem of illegal aliens is now the deluge of illegal aliens. The federal machinery that was established to contain the tide has failed. Each year INS agents arrest and deport more than five hundred thousand illegal aliens,[16] but many soon return. One INS official noted that "the system has collapsed." Organized criminal elements have been quick to take advantage of this situation.

Many U.S. citizens turn away from work that they find demeaning. The high expectations instilled in the population have led many to shun manual labor. But the need for such labor continues and organized crime provides businessmen and farmers with cheap illegal alien laborers. These criminal brokers usually receive large commissions with the result that many aliens become indentured laborers. Thus a new class of serfs has been created.

Unlike American workers, illegal aliens will work for pennies an hour. Economic need has driven millions of Latin Americans, many from Mexico, to come to this country. Some sources put the total illegal immigration figure at over 8 million.[17] This class of laborers poses no problem for the employer; they cannot form unions, nor can they actively fight their poor conditions. The threat of deportation constantly lingers over their heads. In essence they form the slave class of modern America. In many ranches in the Southwest as much as 99 percent of the labor is made up of illegal aliens. The alien is also a victim of the company store. Many aliens are forced not only to work for small wages but also to purchase all their necessities from their employer. These goods usually cost more than they would if purchased through normal channels, as much as twice the standard price. Many illegal aliens are forced to work under hazardous and unsanitary conditions; for example, investigators have found that aliens are often sprayed by pesticides while working on farms. Some aliens are even forced into prostitution and crime. In one year INS agents arrested more than ten thousand aliens for involvement in criminal activity.[18]

The trade in illegal aliens is extremely lucrative; it produces large revenues for its tradesmen. Alien smugglers run little risk of prosecution, for neither the alien nor the employer is likely to inform authorities. Not surprisingly, law enforcement officials are bribed, and a lucrative trade in false identification papers has sprung up. The illegal trade in false documents may run as high as $20 billion annually.[19] False identification papers are used not only to give the alien a legal status but also to bilk businesses of billions of dollars and local governments of millions of welfare dollars. Organized crime has the capability and the talent to manufacture these false documents, which are sold to a captive market of illegal aliens eager to buy them.

In their attempts to reduce the influx of illegal aliens, federal agents have been accused of violating the civil rights of U.S. citizens.[20] While attempting to apprehend illegal aliens, federal agents often arrest permanent residents and citizens of Mexican extraction. Frustrated federal sources have called for the establishment of a national identity card to curtail the effectiveness of false documents.[21] Federal officials also fear that the marketing of false identification documents may increase radically and that illegal aliens may soon constitute a sizable minority.[22] The danger in such an outcome lies in the ability of organized criminal groups to enhance their economic and political power by employing this sizable group to do its bidding.

Various proposals have been put forth to deal with this problem. The Carter administration's plan calls for civil fines for employers who knowingly hire illegal aliens and for amnesty for all aliens who entered this country before 1970. It also proposes an increase in the number of federal agents engaged in the interception of illegal aliens.[23] However, business groups and Americans of Latin extraction argue that employers might use it to discriminate against minorities. In addition, the plan suffers from practical application. How does the government go about determining who entered this country before 1970? Are hearings to be held, thus further crowding the already overworked court system and prosecutorial machinery? Might not this plan create an even bigger black market in stolen and counterfeit documents, as illegal aliens search for some documentation that they entered this country before 1970? Stolen and counterfeit identification papers would make it difficult to prove that the employer knew that his employees were illegal aliens. The prosecution of thousands of employers will only increase the prosecutorial and judicial backlog and further strain our legal system. The problem is too large and too complicated to be solved by the Carter plan. Millions of illegal aliens, thousands of businesses, and millions of American citizens are involved. The Carter plan is sincere but too late and too fraught with political entanglements. It would only provide organized criminal elements with new markets to service and give rise to new schemes to circumvent it.

Organized Crime as Employer

In June 1975 a well-known Chicago Mafia boss was killed in the basement of his house. In November of that same year a federal informer was killed as she was preparing to tell authorities about organized crime interests in Nevada. Almost two years later a well-known California mobster was shot dead as he emerged form a telephone booth.[24] Law enforcement sources speculate that all these informers may have been killed by aliens brought into this country as hired assassins. In Miami law enforcement sources speculate that organized crime employs illegal aliens from the Caribbean to assassinate its opponents.[25] New York police agencies theorize that illegal aliens of Balkan extraction are heavily involved in illegal gambling operations.[26]

The illegal alien trade has provided criminal syndicates a new source of revenue and devoted recruits. The alien criminal works for smaller fees than his American counterpart, and he will handle tasks that American criminals may find too risky or degrading. The alien felon depends on organized crime for his very survival; he escapes prosecution largely because of his criminal contacts. Criminals from southern Europe and Latin America have been employed as enforcers in various roles. Organized crime offers foreign criminals an opportunity to serve it within this country. Criminal syndicates employ these foreign felons in their legitimate businesses, thus giving them the needed cover. Sham marriages are arranged to reward the faithful and ensure their legal residency in this country. The foreign criminal residing illegally in the United States is unknown to law enforcement intelligence units and thus better able to evade detection and prosecution.

Organized crime owns large legitimate businesses that need cheap labor and whose very nature is well suited to employing illegal aliens. Restaurant chains, hotels, entertainment resorts, and the garment industry need unskilled labor. Illegal aliens thus find their way into these mob-owned businesses, providing a competitive advantage over the legitimate sector.

Prosecuting Immigration Crimes

Immigration officials can inspect any alien seeking admission or readmission into this country. They can also exclude aliens. The costs of maintaining and detaining an illegal alien are borne by the owner of the aircraft or vessel in which the alien came. It is illegal to bring in an alien whose visa has expired. Anyone who brings in an illegal alien can be fined up to $2,500 and imprisoned up to five years. However, prosecutors must first show that the defendant knew that the alien entered illegally, that he willfully or knowingly concealed, harbored, or shielded the illegal alien from detection, and that he knowingly or willfully encouraged or induced the alien to enter illegally.[27]

Section 1325 of Title 8 of the federal code makes it a misdemeanor, and provides for fines of up to $500, for an alien to enter this country by making a false or misleading misrepresentation or by concealing a material fact. A deported alien who illegally reenters or attempts to reenter this country is guilty of a felony and can be fined up to $1,000 and imprisoned up to two years. Anyone who brings in an alien for immoral purposes (such as prostitution) can receive a fine of up to $5,000 and up to ten years in prison.[28]

Whoever knowingly forges, counterfeits, alters, or falsely makes any immigrant or nonimmigrant visa, permit, or other document required for entry into the United States be fined up to $2,000 and imprisoned up to five years. The misuse of evidence of citizenship or naturalization is prohibited, and those convicted can receive up to $5,000 in fines and up to five years of imprisonment. Impersonating someone else in a naturalization proceeding is a violation of federal law that carries fines of up to $5,000 and imprisonment for up to five years. Other federal statutes deal with the falsification of citizenship or naturalization papers and provide both fines and prison sentences. Black marketeering in immigration documents is also a violation of federal law. Immigration officials who receive, demand, charge, solicit, or collect bribes from any aliens, or their agents can be fined up to $5,000 and imprisoned for up to five years.[29]

Killing an immigration official engaged in the performance of his duty is a federal crime. A person who makes a false statement under oath, in any matter relating to citizenship, naturalization, or registry of an alien, can be fined up to $5,000 and imprisoned for up to five years.[30]

Immigration officials have an arsenal of legal weapons to enforce immigration laws, but the real problems are the economic plight of many Latin American nations that leads to the deluge of illegal aliens and the refusal of much of the U.S. population to do work it deems menial and demeaning. Organized crime has seen these problems as opportunities to enhance its wealth. It has supplied businesses with cheap labor; it has hired many illegal aliens to man its own business ventures; it has employed smaller numbers in its criminal ventures. The problem of illegal aliens is an economic one. It cannot be solved by increasing the number of border agents or INS investigators. The millions who have crossed U.S. borders illegally constitute a political time bomb that organized crime has helped create and over which it exerts considerable power.

Notes

1. "Illegal Aliens Being Provided on Order, Castillo Says," *Washington Post,* February 13, 1978, p. C-3; see also "Agents Infiltrate 100 Rings Smuggling Illegal Aliens," *Washington Post,* April 2, 1978, p. A-12. Numerous interviews by the author with law enforcement sources have confirmed these allegations.

2. "Addenda," *Washington Post,* March 2, 1978, p. A-9.

3. "More Aliens Caught Since Announcement of Amnesty Proposal," *Burlington Free Press,* August 25, 1977, p. 5A; see also "Mexican Exodus," *Newsweek,* February 6, 1978, p. 13.

4. Dan P. Danilov, "Immigration Today: What the Practitioner Needs to Know," *Trial,* August 1977, p. 45.

5. U.S., Department of Justice, Office of the Attorney General, *An-*

nual Report for 1975 (Washington, D.C.: U.S. Government Printing Office, 1976), p. 167.

6. Barbara J. Leidigh, "Defense of Sham Marriage Deportations," *University of California Davis Law Review* vol. 8 (1975):309; see also Christopher Dickey, "An Immigration Tangle," *Washington Post,* April 4, 1978, pp. C-1, C-4.

7. Maurice A. Roberts, "Marriage—Alien Style," *Interpreter Releases,* June 30, 1975, p. 197.

8. Office of the Attorney General, *Annual Report for 1975,* pp. 163, 165.

9. Ibid., p. 165.

10. Ibid., p. 168.

11. Based on author's interviews with law enforcement sources at the Department of Justice.

12. "More Aliens Caught," p. 5A.

13. "Aliens Are Said Abusing Welfare," *Washington Post,* November 14, 1977, p. A-20.

14. United States v. Anastasio, 226 F 2d 913 (1955).

15. United States v. Montabano, 236 F 2d 757 (1956); see also United States v. Lucchese, 247 F 2d 123 (1957); and United States v. Castello, 275 F 2d 355 (1959).

16. Office of the Attorney General, *Annual Report for 1975,* p. 165.

17. Based on author's interviews with federal investigators.

18. Based on author's interviews with sources within the Department of Justice; see also Office of the Attorney General, *Annual Report for 1975,* pp. 165-166.

19. "U.S. Seeks to Curb Use of False Identities," p. A-12.

20. "Lawsuits on Aliens," *Washington Post,* February 26, 1978, p. A-3.

21. "U.S. Seeks to Curb Use of False Identities," p. A-12.

22. "Carter Unveils Illegal-Alien Proposals; Unions, Businessmen Criticize Package," *Wall Street Journal,* August 5, 1977, p. 5.

23. Ibid.

24. Jack Anderson and Les Whitten, ".22 Pistols Used in Gang Slayings," *Washington Post,* December 6, 1977, p. B-15.

25. Based on author's interviews with Dade County law enforcement officials.

26. Based on author's interviews with New York City law enforcement sources.

27. 8 U.S.C. 1223-1227, 1232, 1251.

28. 8 U.S.C. 1326, 1328.

29. 18 U.S.C. 1421-1428, 1546.

30. 18 U.S.C. 1025, 1114.

12 Infiltration into White-Collar Crime

A major American airline paid over $50,000 to organized crime figures as ransom for more than a thousand stolen blank tickets.[1] The vice-president of a Texas bank was said to have been involved in a major bank-related fraud with organized crime members.[2] In New York a key Mafia figure and several of his associates were charged with conspiring to take over a multi-million-dollar national poultry firm. In Arizona a respected national developer of shopping centers and office buildings is said to be an active business partner of well-known Mafia figures. Chicago underworld figures are suspected of having bought a three-thousand-acre ranch in the Southwest, and a bank whose directors include the brother of a former United States presidential candidate is said to have made loans totaling millions of dollars to mob-controlled businesses.[4]

In the 1890s the American underworld earned much of its income from dock racketeering, extortion, and blackmail. In the 1920s rum-running became the mob's chief source of income. The violence and the gangland killings of these early years led to the 1929 Atlantic City conference of gangland's chief architects. This conference marked the beginning of a new era. Territories were carved up and business fronts were established. It marked the entrance of organized crime into the legitimate business sector. Today it is estimated that between fifteen thousand and fifty thousand domestic business entities, with investments amounting to more than $20 billion, are controlled either directly or through fronts by the syndicate.[5] While law enforcement concentrates on robberies and muggings, the syndicate has infiltrated business and threatens the economy and the consumer's confidence in it.

Penetration of the Legitimate Economy

Prohibition supplied the syndicate with billions of dollars in profits and with the expertise to operate multimillion-dollar ventures. The criminal of the 1890s became the businessman of the 1920s. Prohibition required the gangster to learn the techniques of management and marketing; the gangster had to meet a payroll and delivery deadlines. Prohibition enabled the syndicate to establish a national network of contacts in the legitimate business sector and gave the gangster a semblance of respectability.

183

Gambling, narcotics, and loansharking have provided the syndicate with avenues to legitimate business. One criminal group reportedly owns real estate valued at more than $200 million, and another group controls a large hotel chain.[6] New York crime figures are said to be part owners in some of that city's largest skyscrapers.[7] A giant conglomerate, said to be the biggest corporate sports enterprise in this country, is said to have links to the syndicate.[8] Clearly organized crime has established itself in the business sector. But why would the syndicate enter legitimate business and pay taxes, when its illegal operations enjoy de facto immunity from the Internal Revenue Service? Why go legitimate when there is little reason to fear law enforcement? There are many reasons, and there is every indication that the syndicate will continue to enter the world of business, bringing its criminal behavior. Just as the barbarian tribes brought their violence and traditions, so will the syndicate bring the business mentality that characterized the robber barons of the nineteenth century but which has since been tempered by public outcry. Pressure groups and the press may have an impact on the Madison Avenue executive, but the influence they exert on the syndicate remains dubious.

The mob's entry into legitimate business has been prompted by a number of factors. Every individual wants respectability, at least in the eyes of his peers. The Mafia bosses of Sicily were not revolutionaries; rather they sought to mimic the landed nobility of the mezzogiorno. The syndicate chiefs of this country seek to mimic the businessman, if only to provide themselves and their associates a legitimate cover. The gangster is neither a reformer nor a revolutionary. He is in many respects a caricature of the robber barons of the late nineteenth century; his mentality and outlook are those of an industrial feudalist. The legitimate business sector offers him new avenues for his investments and new opportunities for power and wealth. It opens the world of white-collar crime, in which prosecution is rare and punishment genteel. The gangster can "steal more, and pay less."

The gangster may be part or complete owner of a business. The corporate veil allows him to remain anonymous. The corporation may serve as a vehicle for illegal activities, or it may have legal objectives. It is not the gangster's ownership but his techniques and objectives that make his entry into the business world illegal. Some syndicate-owned businesses continue to prosper, pay their taxes, and behave like legitimate enterprise. But criminal abuse is always a possibility and depends on the whims of the gangster-owner. The business world may temper the syndicate's ways, and some gangsters may become transformed into businessmen, just as the Teutonic tribes eventually settled in Europe and abandoned their warlike ways. However, the gangster, while undergoing this metamorphosis, may destroy the fragile economic fiber. He may also destroy consumer cofidence in the free marketplace. The syndicate has now joined the white-collar felon in pillaging the economy. The robber barons of early industrial America provide him with suitable role models.

A Tradition of Corporate Corruption

The financiers of early twentieth-century America have provided the gangster with both role models and suitable justification for his plunder of the U.S. economy. More than half of the $50 billion in new securities that floated in the American stock market of the 1920s were worthless. In 1927 the National City Company (a subsidiary of the National City Bank) floated three bond issues for the Republic of Peru, for $90 million.[10] The investing public was never told that Peru's budget was unbalanced; within two years the bonds were worthless, and thousands of investors lost their money. About the same time a fraud involving the Libbey-Owens-Ford stock pool cost the investing public millions of dollars.[11] As with most pools, the object was to create fictitious demand for the company's stock, thus breaking the price of the common stock. Among the manipulators were some of Wall Street's most prestigious financial institutions, including the father of a deceased United States president and Walter P. Chrysler, the auto builder.

Stock frauds were so common in the 1920s that the prices of more than a hundred stocks listed in the New York Stock Exchange (NYSE) in 1929 were said to be manipulated. From 1929 through 1933 more than a hundred NYSE member firms (brokerage houses) participated in stock frauds.[12] Among those involved in these financial frauds were highly acclaimed financial institutions such as the Chase National Bank, the Sherman Corporation, and the J.P. Morgan Company. Also involved were the well-known business figures Arthur W. Cutten, a member of the Chicago Board of Trade, Raleigh T. Curtis of the *New York Daily News*, and Charles F. Adams, secretary of the Navy. These frauds eventually led to an investigation by the U.S. Senate, in December 1931. The Securities Act of 1933, an outgrowth of that Senate's investigation, was the first serious attempt to curtail the financial frauds that permeated America's business community. When the millionaire J.P. Morgan was asked by Senate investigators whether he had paid any taxes in 1930, he replied, "I cannot remember."

The numerous federal statutes enacted to curtail the financial frauds of corporate America were poorly designed, and the frauds have continued virtually uninterrupted. The regulatory agencies established to police the business world were riddled with red tape and fell under the control of the very industries they were to police. The watchdogs became the captives. For example, in 1950 Walter F. Tellier's firm (Tellier and Company) specialized in penny-stock manipulations. In a five-year period Tellier and Company took in more than $5 million from stock-related frauds. In 1956 alone boilerroom swindles cost the investing public more than $100 million, and more than 30 million shares of worthless securities were dumped on investors, who lost over $60 million. These operations were soon to attract the interest of organized crime. Stock fraud artists were quick to turn to the mob for assistance; in return the mob became a partner. Firms like Lincoln Securities and Russell Securities soon fell under the sway of the mob.[13]

In 1977 the president of an Ohio bank was convicted in federal court of conspiring to misapply more than $300,000 in bank funds.[14] He was alleged to have approved a large loan to a real estate firm in return for 10 percent ownership. A study of small investors found that more than 50 percent of them distrusted Wall Street and believed that the financial community was riddled with fraud.[15] Given such an environment and the history of corporate corruption, it is little wonder that organized crime has made its way into legitimate business. In some cases it has entered as a welcome partner; in others it has bought or extorted its way into partnership. Organized crime has essentially adopted the strategy and modus operandi of the white-collar felon. However, it has also brought violence and a feudal outlook on society.

Business-Related Frauds

A Maryland construction executive, subpoenaed by a federal grand jury investigating racketeering in the construction industry, was found shot to death in a motel room.[16] The acting executive director of Pennsylvania's crime commission disclosed that the resort industry in the northeastern part of the state had been infiltrated by organized crime. Four of these resorts were operated by a Los Angeles-based firm alleged to have organized crime ties; two were owned by a Miami lawyer said to be an associate of Meyer Lansky.[17]

The United States Justice Department has received allegations of syndicte activity in the coal industries of West Virginia, Kentucky, Alabama, Illinois, Georgia, Pennsylvania, California, and Virginia. The death of a Virginia businessman was linked to organized crime. Virginia's governor, in a press conference, charged that organized crime was behind numerous corporate-related crimes, including insurance fraud and the fencing of valuable stolen mining machinery. The head of Virginia's state police told the state's crime commission that the syndicate had also been dealing in fraudulent coal leases and fraudulent loans and may have been involved in an international network that exchanged valuable coal for drugs in foreign markets.[18] Virginia's coal fields are not the only victims of organized crime. The mob has infiltrated all areas of legitimate business and has bilked legitimate firms of billions of dollars.

Bankruptcies have often been used by legitimate businessmen to avoid payment of liabilities. Criminals have discovered how easy it is to use bankruptcy to bilk creditors and stockholders of publicly held firms of millions of dollars.[19] Criminal prosecutions in cases of bankruptcy fraud are few. One such case, involving more than $100 million, culminated in a suit by the bankruptcy trustees against officers of the defunct firm, charging them with manipulating the firm's assets and concealing from investors and creditors the firm's poor financial condition.[20] Bankruptcy frauds, also known as scams or bustouts, account for losses of more than $50 million annually. Businesses that handle goods with a high turnover potential are usually more attractive to criminals.

Scams take several forms. If organized crime gains control of an old and established company, it is rather simple for the manipulators to gain the confidence of creditors and financial institutions. If they cannot gain control of an existing company, the operators may establish a firm of their own, possibly with a name similar to that of an old and respected company in the same area. Once the syndicate gains control over a business, it begins to fleece the public and creditors. At first the syndicate-controlled business places only moderate orders with suppliers and makes payments in full. Eventually credit is established, and as the operators gain the confidence of the creditors, credit is expanded. The manipulators then sell the goods and conceal the proceeds. When the creditors press their claims, the operators either declare bankruptcy or clean out the firm and leave town. The creditors and the public are left to absorb the loss. Antiquated bankruptcy laws and lax prosecutorial enforcement are largely responsible for these frauds.

A West Coast ring of as many as 180 individuals may have bilked California insurance companies of more than $300,000. Members of this ring made fraudulent claims in the millions of dollars based on rigged auto accidents. In the Midwest the ring may have been behind more than $5 million in arson claims.[21] A Maryland ring of more than twenty individuals was the focus of a federal grand jury probe into insurance frauds.[22] Arson frauds have grown into a multimillion-dollar industry. Professional arsonists known as torches earn over $100,000 a year.[23] In New York more than twenty thousand fires in the last several years were said to be of suspicious origin.

Insurance frauds are big business; the cost to the public may exceed $3 billion annually. These frauds take various forms and their operation may be domestic or international. The fraud may be directed at the insured or the insurer; the victim may be an individual or a corporation. Frauds against the insurer take the form of phony and inflated claims for injuries, loss of property, or loss of wages. Frauds by the insurer may take the form of false or exaggerated policy claims, a failure to honor claims, or partial payments. The loose structure of insurance laws makes it easy for manipulators to establish a phony insurance company, usually outside the United States, collect premiums from the insured, and then vanish. Domestic manipulators have used similar tactics to bilk policyholders and fraudulent reinsurance schemes to bilk other insurance companies, as in the case with the massive Equity Funding scandal.[24] Organized crime has defrauded both the insured and the insurer.

More than 80 percent of the volume of business in the United States is done by check. Over 20 billion checks are drawn annually on approximately 80 million checking accounts, at more than ten thousand banks. According to federal sources, check-related frauds may account for more than $1 billion in annual losses to business and consumers.[25] Credit card-related frauds are also a growing problem. More than 50 million credit cards have been issued by hundreds of department stores, merchants' associations, and gasoline companies, and frauds connected to credit cards may account for annual losses in excess of $10 billion.[26] Stolen and phony credit cards have been used in welfare frauds, check-kiting schemes, and numerous other frauds. In Washington a federal grand jury indicted more than a dozen individuals said to be involved in a multimillion-dollar credit card fraud.[27] For fees ranging from $300 to $800 the ring would alter the credit history of any individual according to his request.

The syndicate has made its way into credit card and check fraud. Department stores are bilked with fraudulently obtained credit cards, and stolen credit cards are used to obtain services, vacations, and obtain cash advances from banks. The merchant may be a coconspirator, thus playing the role of a willing victim. Merchants have been known to conspire with felons by authorizing purchases on stolen credit cards and splitting the gains. Sixty percent of all credit card-related frauds are said to result from lost or stolen cards, 20 percent are due to cards issued on false applications, and the remaining 20 percent on cards issued but never received by their rightful owners.[28]

Check frauds are a growing and national problem. The techniques employed by criminals vary. Criminals may set up a corporate shell and issue bogus checks. They may use a firm's blank checks and its check-writing machine to issue checks to themselves. One felon wrote himself checks worth more than $1 million.[29] Criminals have been known to open several bank accounts with phony checks and then withdraw most of the cash before the scheme is uncovered. Criminals have impersonated bank officials, government officers, and others in numerous check-related frauds. Felons have forged the signatures of rightful owners on checks that they stole or purchased from a fence. Stolen credit cards and checks have found a favorable market with syndicate fences.

Securities-related frauds may account for more than $4 billion in annual losses.[30] Lost, stolen, or missing securities may account for as much as $50 billion in security certificates.[31] Organized crime has made its way into Wall Street. One United States senator, speaking before the Senate, put it this way:

> Organized Crime figures operate at every level of the financial community. They are employed in the backroom of brokerage houses, in large financial firms on Wall Street and in lending institutions throughout the Nation.[32]

Stolen and counterfeit securities are used by the syndicate as collateral for loans and other financial transactions. With these loans the syndicate finances other ventures. Stolen or bogus securities may also be extended as a loan to a company or businessman, who then uses these securities as collateral for loans. Stolen and bogus securities are used by dishonest businessmen to bolster the sagging net worth of their firms. One dishonest businessman rented stolen securities from the syndicate for $70,000 and used them to obtain a large loan from a bank. Syndicate fences play a key role in stolen and bogus securities. One fence bought more than $2 million in stolen securities from a small-time operator, in return for a new car.[33] A key member of organized crime was involved in the fencing of more than $500,000 of stolen securities.[34]

Organized crime has also been involved in a number of other securities-related frauds. Syndicate-controlled brokerage firms have been involved in boiler-room operations and stock manipulations. Members of the unsuspecting public are induced through false and misleading information to buy stock in unknown companies. The investor is led to believe that for a relatively small investment he can triple his money. The company is usually a shell, perhaps an offshore bank or an insurance firm with virtually no assets. Syndicate-controlled brokers have been known to trade inside information and to engage in unauthorized trading in clients' accounts.[35] One government source said: "The most significant feature of . . . [these] . . . schemes is the tremendous amounts of money manipulators are able to amass in short periods of time."[36]

Bribes, kickbacks, and payoffs are estimated to account for more than $2 billion annually and to affect every facet of the economy.[37] A large telephone company has admitted making secret payoffs to numerous individuals in several states.[38] A large liquor wholesaler has disclosed that it provided more than $4 million in goods and services to induce other businesses to buy its brands.[39] In New York City a company received a $100,000 kickback on a $1 million contract.[40] Bribery, kickbacks, and payoffs are pervasive in American business.[41] Organized crime neither invented them nor introduced them to the world of business. It found an atmosphere of corruption and took advantage of it. Syndicate figures and mob-owned businesses extort bribes, payoffs, and kickbacks from legitimate business as a price for doing business in syndicate-controlled industries and localities.[42] The outcome is higher prices and costs to the consumer.

Victimizing the Consumer

Consumers are victimized yearly of more than $20 billion.[43] Federal officials estimate that of more than $40 billion spent annually by consumers on auto repairs, over $10 billion may be for unnecessary work.[44] Hundreds of categories of consumer fraud have already been identified: phony charities, work-at-home ploys, and energy-saving schemes. Syndicate-run land frauds in the Southwest have bilked consumers of more than $100 million, and a syndicate-controlled Florida firm attempted to sell swampland to consumers by mail.[45] The mob has also made its way into the multibillion-dollar nursing home industry.[46] The consumer, whether an individual or a corporation, is a target of the syndicate. Consumer fraud is big business, and it touches every class.

One of the fastest-growing consumer frauds is in the energy-saving field. Energy consultants and energy-saving devices have sprung up everywhere. Consumers are bombarded with false advertising. They are promised large savings if they install X in their car and device Y in their home heating unit. For a small investment they are promised large returns. The energy crisis enables criminals to bilk the public of millions of dollars.

Home improvement frauds have traditionally been one of the syndicate's more popular ways of bilking the consumer. The home owner is promised low-cost renovation and quality work; he is even shown phony letters from satisfied customers. The consumer is asked for an initial down payment; work is slow and shoddy. One home improvement scheme bilked home owners of more than $4 million over a period of several years.[47]

Real estate swindles have also robbed the public of billions of dollars. Consumers are given brochures that describe in great detail the retirement home of their dreams. They are told that for a few dollars a week can buy hundreds of acres of land, which can be converted into residential or vacation property. The swindlers promise large profits within a brief period; land, the consumer is told, is the best investment in the world. Several such fraud rings operating from Arizona have bilked consumers of millions of dollars.[48] The buyer eventually finds that the land is worthless desert or swampland. The consumer learns painfully and inevitably that the land is unusable. One buyer found that he had bought swampland and that the nearest golf course was several hundred miles away.

The syndicate has perpetrated work-at-home frauds. Consumers are told that they can make large profits by running businesses from their homes. For a small investment they can buy the needed equipment from the operators, and they are promised buyers for their products and services. Such schemes vary from growing rare flowers in home gardens to raising chinchillas. The investor soon finds that there are no buyers and no demand for his home-manufactured goods.

Self-improvement schemes have also proven attractive to the syndicate. Relying on fears and psychological needs, the promoters advertise courses and training programs to make the individual a more productive and confident person. Long-term memberships are sold in health spas, beauty schools, health clinics. The promoters may even supply phony letters from satisfied customers. The objective is to obtain as much money as possible from the unsuspecting consumer for nonexistent or unnecessary services.

Charity frauds rely on the inner weaknesses of their victims; the promoters play on guilt or superstition. Consumers are told that a small donation will save thousands of young children in other countries or help erect a library or monument in memory of a well-known leader. In one case promoters raised large sums of money by promising to build a library in New York City in memory of a slain civil rights leader.

The syndicate has made its way into numerous other areas of consumer fraud. Mob figures have been behind repair frauds, franchise swindles, advanced-fee schemes, and pyramid operations. Prosecution in consumer fraud cases is rare, and when it does occur it usually takes the civil route. Most cases are settled out of court, with the operators promising to make some restitution. Criminal prosecution is often difficult because the operators can usually claim business error. Judges are often reluctant to impose severe sanctions on these operators. The syndicate has taken advantage of a long history of corporate corruption and abuse aimed at the consumer, who has little cause to suspect the syndicate's real role.

Environmental Crimes

Tough environmental laws have given rise to a new and growing business for the syndicate: the illegal disposal of chemical wastes. In industrial states with tough air- and water-pollution controls, the disposal of chemical wastes has become an expensive undertaking. Organized crime has already made inroads in this area. In New England local prosecutors are investigating the illegal dumping of chemical wastes by the syndicate. New Jersey police arrested the driver of a tank truck who was attempting to dispose of several thousand gallons of chemical wastes. In one New Jersey town the water supply was polluted when containers rotted and released the illegal chemical wastes into the town's drinking water.

The cost of disposing of dangerous and toxic chemicals will continue to increase. Some of these wastes have been shown to cause cancer. But industry, especially in the industrialized eastern states, finds it increasingly difficult to dispose of these wastes at an acceptable cost. Syndicate-owned waste-disposal firms provide the unscrupulous with a cheap, albeit illegal, alternative. It is a growing business and one that organized crime is well equipped to handle. Even if illegal dumping is discovered and prosecuted, courts have been reluctant to impose harsh penalties. Most cases culminate with a mild fine. The syndicate has assumed the cover of legitimate business, uses similar techniques, and relies on the same defense when caught. Unlike the legitimate business sector, however, it takes an amoral view of life and society that may prove dangerous not only to the legitimate business sector and the consuming public but also to the survival of the environment.

Notes

1. Based on author's interviews with law enforcement sources. The airline in this case was Pan American Airways.

2. "How the Mafia Invades Business," *U.S. News & World Report*, June 13, 1977, p. 21.

3. Morris Kaplan, "A Reputed Mafia Figure Accused with Seven Others of a Plot to Seize Bronx Concern," *New York Times*, August 26, 1977, p. A-13.

4. "Mob Shakes Money Tree in Arizona," *Washington Star*, March 27, 1977, p. A-8.

5. "Infiltration into Legitimate Business," in *An Economic Analysis of Crime*, ed. Lawrence J. Kaplan and Dennis Kessler (Springfield, Ill.: Charles C. Thomas, 1976), p. 275.

6. Chamber of Commerce of the United States, *Deskbook on Organized Crime* (Washington, D.C., 1972), pp. 10, 11.

7. Paula A. Weinstein, "Racketeering and Labor: An Economic Analysis," in *An Economic Analysis of Crime*, p. 269.

8. Jack Anderson and Les Whitten, "The Slaying of Bolles," *Washington Post*, June 28, 1976, p. B-11.

9. Hillel Block, *The Watchdogs of Wall Street* (New York: William Morrow, 1962), pp. 4, 5.

10. Frank Carmier, *Wall Street's Shady Side* (Washington, D.C.: Public Affairs Press, 1962), p. 3.

11. Block, *Watchdogs of Wall Street*, pp. 5, 6.

12. Ibid., pp. 6, 61-63, 77.

13. "Northern Ohio Bank Ex-Official Convicted of Misapplying Funds," *Wall Street Journal*, December 27, 1977, p. 19.

14. Gene G. Marcial, "Poll Says Individual Shareholders Resent Companies Well as Distrust Wall Street," *Wall Street Journal*, December 28, 1977, p. 10.

15. Elizabeth Becker and Judith Valente, "Builder Subpoenaed in Maryland Rackets Probe," *Washington Post*, May 10, 1978, p. A-1.

16. "Pocono Resorts, Crime Figures Linked," *Washington Star*, April 17, 1978, p. A-2.

17. Wilson Morris, "Dalton Requests FBI Probe of Coal-Crime Link," *Washington Post*, June 1, 1978, p. A-4.

18. August Bequai, *White-Collar Crime: A Twentieth Century Crisis* (Lexington, Mass.: Lexington Books, D.C. Heath, 1978), pp. 33-36.

19. "Four GAC Officers Manipulated Funds, Trustees Charge," *Washington Star*, September 1, 1977, p. A-14.

20. Ron Roach, "Arabs on Student Visas Charged in Fraudulent Insurance Claims," *Washington Post*, February 16, 1977, p. D-16.

21. Based on interviews with federal investigators.

22. Larry Kramer, "Arson Costs U.S. $2B a Year," *Washington Post*, January 5, 1978, p. D-2.

23. Bequai, *White-Collar Crime*, pp. 80-81.

24. U.S., Department of Commerce, *Crime in Service Industries* (Washington, D.C.: U.S. Government Printing Office, 1977), p. 109.

25. Robert Meyers, "Credit Card Theft Racket Is a $10B Business," *Washington Post*, December 8, 1976, p. C-1; see also Chamber of Commerce of the United States, *White-Collar Crime* (Washington, D.C., 1974), pp. 34-35.

26. Timothy S. Robinson, "Northeast Man Convicted of Credit Fraud Scheme," *Washington Post*, September 21, 1977, p. B-3.

27. Florida Organized Crime Control Council, *Annual Report for 1976* (Tallahassee, Fla., 1977), p. 2.15.

28. Ibid., p. 2.16; also U.S. Chamber of Commerce, *White-Collar Crime*, p. 37.

29. U.S. Chamber of Commerce, *White-Collar Crime*, p. 6.

30. U.S. Senator Jackson speaking for an Amendment of the Securities Act of 1934, S.6186, before the 94th Cong., 1st sess., April 17, 1975.

31. Ibid.

32. U.S. Senator Jackson speaking on Notice of Hearings on Organized Crime in Stolen Securities, S. 16477, before the 93rd Cong., 1st sess., September 13, 1973.

33. Jack Anderson, "A 'Classic Study' in Labor Rackets," *Washington Post*, May 25, 1978, p. DC-9.

34. Bequai, *White-Collar Crime*, pp. 25-27.

35. "Securities Theft and Fraud," *Investment Dealers Digest*, July 9, 1974, p. 28; see also Matthew G. Yeager, "The Gangster as White-Collar

Criminal: Organized Crime and Stolen Securities," *Issues in Criminology* 8, no. 1 (Spring 1973):49-70.

36. U.S. Chamber of Commerce, *White-Collar Crime*, p. 6.

37. John F. Berry, "Southern Bell Will Disclose Cash Payments," *Washington Post*, June 6, 1978, p. D-9.

38. Hobart Rowen, "Kickbacks Are Not Kid Stuff," *Washington Post*, July 22, 1976, p. A-15.

39. James Mateja, "How Firms, Laws Open the Way for White-Collar Crime," *Chicago Tribune*, October 3, 1977, sect. 6, p. 11.; see also, Jules B. Kroll and Sanford E. Beck, "Security's Role in Combatting Commercial Bribery," *Security Management*, July 1978, p. 6.

40. Mark Green, "Crime Up in Big Business Too, SEC Discovers," *New York Times*, May 11, 1975, p. E-5.

41. Jonathan Kwitny, "Pizza's Big Cheeses Find Competition Is Heating up a Lot," *Wall Street Journal*, January 10, 1978, pp. 1, 14.

42. U.S. Chamber of Commerce, *White-Collar Crime*, p. 6.

43. Gerald F. Seib, "Dallas Ordinance against Fraud in Car Repairs Help Consumers Recover Nearly $3,000 a Month," *Wall Street Journal*, September 13, 1977, p. 46.

44. John Bradshaw, "The Death Of a Reporter Who Knew Too Much," *New York*, September 6, 1976, pp. 34, 36.

45. "U.S. Action Urged to Bar Mafia from Private Health Care Units," *Washington Post*, May 19, 1978, p. A-8.

46. Jay Mathews, "Fraud Figure's Deals Stir Complaints," *Washington Post*, March 8, 1975, p. A-4.

47. Albert J. Sitter, "Valley Loan Frauds Probed as Part of Nationwide Ring," *Arizona Republic*, November 7, 1978, pp. A-1, A-22.

13 Electronic Crimes: Advent of the Computer Age

One of the most bizarre criminal cases took place in the early 1970s. Over two hundred boxcars belonging to one of the nation's largest railroads were discovered in an isolated yard near Chicago; they had been routed from the company's yards almost a thousand miles away. The original markings on the boxcars had been painted out. Investigators concluded that organized crime had gained access to the company's computer and instructed it to route the boxcars to another yard. A grand jury was told that as many as two thousand boxcars may have been misrouted.[1]

A West Coast computer programmer had fallen behind on his gambling debts. Organized crime figures offered to repay his debts if he agreed to disclose sensitive programs to them. In another case a major midwestern gambling czar had used a university's computer to keep track of his handicaps.[2]

Law enforcement officials have been warning for several years that organized crime has infiltrated the computer field. This is only an evolutionary process; organized crime has shown itself sufficiently flexible to keep abreast with technology. Its infiltration has been facilitated by the computer system itself and by lax security measures.

Defining the Computer

In 1946 researchers at the University of Pennsylvania built a giant calculator to help them solve problems in nuclear physics. This calculator contained more than fifteen thousand vacuum tubes and performed several thousand additions per second. Its inventors named it the Electronic Numerical Integrator and Calculator (ENIAC). In the early 1950s the federal government purchased two computers; by 1960 the government had four hundred. Now the federal government has more than ten thousand computers. Private industry uses more than eighty thousand, and more than a hundred thousand minicomputers are in use. These computers are manned by more than 2 million operators, programmers, and technicians.[3]

The role of the computer in the private and public sectors is increasing. New technological breakthroughs have stimulated its growth in every facet of our lives. Semiconductors have made it possible to provide the calculating power of a room-sized computer in a microprocessor less than

195

an inch long.[4] In the near future almost everyone will be able to purchase a small computer at a very reasonable cost. The computer, like the television, may be found in almost every household.

The computer is an electronic calculator. It performs mathematical calculations on the data it has been supplied, and it does so with extreme efficiency and rapidity. It can process only the data it has been fed and in the manner in which it has been instructed.[5] The computer system consists of software (programs) and hardware (the mechanical devices employed to process the data fed into the computer).[6] Computers are usually employed in one of two functions: general (digital) or special (analog). General-purpose computers are the more common type; the special-purpose computer is used for specialized purposes such as controlling an airplane, a guided missile, or another machine.[7] Computers employed in both roles are called hybrids.

Crimes by Computer

New and bizarre crimes have come into being with the advent of computer technology. Organized crime has been directly involved in some of these crimes; the new technology offers it unlimited opportunities. There are eight categories of crime by computer: data crimes, theft of services, property-related crimes, industrial sabotage, politically related sabotage, vandalism by employees, crimes against the individual, and financially related crimes.

Imperical Chemical Industries (ICI) is one of Europe's industrial giants, with sales that exceed $5 billion annually. ICI makes much use of computers; the financial data stored in these electronic brains could prove extremely valuable to thieves and competitors. One weekend an ICI programmer stole from ICI's headquarters several hundred computer tapes containing ICI's most valuable financial data.[8] Just to recompile the stolen data would have cost ICI more than $100,000. In Sweden two employees sold competitors confidential data from their employer's computer bank; in New York City an employee attempted to sell a valuable list of customers to his firm's competitors.[9]

These are examples of the growing problem of computer crime. Theft of data, or data crime, has attracted the interest of organized criminal syndicates. This is usually the theft or copying of valuable computer programs. An international market already exists for computerized data, and specialized fences are said to be playing a key role in this rapidly expanding criminal market. Buyers for stolen programs may range from a firm's competitors to foreign nations. As computers become even more important to business and government, and as more valuable information is stored in them, data crimes will increase.

Another category of computer crime is the theft of services. Employers have used computers to run their own businesses. Members of organized crime have used company computers to keep track of their illegal investments. Two Philadelphia programmers were indicted for using their employer's computer to turn out musical arrangements.[10] They had also used it to do their billing and to run their business, at great cost to their employer. Computer security is so lax that a New Jersey high school student used an outside terminal to break into a major computer system; he left his calling card: The Phantom.

The theft of computer services is likely to increase. Lax security measures and the lack of investigative tools at the local level ensure the thieves de facto immunity from prosecution. Organized crime has shown great ingenuity in adapting to changing technology; they should be able to make their presence felt in computer crime as well.

In Los Angeles a young university student bilked that city's telephone company of more than $500,000 in property. Having obtained the company's secret computer entry code, he simply used a pushbutton telephone to order valuable electronic equipment. He then established a front through which he sold this equipment to smaller firms. In South Korea American army computers were said to be used to defraud the American military of more than $10 million in valuable equipment annually.[11] The South Korean underworld and American criminal groups were said to have cooperated.

These are examples of a third area of computer related crimes: theft of property. By manipulating a business's computer, a felon can steal valuable property. Computers can be instructed to have merchandise shipped to given locations. Computer components are valuable property in their own right. A federal grand jury in Miami convicted two spies of attempting to export computer components.[12]

A fourth category of computer crime is industrial sabotage; the cost to business and government may run into the millions of dollars annually.[13] A competitor sabotages a company's computer system to destroy or cripple a firm's operational ability, thus neutralizing its competitive capability either in the private or the government sector. Computer sabotage may also be tied to an attempt by affluent investors to acquire the victim firm. With the growing reliance by firms on computers for their recordkeeping and daily operations, sabotage of their computers can result in internal havoc, after which the group interested in acquiring the firm can easily buy it at a substantially lower price. Criminal groups could easily sell their sabotaging services to competitors or potential buyers. They could also resort to sabotage if the company is a competitor of a business owned or controlled by organized crime.

Politically motivated attempts to destroy a business- or government-owned computer constitute the fifth category of computer-related crimes:

political sabotage. Several attempts have already been made to destroy the computer facility at an air force base. A university computer facility involved in national defense work suffered more than $2 million in damages as a result of a bombing. A major computer system located at the Pentagon was attacked and suffered extensive damange.[14] In England terrorists have made repeated attempts to blow up police computers.[15] In Africa saboteurs successfully attacked and destroyed a computer facility, killing several of its employees in the process.[16]

Politically motivated sabotage is on the increase; political extremist groups have sprouted on every continent. Sophisticated computer technology arms these groups with awesome powers and opens technologically advanced nations to their attack.[17] In the 1960s and early 1970s extremist groups turned to the airline industry. With the growth of computer technology and the proliferation of computers, these groups may well turn to computer sabotage. Computer systems may even be held for ransom someday.

Computer vulnerability has been amply documented.[18] One congressional study concluded that neither government nor private computer systems are adequately protected against sabotage.[19] Organized criminal syndicates have shown their willingness to work with politically motivated groups. Investigators have uncovered evidence of cooperation between criminal groups and foreign governments in narcotics. Criminal groups have taken part in attempts to assassinate political leaders. Organized crime has the know-how and the contacts to assist political groups. Both sides have shown sufficient flexibility to work together in an alliance of convenience that may result in coordinated efforts in computer crime.

Vandalism by irate employees constitutes the sixth category of computer crime. Employees have set fire to computer facilities and flooded computer centers; at least one employee has shot a computer. One computer operator destroyed the billing information he was to enter into the computer, an attack that cost his employer several million dollars in unpaid bills.[20]

Most employee attacks have been sparked by personal grievances against the company. However, members of criminal groups could easily recruit an irate employee to manipulate or sabotage a company's computer.

Computers may be used in crimes against the individual. Computers are used in hospital life-support systems, in laboratories, and in major surgery. Nuclear missiles and other tools of modern destruction are controlled by computers. Criminals could easily turn these computers into tools of devastation. By sabotaging the computer of a life-support system, criminals could kill an individual as easily as if they had used a gun. By manipulating a computer, they could guide awesome tools of terror against large urban centers. Cities and nations could become hostages. Homicide could take a new form. The computer may become the hit man of the twentieth century.

A bizarre story unfolded in a lawsuit filed in a large eastern city. The plaintiff alleged that an associate, a known member of organized crime, had introduced him to an officer of a large and prestigious brokerage firm.[21] The officer told him how easy it was to manipulate his firm's computer and instruct it to forward payments to fictitious accounts. In a separate case a well-organized criminal group recruited agents in major financial institutions to manipulate their firms' data banks.[22] For a fee the organized crime group provided the agents with fictitious credit histories and phony references. Numerous businesses and banks, relying on these phony credit histories and references, lost large sums of money.

These examples illustrate a growing problem in computer crime: financial crimes. These crimes usually involve the manipulation of payrolls, accounts payable and receivable, and other financial data. Financial crimes can easily be planned by criminal groups and carried out by their agents, usually employees of the target company. Fences may also play a key role. These financial crimes can take numerous forms. For example, organized crime members can easily mislead creditors into believing that a firm is financially sound, thus setting the stage for bankruptcy fraud.

The computer opens vast areas of crime to organized criminal groups, both national and international. It calls on them to pool their resources and increase their cooperative efforts, because many of these crimes are too complex for one group to handle, especially those requiring a vast network of fences. Although criminals have adapted to computer technology, law enforcement has not. Many still think in terms of traditional criminology.

Computer Vulnerability

A democratic society, unlike a totalitarian one, allows a citizen great freedom of movement. The individual's right to privacy is highly cherished and is balanced against the needs of the state. The computer, however, opens the individual's privacy to attack not only from the state but also from criminal groups. Security measures are needed to protect computerized data from criminal attack and manipulation. Organized crime poses a serious and growing threat to the individual's privacy.

The computer is vulnerable to attack from insiders. Computer personnel can easily be employed by criminal groups to attack or manipulate a computer. Employees have been known to steal valuable programs at the instruction of criminal elements. Clearly there is a real need for personnel security.[23] Several steps can be taken to safeguard the computer from dishonest employees.[24]

The computer facility itself should be isolated from the other divisions of the firm or government agency. Access to and from the computer center should be regulated and logged. Only employees with a clear need should have access to the facility and its data banks. Guards should be employed where necessary to ensure that only authorized personnel have access to the system. A daily log should be kept of all individuals who have had access; their time of entry and departure should be recorded. Low-echelon employees should not have access to every operation of the computer system. Personnel at the computer center should be routinely rotated without advance notice.

Errors in the system or the data should be reported immediately to responsible officials within the firm or government agency. A detailed accounting system should be employed for documents sent to the computer center. Where possible original documents should be retained for a period of time rather than destroyed immediately after being computerized. Suspicious deviations from normal operation should be immediately reported and investigated. If a crime is suspected, the authorities should be called in as soon as possible.

Security measures should be periodically reviewed and revised, and a security director should be charged with overall responsibility for ensuring that these measures are adequate. The private sector should be encouraged to press for prosecution once a crime has been discovered. The best personnel security measures are meaningless if prosecutors hesitate to act; many private sources often complain that both local and federal prosecutors are lax.

Criminal groups play on the weaknesses of their victims. Control of a vast empire of illegal ventures, ranging from narcotics to gambling and loansharking, ensures criminal syndicates that some computer personnel can be made pawns of organized crime. Security measures are of limited value; nevertheless they are a badly needed first step.

Related to the need for personnel security is the need to develop security measures for the computer system itself. The operational stages of the system are open to attack. Criminals can sabotage a computer at any one of the following stages: input, programming, central processing unit, output, and communications.

The input stage is the first phase of a computer operation. At this point data are translated into a language understandable to the computer. Criminal elements with access to this stage can easily alter or falsify the data. False accounts, fictitious assets, ghost employees—even fictitious earnings—can be fabricated at this stage. Financial crimes usually take place at the input stage.

Each computer is supplied with programs, logical sequences of step-by-step instructions. Criminals have been known to steal, copy, and alter programs; they have even held programs for ransom. Competitors and foreign powers could be interested in valuable programs. Financial crimes, data crimes, and thefts of property may take place at this stage of a computer's operation.

The central nervous system of the computer is the central processing unit (CPU); it is analogous to the brain. Destruction of the CPU can cripple a computer system. Lax security measures are largely responsible for attacks against CPUs. Attacks against the computer may take the form of industrial or political sabotage or vandalism by employees. Criminal groups could easily sell their services to the highest bidder. New forms of extortion may soon appear.

Computerized data becomes intelligible at the output stage. Criminals can steal, copy, or destroy output data. Theft of data usually occurs at the output stage. Valuable data can be sold to domestic or foreign buyers; military secrets can be sold to foreign agents. Dishonest employees have been known to sell mailing lists to competitors. Theft of output data is a growing and lucrative business in which organized crime has assumed a key role.

During the communication stage data are forwarded from one computer to another or from a computer to a terminal. During the communication phase data are vulnerable to electronic interception; computers are especially vulnerable to electronic attack. Encryption is one method of preserving the integrity of the data.[25] But encryption is limited by the need to change codes constantly, and criminals have been able to gain access to secret codes. Further, to be effective against electronic interception, encryption must be uniformly employed. Only a handful of firms now employ encryption.

The computer system is open to taps applied directly to communication lines between computers or between computers and terminals and to unauthorized entries through terminals. There are electronic tools that can intercept the heat or radiation emitted by a computer and convert it into an intelligible language. Microwave communications can also be intercepted, and computers can be employed to make them intelligible. Data transmitted between user and computer can be electronically intercepted and altered. Computer facilities themselves can be bugged and thus compromised.

Computer technology is here to stay; its uses grow daily. More than 2 million men and women operate more than a hundred thousand computers throughout this country. Technology has developed tools that make the computer vulnerable, and lax security measures open it to attack from those that operate it. Law enforcement is still unequipped to deal with this new technology. Although some training programs have been established, they are too small to be effective within the near future.[26] Organized crime now operates with impunity and the knowledge that it enjoys de facto immunity from prosecution.

Notes

1. Gerald McKnight, *Computer Crime* (New York: Walker, 1973), pp. 152-154; see also August Bequai, *Computer Crime* (Lexington, Mass.: D.C. Heath, 1978), pp. 19-23; Robert S. Becker, *The Data Processing Security Game* (New York: Pergamon Press, 1977), pp. 17-24.

2. U.S., Congress, Senate, Committee on Government Operations, *Problems Associated with Computer Technology in Federal Programs and Private Industry* (Washington, D.C.: U.S. Government Printing Office, 1976), p. 346.

3. Marc Leepson, "Computer Crime," *Congressional Research Report*, January 6, 1978, pp. 3, 9.

4. "Coming: Another Revolution in Use of Computers," *U.S. News & World Report*, July 19, 1976, p. 54; see also, Victor Dricks, "Electronic Crime Poses New Challenge," *Star-Telegram*, November 27, 1977, p. 1.

5. Jerome J. Roberts, "A Practioner's Primer on Computer-Generated Evidence," *University of Chicago Law Review* 41 (1974):258; see also James A. Sprowl, "Evaluating the Credibility of Computer-Generated Evidence," *Chicago-Kent Law Review* 52 (1973):547.

6. Peter Hamilton, *Computer Security* (Philadelphia: Auerbach, 1973), pp. 24-25.

7. U.S., Department of the Treasury, Federal Law Enforcement Training Center, *White-Collar and Computer Related Crimes* (Washington, D.C., 1977), p. 20.

8. Bernard D. Nossiter, "Scotland Yard Deprograms Great Computer Tape Heist," *Washington Post*, January 14, 1977, p. A-15.

9. Stephen W. Leibholz and Louis D. Wilson, *Users' Guide to Computer Crime* (Radnor, Pa.: Chilton Book Company, 1974), pp. 36, 37.

10. "Crash Course in Computer Science Enables FBI to Nab Brainy Crooks," *Crime Control Digest*, June 27, 1977, p. 5.

11. "South Korean Thefts from Army Probed," *New York Times*, August 5, 1977, p. A-8.

12. "Two Convicted in Miami Conspiracy to Sell Secret Navigation Devices," *Washington Post*, November 12, 1977, p. A-8.

13. Based on interviews with individuals at the American Society for Industrial Security.

14. U.S., Congress, Senate, Committee on Government Operations, *Problems Associated with Computer Technology in Federal Programs and Private Industry* (Washington, D.C.: U.S. Government Printing Office, 1976), p. 8.

15. Hamilton, *Computer Security*, p. 17.

16. "For the Record," *Washington Post*, December 31, 1977, p. A-6.

17. Philip Manuel, a well-known investigator with the U.S. Senate Committee on Government Operations, notes that we may only be looking at the tip of the iceberg with regard to the entire problem of computer crime. See also Nan Randall, "If the Unthinkable Happened Here," *Washington Post*, January 29, 1978, p. C-1.

18. "Data Communications Security," *Assets Protection Magazine* 2 (Winter 1977):9-13.

19. Senate, Committee on Government Operations, *Problems With Computer Technology*, pp. 7-10.

20. Leepson, "Computer Crime," p. 5.

21. "John Doe Sues Dean Witter in Anonymity Necessitated by Mafia Tie, Fraud Effort," *Wall Street Journal*, January 28, 1977, p. 14.

22. G. Christian Hill, "Large Loan Swindles Spread with Reliance on Central Data Banks," *Wall Street Journal*, March 12, 1976, p. 1; see also "Six Accused of Manipulating Credit Data Bank on Coast," *New York Times*, September 3, 1976, p. 1.

23. Lindsay L. Baird, Jr., "Auditing the Computer Center," *Risk Management*, August 1976, p. 50; see also U.S., Federal Deposit Insurance Corporation, Division of Management Systems and Financial Statistics, *A Guide to EDP and EFT Security Based on Occupations* (Washington, D.C., 1977), pp. 11-13.

24. August Bequai, "Litigation in the Cashless Society," *Case and Comment*, November-December 1976, p. 37.

25. E.K. Yasa, "Encryption Algorithm: Key Size Is the Thing," *Datamation*, March 1976, pp. 163-168.

26. Peter J. Shurn, "Electronic Funds Transfer Systems: A Need for New Law," *New England Law Review* 12 (1976):111.

14 Traditional Tools: A Need for a New Approach

A federal prosecutor has said that the criminal investigatory apparatus is "out of step" and brings "insignificant cases to prosecutors."[1] A Maryland county police chief has charged that city police fail to give county investigators information developed in joint cases. Federal law enforcement agencies charge that state police units do not cooperate and coordinate efforts with them.[2] In Nevada a candidate for the office of governor acknowledged that he has received political contributions from casinos with possible links to organized crime.[3] In the Midwest a key federal prosecutor is said to have received a secret loan from a defense attorney who represented many criminal defendants in cases handled by that prosecutor.[4]

The United States has more than forty thousand police agencies; of these approximately thirty thousand employ fewer than five full-time officers.[5] With the exception of police departments such as those in New York, Los Angeles, Miami, Philadelphia, Baltimore, and the District of Columbia, local police forces have no specialized units to deal with organized crime. Even in the large local police departments, the expertise and specialized know-how to tackle organized crime are either poor or nonexistent. New York City, for example, has only one specialist handling stolen art investigations.[6] Serious questions have been raised about the ability of local police forces to handle frauds such as the National Student Marketing case, which cost stockholders more than $300 million in losses within a three-month period, or the Four Seasons Nursing Centers case, which left stockholders with more than $100 million in losses.[7] One national study concluded: "With the function of police becoming more technical and with the high mobility of the modern criminal, these small departments find it increasingly difficult to meet generally accepted police standards."[8] The prosecutorial structure, highly fragmented and dependent on local police agencies for criminal referrals, suffers similar drawbacks. Yet these are the tools available for curtailing organized criminal activity.

Evolution of U.S. Police Forces

In less developed societies the individual had to rely on his family, clan, and friends to avenge wrongs to him or his relatives. Organized societies soon made efforts to replace the role of the family and clan in enforcement matters. Policing became a responsibility of the state. In ancient Mesopotamia King Hammurabi (1792 B.C.-1750 B.C.) had more than two hundred laws engraved on a pillar of stone for all the citizens to see. When China was unified under the Chous in 221 B.C., the new rulers enacted a system of unified laws for the entire country. In ancient Athens aggrieved individuals took their cases before juries of Athenian citizens (the Leliaea). In Rome a system of Quaestores (inquirers) investigated criminal cases and brought their findings to the attention of the city's magistrates. In the ninth century the Carolingians of France established one of the first police forces since the fall of Rome.

In England the first national police structure took shape under King Alfred the Great (849 A.D.-899 A.D.). Present law enforcement has its roots in Alfred's mutual pledge. Villages and towns were divided into tithings, clusters of ten families. The tithing had the responsibility for investigating crimes against its members and for arresting culprits. Ten tithings were organized into the hundred. This body fell under the direct control of the local noble, who was responsible for maintaining law and order in his lands. Each hundred had a constable who had control over all the weapons in the hundred. This structure was later replaced by the shires, similar to U.S. counties. Law enforcement within the shire was the function of the sheriff. The large towns developed a system of watches; citizens patrolled the streets at night to ensure peace and look out for fires. In 1361 passage of the Justices of the Peace Act codified a police system based on a working relationship between constables, sheriffs, and justices. This police system, highly fragmented and resting on the localities, served England through the early nineteenth century.

By the eighteenth century the police forces in England had gained notoriety for their corruption. Some citizens openly questioned whether there were any differences between local police forces and the criminals they were hired to arrest. In 1750 Henry Fielding formed a small professional police force known as the thief-takers whose task was to maintain peace and order in London. In London, rich in commerce, organized criminal bands preyed on the piers. In 1800 Parliament established a small police force to patrol the piers. Policing continued to be a fragmented and highly localized institution. Constables, thief-takers, sheriffs, and justices were all charged with enforcing the laws; as a result, chaos reigned and crimes went undetected. In 1829 Parliament enacted the Metropolitan Police Act, which gave London a professional police force under the command of a commissioner. Scotland Yard was born. The police commissioner had to be nominated by Parliament and appointd by the crown.

The Act of 1829 had a profound impact on future police models. The reformers took pains to define the role of a modern police department. Police forces were organized along military lines, and the efficiency of a police agency was measured by the crime rate in its jurisdiction. The focus from the first was traditional crime. Organized crime was viewed as too immersed in politics to be of concern to the police. Policemen were instructed to dress and behave with dignity; good conduct was a tool for gaining respect. Police forces were trained, armed, and made efficient. The concern of the Act of 1829 was street crime. The newly created police forces were given the task of ensuring that London's streets were safe for the citizenry and commerce.

The American colonies followed the English example. A system of constables and night watches was formed to deal with street crime and fires. At first each member of the community was expected to act as night watchman; it was a voluntary position. Eventually the night watchman became a salaried employee. The objective of these volunteer police forces was to ensure that visible crimes were detected and brought to prosecution and to enforce the community's code of morality. Drinking, gambling, and other vices were viewed as crimes against God. In the frontier areas the citizenry took the laws into its own hands.

The Industrial Revolution and the great migrations to the cities brought calls for a professional police force similar to the London force. The watch system was unable to meet the needs of an increasingly urbanized society.

By the midnineteenth century cities like New York and Philadelphia established unified police forces. Unlike England, where the London police recruited on the basis of ability, America's cities sold the job to the highest bidder. The local political machines viewed these positions as rewards for party loyalty. Corruption was thus associated with the police force from its inception. New York's Boss Tweed appointed only his supporters to high police offices. Clashes between New York City police and the state militia were prompted by political differences between Tammany bosses and their upstate rivals. The police agencies became tools of the political machines. While England continued to professionalize police agencies, America's police forces became highly politicized. The role of local police forces was to curtail street crimes and to serve the needs of the local political bosses.

America's Civil War further hindered the development of a professional police force. Many of the Southern states, once occupied by Northern troops, fell under military control. Their police forces were disbanded, and policing became the responsibility of the North's army. Corruption reigned. Criminal activities took on an organized form, but the military was illprepared. In New Orleans the Mafia began to grow in the late nineteenth century; yet there were no police forces to check its activity. New Orleans had no police force until 1891 (its local police force had been disbanded in 1861, when the city fell to the Union army). Many cities in both the South and West organized vigilante groups; powerful businessmen hired private forces. Save for the East, where policing was controlled by local political machines, the country had no police forces. Either the military performed that function, or took the law into their own hands.

Attempts by state governors to centralize police functions under state governments met with opposition from local political machines. In 1868 the Democratic party openly called for restoration of police functions to the localities. There were no sizable federal police agencies; the attorney general's job was still a part-time position. In 1893 a police chiefs' convention in Chicago called for greater cooperation and coordination among fragmented police agencies. In 1905 Pennsylvania created the first professional state police force in this country. In 1908 the first police training academy was created in California. During the late nineteenth century several federal agencies were formed to police and curtail corporate abuses. In the early years of this century there was little effort to develop a strategy or coordinate efforts in the war against organized crime. Whatever efforts were made were small and local in nature.

In 1916 August Vollmer established the first college curriculum for the training of police forces. Vollmer's definition of the role of a police agency dictates policy and strategy to this day. Vollmer emphasized prompt investigation of all complaints and model conduct by the police. He spoke of the need for a code of ethics and for training programs in both specialized and public-related areas. Like others before and since, however, Vollmer did not address the role of police agencies in white-collar or organized crime. The Prohibition era and the financial frauds that resulted in the 1929 crash led the Wickersham Commission to call for the eradication of corrupt practices in the police departments.

During the 1930s the federal police agencies began to emerge as distinct entities. The Federal Bureau of Investigation (FBI) was established in 1924; the Securities and Exchange Commission (SEC), as well as a number of other federal regulatory agencies, was established in the early 1930s. Under J. Edgar Hoover the FBI captured notorious criminals such as Pretty Boy Floyd and John Dillinger. Like local law enforcement, the federal agencies devoted few of their resources to the investigation and prosecution of organized crime figures. During the 1940s, with America's attention drawn to war, black marketeering and other mob-related activities continued unchecked.

In the 1950s law enforcement was still decentralized and fragmented as it had been in the early part of the century. The more than a hundred federal agencies that had been created to deal with economic abuses continued the traditional policy of fragmentation and decentralization. The SEC and FBI showed little desire to work together. The Internal Revenue Service (IRS) showed even less interest in cooperating with state and city tax units. Although technology had given law enforcement new tools for investigating organized crime, the old strategies and policies dominated.

Present Police Forces

Local police agencies not only enforce local laws and ordinances but also provide social services. They help locate lost persons, assist the ill and dying, and mediate family disputes. Local law enforcement has received little training in dealing with commercial and organized crime. Local police have received no training in the identification of securities frauds, consumer-related abuses, planned bankruptcies, and the countless other crimes that mob figures may be engaged in. Instead many local police officials view the syndicate as their predecessors did in the 1920s. Outdated strategies are often used, and police personnel are trained for an era that no longer exists. The criminal has refined his techniques, but local law enforcement officers are still trained the old way.

In 1967 the President's Task Force Report on the Police recommended ways of improving police performance: Lines of authority must be clear and defined, work must be distributed equitably, and efforts must be coordinated.[9] The report did not mention training aimed at combating more sophisticated crimes in commerce and business. It did not call for the training of specialized units or the development of new policies and strategies to combat organized crime.

A more recent study of the problem concluded that organized crime has made important advances in the last several years and that the progress made by local law enforcement agencies has been offset by the syndicate's gains.[10] Local police are hampered by antiquated strategies and laws. They are poorly organized and ill-trained to combat a progressive and resourceful enemy. If local police forces appear to be making significant gains, the syndicate simply moves its activities to another state or county. In a era of mobility law enforcement is static and hindered by jurisdictional limitations. Petty jealousies, rivalries, and political disputes hinder coordinated efforts against a national enemy. Local law enforcement has to rely on the federal apparatus.

Federal Police Forces

One of the oldest federal police agencies is the U.S. Marshals Service (MS), with an office in each of the ninety-four judicial districts. The MS, a bureau within the Justice Department, has a staff of more than fifteen hundred deputies and administrative personnel.[11] The MS is charged with court security and with the transportation of federal prisoners. MS personnel also serve warrants and civil and criminal court orders to persons as well as corporations. Title V of the Organized Crime Control Act of 1970 gives the attorney general authority to provide security for government witnesses who testify against syndicate figures. The attorney general has assigned this responsibility to the MS. The federal witness program encompasses security and "maintenance" for the witnesses and their families. The witness and his family are provided with new identities, and are relocated to new geographic areas away from the threat of the syndicate.

The MS has come under sharp attack for its handling of the witness protection program. Critics, among them federal prosecutors, have charged that MS personnel are poorly trained for the task and that some MS personnel have leaked information on the whereabouts of key witnesses to the syndicate. The MS has also been criticized for its poor training in organized crime. Serious charges of corrupt practices by some MS personnel have been made, and some MS regional offices are said to have been infiltrated by the syndicate.

The Bureau of Customs, created in 1927 and redesignated the U.S. Customs Service in 1973, has played a key role in the federal law enforcement strategy against organized crime. Customs conducts inspections at piers, airports, and other landing areas. Its mission is to intercept and seize contraband, including narcotics and illegal drugs. It also assesses and collects customs duties, excise taxes, fees, and penalties due on imported merchandise. The service has charged a large multinational firm with conspiring to evade duties on computer parts assembled at the firm's plants in Mexico.[12] The service is also charged with enforcing the Currency and Foreign Transactions Reporting Act and other federal criminal laws.[13] Customs Service special agents receive training in areas related to organized crime. The service has the potential to play a significant role against organized criminal activity, but rivalries between it and other enforcement agencies have hindered its efforts, especially in the control of narcotics.

The Internal Revenue Service (IRS), created in 1862 and known then as the Office of the Commissioner of Internal Revenue, is a part of the Treasury Department; it is also one of the largest federal enforcers. The mission of the IRS is to administer and enforce the revenue laws of this country. The Intelligence Division (ID) of the IRS is charged with identifying and bringing to prosecution tax evasion schemes. Organized criminal activity that involves a violation of the federal tax laws falls under the jurisdiction of the ID. These tax laws allow the IRS to play a key role in the war against organized crime. Attempts to evade the tax laws could result in fines of up to $10,000 and prison terms of up to five years. Willful failure to file a tax return, supply the IRS with requested information, or pay taxes can bring fines of up to $10,000 and prison terms of up to twelve months.[14] However, the coordination with other federal and state agencies needed to enforce these laws is lacking. The IRS itself has come under attack for its failure to take a more aggressive posture against organized crime.

The Bureau of Alcohol, Tobacco, and Firearms (ATF) was established by the Treasury Department in 1972. The ATF's jurisdiction includes enforcement of the tobacco and liquor tax laws. The 1934 National Firearms Act, passed in response to the gangland violence of the 1920s, imposes a tax and registration requirement on the possession of machine guns, short-barrel shotguns, and similar weapons. The act was amended by Title II of the Gun Control Act of 1968 (which amended the Omnibus Crime Control and Safe Streets Act of 1968). Title I strengthens licensing requirements for gun dealers, prohibits the importation of certain types of handguns, and makes it a crime for convicted felons to possess or transport firearms in commerce. The ATF is also charged with enforcing Title VII of the Safe Streets Act and Title XI of the Organized Crime Control Act of 1970. In 1974, the ATF also assumed responsibility for enforcing the wagering tax laws. Although well staffed and funded, the ATF has suffered from poor leadership and lack of strategy for dealing with organized crime.

The Federal Bureau of Investigation (FBI), with more than fifty domestic field offices and some fifteen foreign field offices, is staffed by more than nineteen thousand special agents and clerical personnel. It is the closest thing the United States has to a federal police force. The FBI's jurisdiction is broad. It investigates electioneering frauds, frauds against the government, crimes against federally insured banks, bankruptcy frauds, fraud by wire, interstate transportation of stolen property, obscene matter, and gambling devices, and the interstate transportation of persons for fraud. The FBI has other potent weapons for fighting organized crime. It can investigate interstate travel or transportation in aid of racketeering enterprises and the interstate transmission of wagering information and paraphernalia.

Thus it is not lack of weapons but lack of strategy and coordinated effort with other federal and state agencies that has hindered the FBI's efforts to eliminate organized crime. A General Accounting Office (GAO) study revealed that only 16 of the 676 cases investigated by the FBI were prosecuted, and that of these only four led to convictions.[15] The FBI has been accused of attempting to neutralize its critics, in some cases by using organized crime itself.[16] The FBI must be encouraged to develop a sophisticated strategy for fighting organized crime and to coordinate its efforts with other law enforcement agencies. The FBI has the staff, ability, and funds to play a significant role against the syndicate.

Equally important in the investigation and prosecution of organized crime are the Interstate Commerce Commission, the Civil Aeronautics Board, the Securities and Exchange Commission, the Commodity Futures Trading Commission, and more than a dozen other bodies. Similar regulatory agencies at the state level can investigate and prosecute organized crime, but their role has often been neglected. In some instances even their staffs do not view their roles as those of policemen. Yet, with large staffs, many years of expertise in key economic areas, and jurisdiction over business and industry, the regulatory agencies are being called on more frequently to help stop organized crime.

The agency model took shape in the late nineteenth century, in response to the abuses of business and industry. The first of the regulatory agencies was the Interstate Commerce Commission (ICC), followed by the Federal Trade Commission (FTC) and the other regulatory bodies. After an investigation has been concluded, the agency can refer cases to the Justice Department for criminal prosecution, take civil action on its own, or handle cases administratively.[17]

All investigations by the agency staff are ultimately brought before the regulatory agency's decision-making body. This body goes by different names within each agency, and its membership varies from several to as many as twelve individuals. The members of this commission are appointed by the executive branch with the consent and advice of the Senate and serve for fixed terms. Commissioners are usually selected because of their political contacts, rather than their knowledge of police functions. Many commissioners have had no experience in criminal justice, yet they make decisions that have profound ramifications for the handling of commercial crime. They handle criminal violations of the securities or consumer laws and decide whether to prosecute.

Few investigations by regulatory agencies culminate in criminal prosecutions; most are treated as civil or administrative matters. Fewer than 5 percent of all cases are referred to the Justice Department for criminal disposition.[18] Red tape and rivalries between the regulatory agency's staff and the Justice Department often prevent the successful prosecution of organized crime cases. The agencies, with their specialized know-how in complex areas of the economy, are indispensable to the prosecution of syndicate activities, yet their full powers are rarely used. One former agency official noted that "it rarely happens . . . [that] securities crooks" are put away.

In taking the civil route many agencies resort to the consent decree. This is an agreement between the agency and the defendant, ratified by the court, in which the defendant neither admits wrongdoing nor claims innocence, but merely promises not to violate the specific statutes again. Should he fail to abide by his agreement, then the agency's staff can seek a civil contempt ruling. But agencies who enter into consent decrees rarely follow through to ensure compliance. There is no probationary status, nor is there an attempt to monitor the defendant's activity. Consent agreements have little civil value for the victims. Since these agreements are not admissions of wrongdoing, the victims cannot employ them in civil cases against the defendants.

If the agency takes administrative action, a hearing is held by an agency judge (a hearing examiner, or administrative law judge) to determine whether there were in fact violations of statutes that the agency has been charged with enforcing. If the defendant has violated a statute, the examiner can fine, suspend, or permanently bar the defendant from further involvement in that industry. Since the sanctions are noncriminal, administrative proceedings, like civil rulings, are of little value in combating organized crime. Since syndicate figures usually employ underlings (often nonsyndicate criminals) in their frauds, the underling rather than the syndicate figure becomes the target of the agency's action. In securities-related frauds, a brokerage firm that becomes a tool of the syndicate may find itself censured or barred by the SEC while the mob figures escape untouched. Since the syndicate member is not directly involved with the securities industry, his attorneys can easily argue that the SEC has no jurisdiction over him and that barring or censuring him would thus be outside the agency's powers.[19]

The regulatory agencies, first established to investigate and prosecute abuses by business and industry, have now unwittingly become key instruments in the war against organized crime. Their effectiveness has been seriously curtailed, however, by the ease with which their investigations can be manipulated by political insiders. Many agency personnel are reluctant to refer cases for criminal prosecution, because the Justice Department rather than the agency would receive the laurels from a successful prosecution. Regulatory agency attorneys often resent the fact that criminal prosecutions are the exclusive province of the Justice Department when the agency attorneys often have a better grasp of the case.

The agencies have not met the expectations of Congress or the public. Some of the agencies have become the puppets of the very industries they were established to regulate.[20] In at least one agency prosecutors are investigating allegations that key staff members may have leaked confidential data to syndicate agents.[21] The mob has proven quick to take advantage of the loopholes and corrupt influences that business and industry have employed for so long.

A Need for New Tools

Better training and more funds have been suggested as the answers to curtailing organized criminal activities. Billions of federal dollars have been spent in the last several years, yet syndicate-controlled activities have become more aggressive. Academics, law enforcement sources, and many studies have suggested that making the investigatory apparatus less political and giving it new technological tools will improve its performance. Increased use of electronic surveillance, it is said, will do much to curtail organized criminal activity. Granting recalcitrant witnesses greater protection and immunity, we are told, will also assist in the battle against organized crime.[22]

Many other recommendations have been put forth, but they differ little from one another.

A greater commitment of funds and manpower will not turn the tide against organized crime. We need to streamline our present investigatory tools. We need to depoliticize the federal regulatory agencies and disband those that are obsolete. Few can justify the law enforcement value of outdated agencies like the ICC and the Federal Maritime Administration. There are too many obsolete police agencies and too many laws that work at cross-purposes. The problem is not too few means but poor use of those that exist.

Notes

1. "Prosecutor Says FBI Out of Step," *Washington Star,* July 4, 1976, p. A-8.

2. Judith Valente, "The Little City—Big County Police Feud," *Washington Post,* August 20, 1978, pp. B-1, B-3.

3. Lou Cannon, "Shadows of Federal Crime Probe Clouds Nevada Campaign," *Washington Post,* August 26, 1978, p. A-5.

4. "Meet Mr. Manipulator," *Overdrive,* January 1975, p. 61.

5. William H. Hewitt, "Contemporary Law Enforcement: Issues and Problems," in *The Fundamentals of Criminal Justice: A Syllabus and Workbook* (Geneva, Ill.: Paladin House Publishers, 1977), p. 125.

6. Ann-Byrd Platt, "It Takes More than a Thief to Catch Crafty Art Thieves," *Wall Street Journal,* February 16, 1978, p.1.

7. "Who Protects You against Stock Market Frauds," *Changing Times,* April 1974, p. 38.

8. August Bequai, "The Impact of EFTS on Our Criminal Justice System," *Federal Bar Journal,* Summer-Fall 1976, p. 201.

9. President's Commission on Law Enforcement and Administration of Justice, *Task Force Report: Corrections* (Washington, D.C.: U.S. Government Printing Office, 1967), p. 45.

10. Orr Kelly, "How Much Is Mafia Hurting," *Washington Star,* October 3, 1975, p. A-16.

11. U.S., Department of Justice, *Annual Report of the Attorney General of the United States* (Washington, D.C.: U.S. Government Printing Office, 1976), p.29.

12. G. Christian Hill, "Customs Service Hits Multinational Firms for Import Violations," *Wall Street Journal,* November 6, 1974, p. 1.

13. See 31 U.S.C. secs. 1051-1122, and 18 U.S.C. secs. 541-552.

14. Internal Revenue Code, secs. 7201, 7203.

15. "Much FBI Work Held Ineffective," *Washington Post,* September 25, 1975, p. A-12.

16. Rob Warden, "Files Show Hoover Sought to Neutralize Black," *Washington Post,* March 10, 1978, p. A-2.

17. August Bequai, "White-Collar Crimes Require a New Enforcement Strategy," *Prosecutor's Brief,* July-August 1978, p. 13.

18. August Bequai, "White-Collar Crime, The Losing War," *Case and Comment,* September-October 1977, p. 3.

19. August Bequai, "White-Collar Plea Bargaining," *Trial,* July 1977, p. 38.

20. John F. Berry, "Payoffs by Beer, Liquor Companies Reported," *Washington Post,* April 10, 1976, p. F-1; see also John S. Lang, "Drive to Curb Kickbacks and Bribes by Business," *U.S. News & World Report,* September 4, 1978, pp. 41-44.

21. Larry Kramer, "Influence and Murder Probe of ICC Raises New Questions," *Washington Post,* August 27, 1978, p. K-1.

22. National Advisory Committee on Criminal Justice Standards and Goals, *Report of the Task Force on Organized Crime* (Washington, D.C.: U.S. Government Printing Office, 1976), pp. 148, 152, 154, 156.

15 Prosecuting Organized Crime: Present Problems

In 1205 one of the longest prosecutions in recorded history began in India; it was finally concluded in the 1960s. Another prosecution that began in France in the early 1830s culminated more than one hundred years later.[1] Foreign prosecutions may hold the record for longevity, but American cases hold the lead for costs and number of appeals. A celebrated California case produced more than twenty thousand pages of transcripts and more than five hundred exhibits. It took seventeen weeks to select a jury and may have cost the government more than $2 million.[2] The case is still being appealed. Federal prosecution of a well-known corporate defendant took some fifteen years.[3] Not to be outdone, the Justice Department is presently litigating a case that involves more than 100 million pages of documents, hundreds of witnesses, more than three thousand exhibits, and over forty thousand pages of transcripts.

Prosecutions have become costly and time-consuming, and prosecutors often work at cross-purposes. The twenty thousand attorneys employed in various capacities within the federal structure often take conflicting legal positions.[4] Thus the Justice Department may take one position on a specific case, while attorneys for the Treasury Department may assume the opposite position. Federal prosecution appears to be chaotic at best.

Prosecutions at the local and state levels fare no better. The attorney general for the state of Virginia has said that the local prosecutorial machinery is inadequate for the prosecution of organized crime cases[5] and that local prosecutors are hampered by jurisdictional limitations. He also said that they govern their offices like absolute monarchs, responsible to none. New York's special anticorruption prosecutor found his efforts to prosecute corrupt local officials frustrated by procedural technicalities. As a result, none of the key targets of the investigation was ever prosecuted.

The prosecutorial system is riddled with corruption, ineptness, and red tape. Organized crime, sophisticated and versed in the drawbacks of the system, is adept at taking advantage of its loopholes. The weak and poor meet swift prosecution, while the strong and affluent can circumvent justice by raising procedural delays or by making prosecution so costly and time-consuming that prosecutors either abandon their quest or work out compromise pleas. With their wealth and powerful political contacts, organized crime figures have been able to neutralize and frustrate prosecutors or at least work out attractive plea arrangements. As a result, most people look on prosecutorial instruments with cynicism.

U.S. Prosecutorial Machinery

America's prosecutorial apparatus is a motley of local, state, and federal attorneys. Local prosecutorial machinery includes state, county, and district attorneys. The states have attorney generals, and the federal apparatus has regulatory agency attorneys, Justice Department specialized units, and some ninety-four U.S. attorney offices (twenty thousand federal attorneys in all). Most local prosecutors, including state attorneys general, are elected officials; key federal level prosecutors are political appointees.

Local prosecutors, like local law enforcment agencies, are highly fragmented and limited in their jurisdiction. A county prosecutor has no jurisdiction outside his county; local grant juries have little power over individuals who reside outside their jurisdiction. Organized crime figures can avoid prosecution by staying out of the county or the state. The establishment of statewide grand juries, with jurisdiction to cross county and city borders, has been suggested, but this proposal has been criticized by local prosecutors reluctant to give up their almost absolute power. Local prosecutorial autonomy has seriously undermined the efforts of law enforcement to bring organized crime figures before the courts.

To further complicate matters, local prosecutors are limited by lack of funds, small staffs (save for large cities and counties), and poorly trained personnel. Few local prosecutors have organized crime units; in fact, few are willing to acknowledge that the syndicate may be operating within their jurisdictions. And little can be done to oust a corrupt local prosecutor.

A study of some forty local prosecutorial offices by the National District Attorneys Association (NDAA) found that few of these offices have the capability to investigate complex fraud cases. Fewer than two hundred local prosecutors were assigned to these cases. This small group receives more than one hundred thousand complaints annually. Most complaints involving organized crime go unanswered at the local level. The NDAA study also found that many local prosecutors devoted relatively few of their resources to complicated fraud-related cases.[6]

The efforts of state attorneys general against organized crime fare no better. Only four offices have organized crime units. Colorado assigns only one attorney to its unit, Louisiana assigns five attorneys, and New Jersey has a staff of three. State attorneys general are limited by the borders of their states and by lack of funds. Most state prosecutors have annual budgets of less than $3 million, hardly sufficient to conduct statewide investigations, fly in witnesses, and pay for the statewide (and sometimes out-of-state) travels of their staffs.

Fewer than three thousand full-time attorneys are employed by all the state prosecutors combined. Only eight state attorney general offices employ more than one hundred full-time attorneys. The number of attorneys employed by each state prosecutor ranges from as few as six to over five hundred. Some attorney general offices allow their staff to supplement their income through outside practices. Although the National Association of Attorneys General has indicated that such practices "should be subject to strict controls," only twenty-two states have enacted legislation prohibiting it. Obviously conflicts of interest can easily arise in such an environment.

State prosecutors, like their local counterparts, have come under attack. They have limited funds and manpower, but they have also failed to adapt to the changing criminal environment. Few can train their staffs in organized crime; fewer still have a strategy for dealing with organized crime. Many state prosecutors have only civil jurisdictional roles; thus they have to refer criminal cases to local prosecutors. In New York criminal violations uncovered by the state prosecutor are referred to local prosecutors for criminal action. Efforts to establish a statewide special prosecutor's office to handle political corruption and organized crime cases have consistently met with opposition from county and city prosecutors. The divisions and rivalries common among investigators are also prevalent in the prosecutorial machinery. Local and state levels have no unified strategy to combat organized crime.

The federal prosecutorial machinery, consisting of attorneys from various agencies and the Justice Department, appears to have no unified strategy for combating organized crime. Until the Civil War the Justice Department was small, and the office of the attorney general was a part-time job. Most federal cases were handled by local federal prosecutors (U.S. attorneys), as they are today. Although the Justice Department has a number of highly specialized divisions and units, for example the tax division, (the antitrust division, and more than half a dozen strike forces), much of the prosecutorial work is handled by the U.S. attorneys. The department acts as a clearinghouse. Local federal prosecutors guard their powers with great zeal. Attempts by the department to circumvent their monopoly, for example through the establishment of strike forces, have met considerable opposition from U.S. attorneys. Federal prosecutors consider strike forces to be competitors; the local political machinery, which has traditionally played a key role in the selection of the local federal prosecutor, considers the strike force outside its control. Some strike forces have already been dismantled.[7]

At present some two thousand local federal prosecutors handle more than three hundred fifty thousand criminal and civil cases annually, and the number is increasing. Such small staffs, overworked and faced with increasing numbers of appeals, are hardly sufficient to handle complicated and lengthy organized crime cases. Many local federal prosecutors also lack training in this area. Further, the federal prosecutorial effort, like the local and state efforts, is too fragmented; red tape and rivalries between agencies and between units within the Justice Department have hampered successful prosecution. The efforts of federal prosecutors have been directed at low-level syndicate members, leaving the leadership intact. New and unified policies and strategies are needed at all prosecutorial levels. The prosecution of organized crime, more than traditional felonies, calls for concerted and unified effort at all prosecutorial levels.

A Need for a New Approach

It has been suggested that statewide grand juries should be used for organized crime cases at the local level and that civil sanction should be combined with criminal prosecutions. Temporary restraining orders (TROs), preliminary and permanent injunctions, restitution, and heavy fines could be employed. Since organized crime now operates through corporations, TROs and injunctions could play a key role in the prosecutorial strategy. Jailing syndicate figures is not sufficient to disrupt their activities as long as their financial power base remains intact.

It has also been suggested that a witness protection program be developed at the local and state levels and that the federal witness protection program be revamped to serve the needs of the witnesses. Students of organized crime have pointed out the need to depoliticize the prosecutorial structure to create local, state, and federal special prosecutors to handle politically sensitive cases as well as cases involving powerful syndicate bosses.

An equally potent weapon that has often been neglected by federal prosecutors is the Organized Crime Control Act of 1970. It could be an effective weapon in dealing with takeovers and control of businesses by syndicate members.[8] The act also provides for federal prosecutors to take civil action against organized crime figures who violate its provisions. The federal prosecution and conviction of Maryland's governor Marvin Mandel illustrates the flexibility of this act.

The federal prosecutorial monopoly enjoyed by the U.S. attorney offices must be broken. It makes little sense to leave federal criminal prosecutions in the hands of some two thousand attorneys while another eighteen thousand watch. As organized crime becomes more entrenched in white-collar crime, the expertise and talents of federal attorneys from regulatory agencies will increasingly be needed. The U.S. attorneys lack this expertise. In many complex fraud cases they shelve the case and let it die a bureaucratic death. Both federal and local prosecutorial machinery has shown itself unable to deal an effective blow to organized crime. New prosecutorial tools are needed.

1. "The Cases That Go On and On," *Time*, June 27, 1977, pp. 40-41.

2. "The Longest Trial," *Time*, July 19, 1976, p. 43.

3. "Cases That Go On and On," p. 42.

4. Stuart Auerbach, "New Study Finds Chaotic Use of Federal Lawyers," *Washington Post*, March 27, 1978, p. A-1.

5. Blain Harden, "Combating the Mafia," *Washington Post*, August 5, 1978, p. B-4.

6. National District Attorneys Associations, *Fighting the Forty Billion Dollar Rip-Off* (Chicago, 1976), pp. 6, 7, 12-45.

7. Jack Anderson and Les Whitten, "Official Feud over Crime Units," *Washington Post*, December 11, 1976, p. D-23; see also "Winning the War against Organized Crime," *U.S. News & World Report*, June 5, 1972, p. 63.

8. "Investing Dirty Money: Section 1962(a) of the Organized Crime Control Act of 1970," *Yale Law Journal* 83 (1974):1491.

16 A Look at the Penal Model

A U.S. Senate subcommittee investigating organized criminal activity found that fewer than one-fourth of convicted mob figures receive the maximum prison sentence; 12 percent receive no jail term. A study by the General Accounting Office (GAO) has confirmed this finding. The GAO discovered that organized crime figures receive probation in a substantial percentage of cases. In a study of 1,365 such cases, the GAO staff found that 39 percent of the defendants received probation.[1] The New York State Joint Legislative Committee on Crime studied 1,762 criminal proceedings involving mob figures and found that the rate of dismissals and acquittals for mob figures is five times as high as that for ordinary criminals. The committee also found that 44.7 percent of the indictments brought against syndicate figures were dismissed. When mob figures were convicted, they received only fines or suspended sentences in 46 percent of the cases.[2]

Every organized society from ancient Babylon to the present has employed a penal system to enforce its laws and protect its citizenry. Modern society has replaced the traditional role of the clan and tribe; the state rather than one's family, now takes action to protect the individual. In the war against organized crime, however, the state's instrumentalities have fared poorly. Organized crime constitutes a privileged aristocracy. Its members, even when convicted and sentenced, fare better than other criminals (except white-collar felons). On the average, "major Mafia figures . . . get an even kindlier break from . . . judges."[3] Our penal system has proven ineffective against the criminal cartel.

History of the U.S. Penal Model

In antiquity convicted felons were usually sold into slavery. It was not until the Middle Ages that a penal model began evolving into its present form. The kings of England in the thirteenth century began to employ prisons as a means of pressuring offenders into paying their fines. The Church had also employed incarceration against its critics and heretics. By the sixteenth century convicted felons were sentenced to serve as crews for the galleys of ships. In 1576 the English Parliament enacted legislation creating houses of correction to incarcerate the undesirable elements of English society, usually those from the poorer classes.

223

The seventeenth century also witnessed the rise of prisons in the American colonies. Connecticut was the first colony to establish a prison (1773). By the early eighteenth century in both the United States and Europe a heated debate over penal reform was taking place. With the urbanization of society, prisons became more important mechanisms of control. Those who posed a threat or were viewed as undesirables were usually imprisoned. Incarceration was usually reserved for criminals from the poorer classes. The more affluent and politically powerful members of society rarely saw the inside of a prison.

One of the early pioneers in penalogy was Edward Livingston (1764-1836), a man well versed in the tradition of the Enlightment.[4] Livington left a strong imprint on penalogy on both sides of the Atlantic. He devised a penal model directed at criminals from the lower strata of society. Livingston noted that criminal behavior is learned, the product of a defective environment and subsequent associations. He saw idleness, unemployment, and a defective family structure as principal causes. Livingston called for a penal program that would combine detention with religious instruction in an attempt to stamp out the felon's learned criminal behavior. The felon would be retrained and reeducated, with the hope of making him a productive citizen. Those who showed desire to reform would be given benefits and allowed to reenter society as free citizens.

John Haviland (1792-1852), another American penalogist, was equally influential in the founding of the present penal model.[5] Haviland considered the criminal a sinner; thus incarceration should help return him to God's fold. Haviland was the architect of the midnineteenth-century Pennsylvania system. Haviland's model was influenced by Quaker philosophy. It combined work with solitary confinement. The prisoner was to be completely isolated from his fellow prisoners, thus preventing their corrupting influences from further harming him. In 1821 Haviland's model prison was constructed on the outskirts of Philadelphia. The Pennsylvania system was soon adopted in other states and in Europe.

New York and other states soon found that the continuous solitary confinement of the Pennsylvania system led to numerous problems. Many prisoners became sick; some went insane and committed suicide. New York adopted the Auburn system. Although the Auburn system soon replaced Haviland's model in the United States, European countries continued to build prisons along the Pennsylvania model. Throughout the nineteenth century the penal systems bore a strong imprint of religion; salvation and punishment went hand in hand. The models were geared to traditional crimes by the lower classes.

Alexander Maconochie (1781-1860) developed the Irish system.[6] While living in Tasmania, he came to the conclusion that brutal punishment debases the prisoner and his captor. He called for the abolition of time sentences and advocated the use of indeterminate sentences. Under this system the prisoner was released when he had earned a fixed number of points for good behavior. Thus the prisoner determined when he would be released. By working hard and behaving, he earned points that brought him closer to discharge. Maconochie also called for smaller prisons and strict supervision of discharged prisoners. Maconochie's system had profound implications for the modern penal system.

Present Penal Model

From the Pennsylvania, Auburn, and Irish systems came the modern penal model. Nineteenth-century penologists were concerned with crimes committed by the lower classes. Criminal laws were largely attempts to curtail the antisocial behavior of the poor,[7] while antisocial acts by the upper classes were viewed as political offenses. The objective of the penal model thus became the rehabilitation of the criminals from the lower classes, and sentencing was heavily influenced by the concept of rehabilitation. The indeterminate sentence, with widely separated statutory minimum and maximum, became dominant.[8]

Today's penal model gives judges broad discretion in sentencing. Parole boards enjoy similar broad discretion. Sentencing has become individualized, geared toward the needs of each felon. A federal judge can sentence a felon to as much as five years in prison for driving a stolen car across state lines. A bank robber can receive up to twenty-five years in prison. A Colorado judge can sentence a felon convicted of stealing a dog to as much as ten years in prison. In Iowa burning an empty building can bring a prison sentence of up to twenty-five years.[9] Few mandatory guidelines have been established by the legislature to guide judicial officers in sentencing; this discretionary power has led to numerous abuses.

When a defendant is sentenced, the judge can either imprison the defendant or place him on probation. If imprisoned, the felon is usually considered for parole after he has served an average of one-third of his sentence. The judge and the parole board are influenced by several factors:

1. Whether the offender has a prior criminal history
2. The behavior the offender has displayed since committing his crime or since being imprisoned
3. The offender's current attitude toward society
4. Whether the offender has a history of narcotics use
5. The offender's level of maturity
6. His presentence report or his counsellor's report
7. The offender's employment plans or possibilities after release

8. The offender's family status and stability
9. The type of neighborhood he resides in or plans to reside in
10. Whether resources available to him will adequately care or assist him if he is freed

The use of these factors is an outgrowth of the rehabilitative model developed to address crime by the poor. But these factors are of little value for handling the modern mob figure, especially the younger and better-educated syndicate member who usually has no prior criminal record. The mob figure has become a businessman, and his crime is often a white-collar crime. When apprehended, he explains his crime as a business error. He often travels in the same social circles as members of parole boards and judicial officers. In fact, these decision makers may owe their positions to his political support.

The gangsters of the 1920s have given way to a younger and educated class of felons who operate in the worlds of business and finance. The older and more dangerous criminal ventures have been left to nonsyndicate associates. Judges are reluctant to mete out long sentences to the modern mob figure; often they justify light sentences by noting that his crimes are victimless. Few judges will send a defendant to prison on a gambling conviction; fewer still will imprison a person convicted of consumer-related fraud. A judicial officer who was asked why he had dismissed charges against an alleged member of the syndicate noted that he personally knew the defendant to be a "good citizen and a good father."

The convicted mob figure can find ample support for the court's leniency by citing numerous cases involving prominent businessmen. The vice-president of a large box manufacturer who was convicted of price fixing received a seven-day prison sentence, and an associate's ten-day sentence was reduced to twenty-four hours. A commodity firm executive who bilked investors of more than $50 million received a small fine and a two-year prison term. The president of a large restaurant chain received a four-month prison term for his involvement in a securities fraud. A nursing home operator involved in a $1.2 million Medicaid fraud received a four-month jail sentence. Four executives involved in a $170 million real estate fraud, received only six-month prison terms.[10] The former president of a large bankrupt firm said to have been involved in an $80 million fraud received an eighteen-month prison term; a codefendant received a ten-day jail sentence.[11] A convicted art thief, said to have an IQ of 140, pleaded guilty to stealing thousands of dollars of art and received a two-to-five-year suspended sentence.[12] The judge noted that prisons were not a place for intelligent members of our society.

Penologists often note that the objective of the U.S. penal system is "to inspire self-improvement so that, when they leave, prisoners will be able to take their place in the community of law-abiding citizens."[13] U.S. penal facilities handle an average of 1.3 million offenders daily. Of approximately 460 state and federal penal institutions, more than 20 prisons are over one hundred years old and 61 were constructed before 1900.[14] One U.S. senator has described it as "law without order; crime without punishment." He noted that this situation can only lead to a "loss of public confidence in the integrity of our political, economic and governmental institutions."[15] Organized crime has taken advantage of the penal system's failings. Raymond L.S. Patriarca, the alleged head of the New England crime syndicate, was paroled from prison when powerful local politcal figures came to his assistance. In New York a defendant later convicted of mass murders was recommended for relase on personal recognizance by a social service agency because he had no prior criminal record.[16]

Need for a New Model

Few dispute that the present penal model needs to be reformed.[17] It has been suggested that convicted members of organized crime be given long prison sentences. Several studies have recommended that convicted syndicate members not be placed on probation and that present parole procedures be changed to curtail abuses.[18] Some have even suggested that there be no parole for such convicted felons. But organized crime has changed. The Gambinos and Colombos have died; the leadership are men who act and dress like our more respected businessmen. How does one distinguish the modern syndicate member from the businessman or professional who has ventured into crime? It is no easy matter. In some cases the syndicate figure is the white-collar felon. The mob's change in tactics necessitates a new approach by society. Convicted felons are now sent to prison not for the harm they cause society but for the manner in which they do so. The eighteen-year-old who steals a car receives a long prison sentence; the syndicate member who fences valuable works of art receives probation.

Numerous recommendations have been made to curtail the wide discretionary powers of judicial officials and parole boards. The Twentieth Century Fund (Task Force on Criminal Sentencing) has recommended the adoption of the presumptive sentencing model.[19] This model would curtail the powers of judges and parole boards. The legislature would specify fixed sentences, and judges would have to sentence convicted felons to the terms specified by the legislature.

Under this model the legislature could also provide absolute minimums and maximums within which a convicted defendant would have to be sentenced. Parole boards would have only limited authority to release a convicted felon earlier than prescribed by the judicially fixed sentence. For example, a convicted felon sentenced to thirty months in prison could be released after twenty-seven months only if the legislature had authorized a 10 percent reduction in sentence for good behavior.

Present attempts to reform the federal criminal code have incorporated features of the presumptive sentencing model.[20] The proposed reforms would gradually phase out the indeterminate sentence by requiring that judges hand down fixed sentences. The proposed legislation would also establish a permanent sentencing commission which would fix a narrow range of sentences for each crime. A judge who specifies a sentence that does not meet these guidelines must justify his actions in writing. Both defendant and prosecutor could appeal his sentence. The proposed reforms would apply only to federal courts. Only a handful of states have so far shown any interest in the presumptive sentencing model.

Fixed sentences, by limiting the sentencing power of judges, could curtial abuses involving members of the syndicate. They would suffer the same penalties as traditional felons. The influence of outside political pressures would be minimized. At present the United States has two sentencing models: one for the affluent and powerful, the other for the poor and weak. Organized crime has learned to take advantage of the system. Thus the penal model nullifies the efforts of investigators and prosecutors.

Notes

1. National Advisory Committee on Criminal Justice Standards and Goals, *Report of the Task Force on Organized Crime* (Washington, D.C.: U.S. Government Printing Office, 1976), pp. 163, 165-166.

2. Nicholas Gage, "Organized Crime in Court," in *Theft of the City*, ed. John A. Gardiner and David J. Olson (Bloomington, Ind.: Indiana University Press, 1974), pp. 165-167.

3. Edward Browder, a convicted white-collar felon at the McNeil Island federal penitentiary, has conducted an extensive study of sentencing in both white-collar and organized crime cases and has found that 40 percent of all convicted syndicate figures received no prison sentences.

4. "Edward Livingston," in *Pioneers in Criminology*, ed. Hermann Mannheim (Montclair, N.J.: Patterson Smith, 1973), p. 70.

5. "John Haviland," in *Pioneers in Criminology*, p. 107.

6. "Alexander Maconochie," in *Pioneers in Criminology*, p. 84.

7. William J. Chambliss, "The State and Criminal Law," in *Whose Law, What Order* (New York: John Wiley & Sons, 1976), pp. 66-107.

8. Twentieth Century Fund Task Force on Criminal Sentencing, *Fair and Certain Punishment* (New York: McGraw-Hill Book Company, 1976), p. 11.

9. Marvin E. Frankel, *Criminal Sentences* (New York: Hill & Wang, 1972), pp. 5, 6, 7-10.

10. "Jail Terms Reduced for Paper's Officers," *New York Times*, February 19, 1977, pp. 29-30; Larry Kramer, "Abrahams Gets Jail, Fine for a Probation Violation," *Washington Post*, April 21, 1978, p. E-3; Timothy Robinson, "Former Emerson's Chief Given Four Month Sentence," *Washington Post*, April 26, 1978, p. D-10; "Bergman Sentence under Fire in New York," *New York Times*, June 18, 1976, p. A-7; "Four Get Six Month Sentences in New Mexico Property Scheme," *Washington Post*, March 11, 1977, p. C-26.

11. The case involved officials of the National Student Marketing Corporation.

12. "Genius Art Thief Spared Prison Sentence," *Washington Post*, March 18, 1978, p. A-13.

13. Norva Morris and Jones Jacobs, *Proposal for Prison Reform* (New York: Public Affairs Committee, 1974), p. 3.

14. Chamber of Commerce of the United States, *Marshalling Citizen Power to Modernize Corrections* (Washington, D.C., 1972), pp. 1, 2.

15. Edward M. Kennedy, "Mandatory Sentencing: An Answer to Recidivism," *Security Management*, November 1976, pp. 17, 19.

16. "Crime Figure Paroled," *Washington Post*, January 10, 1975, p. A-10; "Agency Proposed No-Bail Release of 'Sam' Suspect," *Washington Post*, August 19, 1977, p. A-1.

17. Andrew Von Hirsch, *Doing Justice: The Choice of Punishment* (New York: Hill & Wang, 1976), pp. 9-35.

18. National Advisory Committee on Criminal Justice Standards and Goals, pp. 168, 175, 177.

19. Twentieth Century Fund Task Force on Criminal Sentencing, *Fair and Certain Punishment*, pp. 19-29.

20. See the Criminal Code Reform Act of 1977 (S.1437), chaps. 20, 21, 22, 23.

Conclusion

A New Jersey Teamster official reputed to be a Mafia boss was charged with ordering the murder of a union rival. In Miami federal and state investigators are looking into charges that an investment firm based in Coral Gables may have been used by Fidel Castro to launder money from narcotics trafficking. A high Justice Department official testifying before a U.S. Senate investigating committee acknowledged that organized crime exerts control over more than two hundred union locals. A convicted loanshark shocked several of his listeners when he explained how the syndicate had used the Freedom of Information Act to discover the identities of government informers. Such revelations are made daily.

Organized crime, once a pawn of local political machines, has become a power in its own right. It controls multibillion-dollar businesses and elects agents to Congress. It has become a de facto government. In many urban slums it commands greater respect and authority than government. In fifty years the Capones and Lucianos have created America's fifth estate, a criminal confederation bound by political and economic needs and extending into every ethnic and racial group. Jews, Italians, Latins, blacks—all work together in this criminal cartel.

Gambling and fencing operations, traditional provinces of organized crime, continue to grow and provide the syndicate with billions of dollars annually. With the growing interest in legalized gambling, syndicate-owned corporations have already appeared. Labor unions, with more than $50 billion in pension funds, are prime targets of the syndicate. The sacrifices of organized labor have been exploited by the mob and corrupt labor officials to enrich themselves. Loansharking, long a syndicate preserve, has become more sophisticated and now caters to businessmen and professionals. The narcotics trade, after billions of dollars and more than fifty years of attempts by law enforcement to curtail it, has grown into a multibillion-dollar empire. It has turned the cities into jungles and has corrupted police, prosecutors, and judges.

Government itself, with its billions of dollars and 10 million employees, has become a target of syndicate frauds. The General Services Administration has amply illustrated the corruption that riddles government. Federal investigators have uncovered numerous secret bank accounts belonging to GSA employees that were used by government contractors, some of them with possible syndicate ties, to deposit millions of dollars in payoff money to GSA officials. Government investigators have uncovered at least five hundred cases of corruption involving political figures throughout the country. One case involved the mayor of a large southern city alleged to have extorted money from a company doing business with the city. Not to be outdone, U.S. Senate investigators have found that more than $40 million allocated to travel expenditures has been wasted on personal and nongovernmental travel by federal employees. Each day brings new revelations of fraud costing millions of dollars. Yet the public looks to government to bring organized crime under control.

Organized crime survives and grows in this corrupt environment. Investigatory and prosecutorial tools are neutralized, and the penal system ceases to act as a deterrent. The Sicilian Mafia was born in a corrupt environment and nourished by the covert assistance of both political and business leaders. America's criminal cartel could not survive more than a week in an ethical and moral climate.

Numerous recommendations for dealing with organized crime have been made. In many respects, they sound alike. Greater resources, we are told, will bring the syndicate to its knees. Yet the billions of dollars already spent on the war against organized crime have produced few results. Training, specialized investigatory police units, and highly motivated prosecutors can help; so would a reformed penal model.

Where will it all lead, I have been asked. More stable societies have come and gone; republics and democracies are not new. The Roman Republic, unable to curtail growing corruption, fell to the dictatorial yoke of the Caesars. Byzantium, when faced with disaster or reform, chose the former. No democracy can survive if its citizens view the government as corrupt and lose confidence in its ability to govern justly. The strength of a democracy lies in the legitimacy it enjoys in the eyes of the populace. When that legitimacy is undermined, the very fiber of the democratic government withers. The alternative is rule by dictator. This, then, is the real danger that organized crime poses.

Bibliography

Abrahamsen, D. *Crime and the Human Mind.* New York: Columbia University Press, 1944.

_____. *The Psychology of Crime.* New York: Columbia University Press, 1960.

Adamic, Louis. *Dynamite: The Story of Class Violence in America.* New York: Viking Press, 1931.

Allen, David D. *The Nature of Gambling.* New York: Coward-McCann, 1952.

Allen, James B. *The Company Town in the American West.* Norman, Okla.: University of Oklahoma Press, 1966.

Allsop, Kenneth. *The Bootleggers and Their Era.* Garden City, N.Y.: Doubleday and Co., 1961.

Asbury, Herbert. *The Barbary Coast: An Informal History of the San Francisco Underworld.* New York: Alfred A. Knopf, 1933.

Ashman, Charles R. *Finest Judges Money Can Buy.* Los Angeles: Nash Publishing, 1973.

Barbash, Jack. *The Practice of Unionism.* New York: Harper & Row, 1956.

Barzini, Luigi. *The Italians.* New York: Atheneum, 1964.

Bequai, August. *Computer Crime.* Lexington, Mass.: Lexington Books, D.C. Heath, 1978.

_____. *White Collar Crime: A Twentieth Century Crisis.* Lexington, Mass.: Lexington Books, D.C. Heath, 1978.

_____. "Developing A Legal Heroin Maintenance Program." *Police Law Quarterly,* October 1977, pp. 34-46.

_____. "White Collar Crime." *Police Law Quarterly,* April 1977, pp. 5-16.

_____. "Organized Crime: Mentor of Cargo Theft." *Security Management,* August 1978, pp. 36-40.

_____. "White-Collar Crimes Require a New Enforcement Strategy." *Prosecutor's Brief,* July-August 1978, pp. 13-14.

_____. "White-Collar Plea Bargaining." *Trial,* July 1977, pp. 38-43.

Bloch, H.A. *Crime in America.* New York: Philosophical Library, 1961.

Blok, Anton. *The Mafia of a Sicilian Village, 1860-1960.* New York: Harper & Row, 1975.

Buck, Frederick. *Horse Race Betting: A Complete Account of Parimutuel and Bookmaking.* New York: Greenburg, 1946.

Burns, Walter Noble. *The One-Way Ride: The Red Trail of Chicago Gangland from Prohibition to Jake Lingle.* Garden City, N.Y.: Doubleday, Doran and Co., 1931.

Chamber of Commerce of the United States. *Marshaling Citizen Power Against Crime*, Washington, D.C., 1970.

Chandler, David L. *Brothers in Blood: The Rise of the Criminal Brotherhoods*. New York: E.P. Dutton & Co., 1975.

Clinard, Marshall. *The Black Market*. New York: Rinehart Co., 1952.

Cook, Fred. J. *The Secret Rulers*. New York: Duell, Sloan, & Pearce, 1966.

Crawford, Francis M. *Rulers of the South*. London: MacMillan, 1900.

Cressey, Donald R. *Theft of the Nation*. New York: Harper & Row, 1969.

DeFranco, Edward J. *Anatomy of a Scam: A Case Study of a Planned Bankruptcy by Organized Crime*. Washington, D.C.: U.S. Government Printing Office, 1973.

Demaris, Ovid. *Captive City*. New York: Lyle Stuart, 1969.

Dinnean, Joseph F. *Underworld U.S.A.* New York: Curtis Publishing Co., 1956.

Dirks, Raymond L., and Gross, Leonard. *The Great Wall Street Scandal*. New York: McGraw-Hill, 1974.

Douglas, Cathleen H. "Police in the People's Republic of China." *Police Law Quarterly*, April 1977, pp. 36-40.

_____. "Media: Whose Message." *Trial*, May 1978, pp. 26-32.

Egen, Frederick W. *Plainclothesman: Handbook of Vice and Gambling Investigation*. New York: Arco Publishing Co., 1959.

Evans, M.S., and Moore, M. *The Lawbreakers*. New York: Arlington House, 1968.

Feder, S., and Joesten, J. *The Luciano Story*. New York: David McKay, 1955.

Fleisher, B.M. *The Economics of Delinquency*. Chicago: Quadrangle Books, 1966.

Frasca, Don. *Vito Genovese: King of Crime*. New York: Avon Books, 1963.

Freedman, Lewis. "Crime Commission Wants to Leave Legacy." *Times-Union and Journal*, April 9, 1978, p. A-10.

Gage, Nicholas. *Mafia U.S.A.* New York: Dell Publishing Co., 1972.

Gardiner, John A. *The Politics of Corruption: Organized Crime in an American City*. New York: Russell Sage Foundation, 1970.

Gartner, Michael, ed. *Crime and Business*. Princeton, N.J.: Dow Jones, 1971.

Gasser, Govert L. "The Confidence Game." *Federal Probation*, December 1963, pp. 47-54.

Glick, Rush G., and Newsom, Robert S. *Fraud Investigation*. Springfield, Ill.: Charles C. Thomas, 1974.

Graham, H.D., and Gurr, T.R. *Violence in America*. New York: Bantam Books, 1969.

Graziano, John V. "Department of Agriculture: The Third Largest Criminal Investigative Force in the Federal Government." *Police Chief*, July 1975, pp. 54-55.

Halper, Albert, ed. *The Chicago Crime Book*, Cleveland, Ohio: World Publishing Co., 1967.

Heckerthorn, Charles. *The Secret Societies of All Ages and Countries*. New Hyde Park, N.Y.: University Books, 1965.

Herman, Robert D. *Gambling*. New York: Harper & Row, 1967.

Hill, Albert F. *The North Avenue Irregulars; A Suburb Battles the Mafia*. New York: Cowles Publications, 1968.

Hobsbawn, Eric J. *Social Bandits and Primitive Rebels*. Glencoe, Ill.: Free Press, 1959.

Homer, Frederick D. *Guns and Garlic*. West Lafayette, Ind.: Purdue University Press, 1974.

Hutchison, John. "The Anatomy of Corruption in Trade Unions," *Industrial Relations,* February 1969, pp. 135-150.

Ianni, Francis A.J., and Reuss-Ianni, Elizabeth. *A Family Business*, New York: New American Library, 1973.

Jenkins, John A. "Working for Uncle Sam: The Flyaway Problem of Federal Attorneys." *Student Lawyer*, April 1977, pp. 48-54.

Jennings, Dean. *We Only Kill Each Other: The Life and Bad Times of Bugsy Siegal*. Englewood Cliffs, N.J.: Prentice-Hall, 1967.

Johnson, Malcolm. *Crime on the Labor Front*. New York: McGraw-Hill, 1950.

Kahn, E.J., Jr. *Fraud*. New York: Harper & Row, 1973.

Katz, Harvey. *Give*. Garden City, N.Y.: Anchor Press, 1974.

Kefauver, Estes. *Crime in America*. Garden City, N.Y.: Doubleday, 1951.

Kennedy, Robert F. *The Enemy Within*. New York: Harper & Row, 1960.

King, Rufus. *Gambling and Organized Crime*. Washington, D.C.: Public Affairs Press, 1969.

Knapp, Whitman. *Knapp Commission Report on Police Corruption*. New York: Braziller, 1973.

Kunnes, Richard. *The American Heroin Empire*. New York: Dodd, Mead & Co., 1972.

Landesco, John. *Organized Crime in Chicago*. Chicago: University of Chicago Press, 1968.

Leiter, Robert D. *The Teamsters Union*. New York: Bookman Associates, 1957.

Lewis, Norman. *The Honored Society*. New York: Putnam's 1964.

Maas, Peter. *The Valachi Papers*. New York: Putnam's 1968.

_____. *King of the Gypsies*. New York: Bantam Books, 1975.

Martin, Raymond V. *Revolt in the Mafia*. New York: Duell, Sloan, & Pearce, 1963.

Maurer, David. *The Big Con*. Indianapolis, Ind.: Bobbs-Merrill, 1940.

McClellan, John L. *Crime without Punishment*. New York: Duell, Sloan, & Pearce, 1962.

Messick, Hank. *Lansky*. New York: Macmillan, 1971.

Milligan, Maurice M. *The Inside Story of the Pendergast Machine*. New York: Charles Scribner's Sons, 1948.

Mori, Cesare. *The Last Struggle of the Mafia*. London: Putnam's, 1963.

Nelli, Humbert S. *The Business of Crime: Italians and Syndicate Crime in the United States*. New York: Oxford University Press, 1976.

Ness, Eliot, and Fraley, O. *The Untouchables*. New York: Messner, Julian, 1957.

Ney, Richard. *The Wall Street Jungle*. New York: Grove Press, 1971.

O'Conner, J.J. *Broadway Racketeers*. New York: Liveright, 1928.

Ottenberg, Miriam. *The Federal Investigators*. Englewood Cliffs, N.J.: Prentice-Hall, 1962.

Pace, Denny F. *Handbook of Vice Control*. Englewood Cliffs, N.J.: Prentice-Hall, 1971.

Pantaleone, Michele. *The Mafia and Politics*. New York: Coward-McCann, 1966.

Peterson, Virgil W. *Barbarians in Our Midst: A History of Chicago Crime and Politics*. Boston: Little, Brown and Co., 1952.

President's Commission on Law Enforcement and Administration of Justice. *The Challenge of Crime in a Free Society*. Washington, D.C.: U.S. Government Printing Office, 1967.

_____. *Crime and Its Impact: An Assessment* (Task Force Reports). Washington, D.C.: U.S. Government Printing Office, 1967.

Randall, Donald A., and Glickman, Arthur P. *The Great American Auto Repair Robbery*. New York: Charterhouse, 1972.

Reckless, Walter C. *The Crime Problem*. New York: Appleton-Century-Crofts, 1961.

Reiss, Albert J., Jr. *The Police and the Public*. New Haven, Conn.: Yale University Press, 1971.

Riordan, William L. *Plunkitt of Tammany Hall*. New York: E.P. Dutton and Co., 1963.

Rubinstein, Jonathan. *City Police*. New York: Ballantine Books, 1973.

Salerno, Ralph. *The Crime Confederation: Cosa Nostra and Allied Operations in Organized Crime*. New York: Doubleday, 1969.

Sann, P. *The Lawless Years*. New York: Crown Publishers, 1957.

Schiavo, Giovanni. *The Truth about the Mafia*. New York: Vigo Press, 1962.

Seidman, Harold. *Labor Czars: A History of Labor Racketeering*. New York: Liveright, 1938.

Sinclair, Andrews. *Prohibition: The Era of Excess.* Boston: Little, Brown and Co., 1962.

Smith, Adam. *Supermoney.* New York: Random House, 1972.

Smith, Dwight C. *The Mafia Mystique.* New York: Basic Books, 1975.

Starr, John. *The Purveyor: Shocking Story of Today's Illicit Liquor Empire.* New York: Holt, Rinehart & Winston, 1961.

Sutherland, Edwin. *The Professional Thief.* Chicago: University of Chicago Press, 1937.

Talese, Gay. *Honor Thy Father.* New York: World Publishing, 1971.

Terrett, Courtenay. *Only Saps Work: A Ball for Racketeering.* New York: Vanguard Press, 1930.

Train, Arthur. *Courts, Criminals, and Camorra.* New York: Charles Scribner's Sons, 1922.

Turkus, Burton B., and Feder, Sid. *Murder, Inc.* New York: Farrar, Straus and Young, 1951.

Tyler, Gus. *Organized Crime in America: A Book of Readings.* Ann Arbor, Michigan: University of Michigan Press, 1962.

Van Cise, Philip C. *Fighting the Underworld.* Boston: Houghton Mifflin, 1936.

Vollmer, August. *The Criminal.* New York: Foundation Press, 1949.

Waller, Irle. *Chicago Uncensored: Firsthand Stories about the Al Capone Era.* New York: Exposition Press, 1965.

Wilensky, H.L. *Organizational Intelligence: Knowledge and Policy in Government and Industry.* New York: Basic Books, 1967.

Williams, John B. *Vice Control in California.* Beverly Hills, Calif.: Glencoe Press, 1964.

Wyden, Peter. *The Hired Killers.* New York: William Morrow, 1963.

Zeiger, Henry A. *The Jersey Mob.* New York: New American Library, 1975.

Index

About the Author

August Bequai is a practicing attorney in Washington, D.C., specializing in legal aspects of technology and crime. A former federal prosecutor and chairman of the Federal Bar Association's Subcommittee on White Collar Crime, he has also been vice-chairman of the Federal Bar Association's Committee on Criminal Law and vice-chairman of the District of Columbia's Bar Committee on Regulatory Agencies.

Bequai holds a J.D. from The American University Law School and the LL.M. from the National Law Center at The George Washington University. He is an adjunct professor of criminal law at The American University and has lectured widely before numerous law enforcement, business, and professional groups such as the FBI Academy, the Institute on Organized Crime, the Federal Bar Association, the American Society for Industrial Security, George Washington University, and the Electronic Funds Transfer Association. He is the author of more than thirty articles dealing with various aspects of the law, as well as a contributor to the *Maryland Jury Instructions in Criminal Cases*. Bequai's *Computer Crime* and *White-Collar Crime: A Twentieth-Century Crisis* (Lexington Books) were published in 1978, and he is currently working on several other books.

August Bequai is a practicing attorney in Washington, D.C., specializing in legal aspects of technology and crime. A former federal prosecutor and chairman of the Federal Bar Association's Subcommittee on White Collar Crime, he has also been vice-chairman of the Federal Bar Association's Committee on Criminal Law and vice-chairman of the District of Columbia's Bar Committee on Regulatory Agencies.

Bequai holds the J.D. from The American University Law School and the LL.M. from the National Law Center of The George Washington University. He is an adjunct professor of criminal law at The American University and has lectured widely before numerous law-enforcement, business, and professional groups such as the F.B.I. Academy, the Institute on Organized Crime, the Federal Bar Association, the American Society for Industrial Security, George Washington University, and the Electronic Funds Transfer Association. He is the author of more than thirty articles dealing with various aspects of the law, as well as a contributor to the *Maryland Jury Instructions in Criminal Cases.* Bequai's *Computer Crime* and *White-Collar Crime: A Twentieth-Century Crisis* (Lexington Books) were published in 1978, and he is currently working on several other books.